MANAGING HUMAN RESOURCES
INTEGRATING PEOPLE AND BUSINESS STRATEGY

THE BUSINESS ONE IRWIN/APICS LIBRARY OF INTEGRATED RESOURCE MANAGEMENT

Customers and Products

Marketing for the Manufacturer   *J. Paul Peter*

Field Service Management: An Integrated Approach to Increasing Customer Satisfaction
Arthur V. Hill

Effective Product Design and Development: How to Cut Lead Time and Increase Customer
Satisfaction   *Stephen R. Rosenthal*

Logistics

Integrated Production and Inventory Management: Revitalizing the Manufacturing Enterprise
Thomas E. Vollmann, William L. Berry and D. Clay Whybark

Purchasing: Continued Improvement through Integration   *Joseph Carter*

Integrated Distribution Management: Competing on Customer Service, Time, and Cost
Christopher Gopal and Harold Cypress

Manufacturing Processes

Integrative Facilities Management   *John M. Burnham*

Integrated Process Design and Development   *Dan L. Shunk*

Integrative Manufacturing: Transforming the Organization through People, Process, and
Technology   *Scott Flaig*

Support Functions

Managing Information: How Information Systems Impact Organizational Strategy   *Gordon B.
Davis and Thomas R. Hoffmann*

Managing Human Resources: Integrating People and Business Strategy   *Lloyd S. Baird*

Managing for Quality: Integrating Quality and Business Strategy   *V. Daniel Hunt*

World-Class Accounting and Finance   *Carol J. McNair*

MANAGING HUMAN RESOURCES

INTEGRATING PEOPLE AND BUSINESS STRATEGY

Lloyd S. Baird
Professor of Management
Boston University

BUSINESS ONE IRWIN
Homewood, Illinois 60430

This publication is designed to provide accurate and
authoritative information in regard to the subject matter
covered. It is sold with the understanding that neither the
author nor the publisher is engaged in rendering legal, accounting,
or other professional service. If legal advice or other expert
assistance is required, the services of a competent
professional person should be sought.

From a Declaration of Principles jointly adopted by a Committee
of the American Bar Association and a Committee of Publishers.

Sponsoring editor: Jeffrey A. Krames
Project editor: Jane Lightell
Production manager: Diane Palmer
Designer: Maureen McCutcheon
Art coordinator: Mark Malloy
Compositor: BookMasters, Inc.
Typeface: 11/13 Times Roman
Printer: Book Press

Library of Congress Cataloging-in-Publication Data

Baird, Lloyd.
    Managing human resources : integrating people and business
strategy / Lloyd Baird.
        p.   cm. — (The Business One Irwin/APICS library of
integrated resource management)
    Includes index.
    ISBN 1-55623-543-7
    1. Personnel management—United States.   2. United States—
Manufactures.   I. Series.
HF5549.2.U5B35   1992
658.3—dc20   91–43744

Printed in the United States of America
1 2 3 4 5 6 7 8 9 0 BP 9 8 7 6 5 4 3 2

*To Coleen (someone who truly knows how to manage human resources)
and our children,
Jennifer, Bret, Tony, Peter, Chris, Matt, Sam, Justin, and Nate.*

FOREWORD

Managing Human Resources is one book in a series that addresses the most critical issue facing manufacturing companies today: integration—the identification and solution of problems that cross organizational and company boundaries—and, perhaps more importantly, the continuous search for ways to solve these problems faster and more effectively! The genesis for the series is the commitment to integration made by the American Production and Inventory Control Society (APICS). I attended several brainstorming sessions a few years ago in which the primary topic of discussion was, "What jobs will exist in manufacturing companies in the future—not at the very top of the enterprise and not at the bottom, but in between?" The prognostications included:

- The absolute number of jobs will decrease, as will the layers of management. Manufacturing organizations will adopt flatter organizational forms with less emphasis on hierarchy and less distinction between white collars and blue collars.
- Functional "silos" will become obsolete. The classical functions of marketing, manufacturing, engineering, finance, and personnel will be less important in defining work. More people will take on "project" work focused on continuous improvement of one kind or another.
- Fundamental restructuring, meaning much more than financial restructuring, will become a way of life in manufacturing enterprises. The primary focal points will be a new market-driven emphasis on creating value with customers, as well as greatly increased flexibility, a new business-driven attack on global markets which includes new deployment of information technology, and fundamentally new jobs.

- Work will become much more integrated in its orientation. The payoffs will increasingly be made through connections across organizational and company boundaries. Included are customer and vendor partnerships, with an overall focus on improving the value-added chain.
- New measurements that focus on the new strategic directions will be required. Metrics will be developed, similar to the cost of quality metric, that incorporate the most important dimensions of the environment. Similar metrics and semantics will be developed to support the new uses of information technology.
- New ''people management'' approaches will be developed. Teamwork will be critical to organizational success. Human resource management will become less of a ''staff'' function and more closely integrated with the basic work.

Many of these prognostications are already a reality. APICS has made the commitment to *leading* the way in all of these change areas. The decision was both courageous and intelligent. There is no future for a professional society not committed to leading-edge education for its members. Based on the Society's past experience with the Certification in Production and Inventory Management (CPIM) program, the natural thrust of APICS was to develop a new certification program focusing on integration. The result, Certification in Integrated Resource Management (CIRM) is a program composed of 13 building block areas which have been combined into four examination modules, as follows:

Customers and products
    Marketing and sales
    Field service
    Product design and development

Manufacturing processes
    Industrial facilities management
    Process design and development
    Manufacturing (production)

Logistics
    Production and inventory control
    Procurement
    Distribution

Support functions
    Total quality management

Human resources
Finance and accounting
Information systems

As can be seen from this topical list, one objective in the CIRM program is to develop educational breadth. Managers increasingly *must* know the underlying basics in each area of the business: who are the people who work there, what are day-to-day *and* strategic problems, what is state-of-the-art practice, what are the expected improvement areas, and what is happening with technology? This basic breadth of knowledge is an absolute prerequisite to understanding the potential linkages and joint improvements.

But it is the linkages, relationships, and integration that are even more important. Each examination devotes approximately 40 percent of the questions to the connections *among* the 13 building block areas. In fact, after a candidate has successfully completed the four examination modules, he or she must take a fifth examination (Integrated Enterprise Management), which focuses solely on the interrelationships among all functional areas of an enterprise.

The CIRM program has been the most exciting activity on which I have worked in a professional organization. Increasingly, manufacturing companies face the alternative of either proactive restructuring to deal with today's competitive realities, or just sliding away—giving up market share and industry leadership. Education must play a key role in making the necessary changes. People working in manufacturing companies need to learn many new things and "unlearn" many old ones.

There were very limited educational materials available to support CIRM. There were textbooks in which basic concepts were covered and bits and pieces which dealt with integration, but there simply was no coordinated set of materials available for this program. That has been the job of the CIRM series authors, and it has been my distinct pleasure as series editor to help develop the ideas and facilitate our joint learning. All of us have learned a great deal, and I am delighted with every book in the series. But the spirit of continuous improvement is built into the CIRM program and into the book series. The next editions will be even better!

Thomas E. Vollmann
Series Editor

ACKNOWLEDGMENTS

This book is about improving performance and morale in organizations. It is a summary of many years of research and consulting trying to help organizations and people not only improve performance but learn and grow from the experience. Some of what is in this book summarizes what is available in other books about human resource management, but from a managerial perspective. Some of the material comes from research and consulting in organizations. The research has been supported by The Manufacturing Roundtable and the Executive Development Roundtable at Boston University. Both are unique organizations that combine the research skills of the academic with the drive for usable answers of the executive. They, along with my associations with human resource professionals through the Human Resources Policy Institute, also at Boston University, have become my source of professional development and truly one of the great pleasures of my work. In addition I have had the opportunity to serve as Executive Director of the Leadership Institute at Boston University. This gives us a chance to share with a broader community what we learn from our research. Much of what is included in this book is a result of the interactions, presentations, challenges, and guidance of my colleagues from the university and the corporations involved in the rountables and institutes at Boston University. It is a much more valuable and usable book because of them.

I also have the opportunity to work with tremendous professionals and support staff. Tanya Phillips organizes and manages my many writing projects. Without her very litte would get done on time. Victoria Selden manages the office; without her juggling none of the many balls would stay in the air. Margret Fischer, ably serving as Director of the Leadership Institute, makes it possible to share our knowledge with wonderful groups of executives. Others who have been crititcal to the research and writing are Holly Fowler and Amy Wetzel.

To them I owe my thanks. I, of course, am responsible for the final product.

I have dedicated this book to my wife and children. Coleen is truly a manager of human resources. Raising ten kids—our nine children plus she counts me as one of the kids—while at the same time completing her graduate work, pursuing her professional art career, writing and publishing children's books, teaching university classes, and serving in the community and church are clear testimonies of her management capability.

Lloyd S. Baird

CONTENTS

CHAPTER 1

PEOPLE AS A BASIC RESOURCE

INTRODUCTION

Operating managers face unprecedented advances in technology, information, and knowledge. Customers demand change constantly. Competition is no longer with someone across the street, but with someone around the world. The demographics of the work force are shifting so quickly that management practices and systems need constant update. Combined, these forces create challenges that can only be met if we recognize the importance of people as a basic resource in the production process. Old assumptions that regard people as instantaneously available in whatever quantities with whatever skills needed are no longer valid. Human resources must be planned and managed with the same care and attention given to technological, material, and financial resources. Those who understand the critical role of human resources and adopt management practices that fit the new environments they face will have sustainable competitive advantages. Let us consider the changing management environment we face and its implications for management practices.

Demographic Trends

America's population is changing dramatically. On average, an American woman gives birth to 1.8 children during her lifetime, down from 3.7 in the 1950s, at the height of the baby boom. A birth rate of 2.1 is necessary to sustain a steady population if the country has no immigration. If the United States is to grow at all, the shortfall must be made up by immigration from other countries.

1

These population demographics have created a bulge of workers currently in their late 30s and 40s, mostly white males who have been working for 15–20 years and are looking for further promotion up the organization hierarchy. Promotions are not likely to come as fast as they expect because ahead of them are workers in their 40s and 50s who have 20 to 30 years left before retirement—if they ever retire.

The ethnic and racial mix of employees is also changing dramatically. Minority populations will grow seven times faster than the population as a whole. This is because in general, minority populations are younger than the U.S. population and because minorities continue to immigrate. In 1990, one in every four Americans is nonwhite. By the year 2000, one in three Americans will be African-American, Hispanic, Asian, or Native American.

We are already seeing these trends in the work force and they are having dramatic effects on the practices of management.

- Fewer young U.S. citizens are entering the American work force; instead, their places in entry level positions are being taken by immigrants for whom English is not the native language.
- An increased number of people over the age of 50 are in the work force. This will provide a rich reservoir of experience, but it also means those over 50 will remain in their positions for many more years, blocking the promotion potential of others.

Increasing the challenges of management are other trends that help create a more heterogeneous work force:

- Women of all ages are joining the work force. In addition to younger women who are choosing careers outside the home, women whose children are grown are also entering the work force.
- An increased number of two-career couples are making joint career decisions. Opportunities must be made available for both before career changes are made.

At the same time that immigrants are filling the ranks of entry level positions, the domestic work force is becoming more educated. This is both an advantage and a challenge. The advantage is that more can be expected from the work force; the challenge is that such employees will expect more from management and from their work experience. The following tendencies increase the complexity of management:

- The level of education of the domestic American work force is projected to increase. Although the potential of the immigrant population is great, their education level is expected to remain low, creating a great disparity between different population groups.
- The number of college graduates is projected to exceed the number of starting jobs for which they are qualified by 20 percent. Consequently, there will be a large proportion of the population who will be overqualified for their jobs.
- Because of the advances in education and the aging work force, if present trends continue, fully one fourth of all working Americans are expected to be overqualified for the jobs they hold.

These demographic projections raise numerous questions that future operating managers will have to answer:

- How do we attract college graduates into jobs in which promotions will not be rapid because older workers still hold higher level positions?
- How do we deal with the excess number of managers the baby boom has generated? Many of them now hold middle level management positions and are expecting promotions.
- What programs do we put in place to help the less qualified but often highly motivated immigrant population gain the skills they need to function at the level their jobs demand?

Value Changes

Economic and social conditions affect the expectations and values people bring to work. Consequently, the new generation of workers is likely to be different from past generations in the following ways:

- People will tend to have more options to choose from and make their choices more often based on individual desires, preferences, and circumstances.
- Based on their advanced training, and on what they have seen other people accomplish, educated workers have very high expectations of what they should receive from work.
- People will place higher value on free time.
- If organizations continue traditional management practices and methods for organizing the work process, people are likely to

grow discontent with the corporate world's ability to deliver the goods and services they want and to provide the work environments they expect.

These changes in values and expectations will lead to the following questions managers will have to answer in the future.

- What values do we need in the organization? Should we hire only persons who have values matching our organization or should we emphasize flexibility, change, and diversity to accommodate many different values?
- What should we do to accommodate the growing importance people place on leisure and flexibility in their schedule without sacrificing the old values of security and predictability?
- How should we organize our activities to match the many diverse values that people bring to the organization?

Socioeconomic Changes

Socioeconomic changes are also having a tremendous impact on organizations. These changes are beyond management's control, but will require management's attention to cope with them productively. Managers must monitor, understand, and adjust to the following changes:

- Increased government regulation of all forms of economic and social activity, such as labor laws, health requirements, and environmental regulations.
- Slower economic growth due to the lack of growth in the population and the need to conserve resources.
- Political instability caused by the massive changes that are now taking place in Eastern Europe and what was formerly the U.S.S.R., plus the continuing dependence of the United States on foreign sources for energy.
- Depletion of our natural resources and the forced need to conserve and prioritize our use of these resources.

As a result of these changes, managers must be prepared to deal with the following questions:

- What effect is the changing economic environment likely to have on our ability to recruit, relocate, train, and develop employees?

- What implications will a slower economic growth rate have for our human resource management (HRM) practices?
- What are the implications of our continuing dependence on other countries for energy on the way we will produce in the future?

Information and Technology Changes

Of all the factors that will affect human resource management in the future, none is changing faster than information and technology. Peter Drucker, for example, describes a shift from control-based to information-based organizations largely devoid of middle management.[1] Knowledge to make informed business decisions will reside primarily at the bottom of the organization in the hands of specialists who direct their own work. Information will be issued for self-guidance, not top-down control. There will be greater reliance on self-discipline and individual responsibility.

Technology will transform the nature of work and challenge employees to use skills they have never had to use before. Relationships between managers and employees will be more intricate and collaborative. Authority will depend more on knowledge than on hierarchical position. As computers integrate information across organizational units, managers and employees will have an opportunity to overcome their narrow unit focus and adopt an overriding concern for the customer. As a result, we can predict the following:

- An increased number of computers that are both faster and cheaper will be used at work and at home.
- Computers and electronic aids will be used in new fields such as education, banking, food purchasing, and home management.
- Office work will become increasingly automated.
- Robots will take over an increasing amount of the boring and monotonous work humans now do.
- Increasingly more time will be spent by both managers and workers on integrating and linking the organization.

These technological and informational advances raise important questions to be addressed by future human resource managers.

---

[1]Peter F. Drucker, "The Coming of the New Organization," *Harvard Business Review,* (January-February 1988) (1), pp. 45–54.

- Which jobs will be eliminated and which should be expanded as a result of technological advances?
- How can we design work for people at home?
- How can we maintain our organization's culture as we go through massive technological changes?
- How can we use robots and automation to improve the quality of work life in our organizations?
- What effect will technological change have on human relations?

Manufacturing Changes

In addition to all these changes, manufacturing organizations are facing unique challenges that will demand new approaches for human resource management. Organizations will become more and more market driven. Manufacturing organizations will be under increasing pressure to produce a wide range of products and be able to customize to customer demands. Global competition will mean that in order to be world class, manufacturing will have to stay current with developments around the world as well as across the street. Continuing financial pressure will force a constant search for efficiency. Competitive pressures will demand ever decreasing time from product development to market introduction. Combined, these forces mean manufacturing organizations will be faced with the following challenges:

- A need to continually improve the production process.
- Pressure to speed up production.
- A requirement to establish mechanisms for monitoring and benchmarking the manufacturing function and processes in other organizations.
- The need to be flexible and adaptable to customer needs, to be able to produce long runs in some products and simultaneously customize others.
- To be able to constantly update production processes to meet ever increasing performance and quality demands.

These pressures rouse interesting human resource management questions:

- How can workers be involved and committed to continuous improvement?

- How can employees' skills be constantly updated to match new production processes?
- How can employees be trained and developed so they have the flexibility to quickly adjust and learn new operating requirements?
- How can a culture of flexibility, adaptability, and risk taking be implemented?
- How should employees be managed so they can take action and quickly solve problems?
- What can be done to get people to constantly stay tuned into not only the customers but what competitors and other organizations are doing to improve the production process?

THE HISTORY OF HUMAN RESOURCE MANAGEMENT

These forces of change create a complex and dynamic world; a world where decisions must be made quickly and implemented competently. It is a world where management of human resources becomes part of everyone's job, most importantly part of the operating manager's job. There is no time to wait for a centralized staff group to tell us what to do. Indeed, any staff group by the very nature of its work will be removed from the day-to-day human resource decisions that must be made to deliver high-quality results on time. The chief human resource managers must be the line operating managers. They are closest to the action and know what needs to be done. Of course, staff groups can provide needed expertise, but line managers are responsible   for understanding current human resource management practices and delivering results. The best way to understand the tools, programs, and procedures available to manage human resources is to review how they were developed. We will then suggest an integrated model that builds on past practices and will serve as a way of answering and managing the complex questions we have posed.

Early Organizations

Management of society and organizations in ancient Rome 2000 years ago is a good example of how early organizations managed people. Management of people was based on several assumptions. First, the Romans assumed that work could best be done by people who were specialists trained in one set of responsibilities. As a result, transportation, government, supplies and materials, military protection, and crafts became the responsibility of groups who were experts in their respective areas. Organizations were structured to create jobs specialists could be trained to do.

Second, management's job was to coordinate the work of the specialists. Coordination was done through an organizational hierarchy in which each person reported to a supervisor, who reported to a manager, who in turn reported to an executive. This formed a chain of command through which all communication and coordination was done. Goldsmiths, couriers, brass workers, potters, soldiers, and flute players each did their assigned jobs. The manager coordinated their work so that the overall objectives of the organizations could be accomplished.

Third, managers were responsible for motivating people to do the jobs they were assigned. Naturally, people would not do the job unless rewards and punishments gave them reasons to work. Managers motivated people by controlling the rewards and punishments subordinates received for performing their jobs. These elements of human resource management—specialization by skill, coordination through hierarchy, and motivation by reward and punishment—prevailed throughout the Middle Ages and into the Industrial Revolution.

The Industrial Revolution

In the early 1800s, Western Europe and North America began to change from agricultural to industrial societies. Prior to the Industrial Revolution, the home and family farm were the centers of activity. Human resource management was done by mom and dad. Small groups of people worked cooperatively in small cottage industries and the family farm produced much of what they consumed. During the 1800s, machinery and factories began to take over the production of goods and services. Factories could produce faster and cheaper than the small home production systems. To run the machinery and the factories, people were brought together and organized according to the traditional principles of human resource management.

When implemented, these principles forced changes in the way work was done. Now, professional managers were needed to coordinate the work of specialists. Because people had to work together, they had to be available to work at a predictable time. Flexible schedules were not possible. Everyone came to work at the same time and went home at the same time. Work was standardized to produce predictable results. Rigorous work rules were established for employees. In contrast to the farm and cottage where everyone worked together and no real social distinctions existed, hierarchies were established in which foremen, supervisors, managers, and executives had to coordinate the work of many people. This increased social distance between people in the organization.

This mode of operation was efficient, but the factory work brought with it such problems as long hours, low wages, child labor, monotony, boredom, and alienation—problems that resulted from the nature of factory work. Rather than training people in crafts and having them work in small groups doing projects from beginning to end, people now operated complex machines, did repetitive work, and were responsible for only a small part of any project.

During this period, labor was viewed as a commodity to be bought, used, and then discarded when it could no longer contribute to the organization. People worked long hours under extremely noisy and dirty conditions. Employees worked an average of 75 hours per week in the United States and 69 hours in England. The long hours and dirty conditions were probably not dramatically different from conditions on the farm or cottage. The difference was that employees lost their flexibility, their control over their own time, their autonomy to make decisions, and the satisfaction of working with close friends and family. They now worked with and for strangers in a controlled environment away from home.

Many practices we consider inhumane today were common during this period. Slavery and indentured servitude were often used to obtain a work force. Some people bound themselves as servants to do whatever their masters wanted for an average of four years, in return for money to pay for their passage to the New World. Among these indentured servants were many of the carpenters, masons, printers, shipbuilders, tailors, and others who were to become master craftspeople. Their experience and expertise made the Industrial Revolution possible. Others came unwillingly in slave ships. Forced from their homes and families, they became the labor force to replace the farm workers who had left. They also took on the undesirable factory jobs.

Children were another source of labor in the factories. They were paid cheap wages and worked long hours. In the coal mines of England, adult miners worked 9 to 11 hours a day and the children worked 14 to 15 hours. In 1829, boys seven and older were employed in Philadelphia factories from daylight until 8 P.M. Child labor was the first abuse of human resources where government began taking an active role. In the early 1800s, both the United States and Britain passed laws forbidding the employment of children under the age of 9 and restricted the hours of older children.

To protect themselves against exploitation, workers banded together in associations to demand better working conditions and higher wages. Initially, these associations or unions met with heavy resistance. In 1806, the cordwainers in Philadelphia were found guilty of criminal conspiracy in their attempts to improve working conditions and raise wages. The Conspiracy Doctrine prohibiting collective action by workers became the law of the land. It was not until 1842 that the Conspiracy Doctrine was overturned and unions were permitted to strike for higher wages. And strike they did. Toward the end of the century, the strikes became violent and often ended in bloodshed.

Scientific Management

From the Industrial Revolution emerged scientific management, which focused on machinery and technology. In the late 1800s and early 1900s, machines dominated the workplace. The challenge in managing people was to help them work as well as possible with machines. Scientific management made the production of goods more efficient by finding the single most efficient way of performing various operations and then making sure workers employed those methods. The most famous person associated with scientific management was Frederick W. Taylor. Taylor was an engineer initially interested in improving the production of steel. He referred to the four underlying principles of management:[2]

1. The development of a true science: The systematic observation, classification, and tabulation of jobs as they are carried out, and then the dividing of the job to be done into the simplest components that could be done by one person.
2. The scientific selection of the workers: Select people with the skills and capacities necessary to carry out efficiently the simple components into which the job was now divided.

---

[2]For a full discussion of principles of scientific management see Fredrick W. Taylor, *Principles of Scientific Management*, (New York: Harper & Row, 1911).

3. The worker's scientific education and development: Train the worker how to do the job the best way. Do not allow workers to develop their own way of doing the job; rather, teach them the best way to do the job, which has been developed from the systematic observation of other people doing the same work.

4. Intimate, friendly cooperation between the management and the worker: Coordinate the worker and the manager. The manager is to plan and organize the work. The worker is to do the job as planned and organized. To be successful, both must understand and cooperate with the other.

Others were also well known for their contributions to the scientific analysis and organizing of jobs. Frank and Lillian Gilbreth made extensive use of motion pictures to record and analyze body movements as people worked. Observing the pictures, they could then develop efficient ways of moving the body so work was done faster and easier. Henry Gantt was Frederick Taylor's assistant during the time he was working at the Midvale and Bethlehem steel plants. Gantt is most known for a chart he developed to coordinate activities so that production schedules could be met, appropriately referred to as the Gantt chart.

Scientific management was the dominating approach to managing people until 1910–20, when managers began to notice that the ''one best way'' did not always work. Many of the problems in organizations and the constraints on production were coming from employees being forced into standardized work. They became bored and many fought back by reducing production and destroying equipment.

Industrial Psychology

The failures of scientific management brought about a recognition of the importance of the individual, the foundation of industrial psychology. An early industrial psychologist who focused on understanding and measuring individual employees so they could be properly placed and trained to perform their jobs was Hugo Munsterberg. He was an experimental psychologist and physician at Harvard University who applied what he knew from these fields to the recruiting, selecting, and training of workers. His most notable contributions were methods for analyzing jobs in terms of their mental and emotional requirements and development of testing devised to help people perform their jobs better.

An example of Munsterberg's work was his experiments in the telephone industry.[3] The work at the switchboards was tedious and fatiguing. Munsterberg constructed a series of tests on space perception, intelligence, and dexterity with a group of switchboard operators and found that those who performed well on the test were also better performers on the job. The conclusion was that the test could be administered to job applicants before they were hired and those who scored well would be the ones hired because they would most likely do better on the job.

Industrial psychologists during this period devoted much of their time to developing tests measuring the mental and physical ability differences among people. World War I provided tremendous impetus to their effort as the military used more and more tests to evaluate recruits to place them in the proper jobs. This was also the period of time when personnel professionals began to emerge, helping managers with such matters as recruiting, safety, training, and health. Usually, there would be no formal personnel department, but these specialists would work directly for managers.

Although industrial psychology shifted the focus of human resource management to the individual, most of the tools and techniques of this period were still oriented toward improving technical efficiency. It was not until the human relations era that the focus shifted from technology to the needs and concerns of individuals.

Human Relations

The human relations approach to managing human resources developed from the interest in people begun by industrial psychology. If engineering the job and then fitting the people to it was not working, then maybe management could improve productivity by determining what people wanted out of work and engineering jobs to fit them. The human relations approach emphasized improving relationships between supervisors and subordinates and between employees and their peers. Management recognized the existence of an informal organization controlled by employees that influenced much of what happened in the organization.

---

[3]Hugo Munsterberg, *Psychology and Industrial Efficiency* (Boston: Houghton Mifflin, 1913).

The human relations era began in the mid 1920s when Elton Mayo, Fritz Roethlisberger, T. North Whitehead, and others at the Harvard Business School were testing the effect of the physical work environment on productivity at the Hawthorne Works of Western Electric in Chicago.[4] Their hypothesis was that lighting and ventilation were directly related to productivity, and that if they could determine the proper amount of each, productivity would increase. In their research, they found that social factors such as group pressure, informal group norms, relationships with supervisors, and other social factors played as much a role in productivity as the physical environment. The motto of this period became "a happy worker is a productive worker." Hence, the focus of management became keeping workers happy.

During this period, formal personnel departments emerged, and with them, increasing emphasis on wages, compensation, benefits to provide for illness, and vacations. Personnel specialists who could develop and implement personnel programs in each of these areas were added to a centralized personnel staff that reported to top management.

Quality of Work Life

In the 1960s after 40 years of dominance by the human relations movement, managers began to realize that the solution to productivity problems did not lie in either the job or the employee, but in a combination of the two. This is referred to as the quality of work life era. During this period, managers endeavored to improve productivity by: (1) restructuring the production process, (2) increasing technical efficiency, (3) selecting or modifying the person to achieve a better job-person fit, and (4) improving human relationships at work.

During this period, government began to exert tremendous pressure on employers to improve the environment within which people worked. Federal laws emphasizing the importance of equal employment opportunity (Civil Rights Act), safety and health (Occupational Safety and Health Act), and the protection of retirement income (Employee Retirement Income Security Act) were passed. At the same time, government was using the laws to affect the nature of work. Employers began to encourage

---

[4]For a summary of their work see F. J. Roethlisberger and W. J. Dickson, *Management and the Worker* (Cambridge, Mass.: Harvard University Press, 1939).

quality circles, productivity improvement programs, quality of work life projects, worker participation programs, and worker councils, all focused on getting the worker involved in solving the productivity problems of organizations. Managers became concerned about both the job and the worker and saw productivity as the result of properly matched jobs and people.

Strategic Human Resources Management

Current demographic, socioeconomic, and technological changes will require new approaches to the management of human resources. Today, we are moving from an industrial society to a service-oriented society. The new industries and products that are likely to emerge will require that organizations work with people in innovative ways.

As we move into a service- and information-based society, the management of human resources will take on added significance. We must anticipate the contributions people can make to our products and services and structure organizations in such as way as to encourage their input. The demands for quick response, quality, and flexibility will require us to organize in project teams, cross-functional work groups, product development groups, task forces, and quality circles. We will have to be constantly concerned with integrating other functional departments and units. These forces combine to create a dynamic and fast-moving environment in which employees will demand much more sophistication in the practices and procedures that manage them.

In the past, human resource programs and procedures could be applied similarly in most organizations with minor modifications. As organizations and employees become more diverse, however, we will have to tailor our programs to fit the unique needs of both the employee and the organization. Also, as organizations and employees change, programs and procedures must also change. We will have to anticipate and prepare for future changes and design programs that will accommodate them. This suggests that we will have to adopt a strategic orientation.

Being strategic means understanding the needs of the business and using those needs as the basis of all personnel practices and procedures. It means that these practices and procedures must fit both the employees and the organization and be able to accommodate change in either. Strategic human resource management also means managers participate fully in developing and implementing the systems to manage people with an eye to productivity and organizational accomplishment. The operating manager becomes the driving force behind good human resource practices.

Adopting a Management Perspective

This book is written to help you manage people in the complex future we all face. Human resource management is becoming more a part of every manager's job, as it should be. We support the increasing status and involvement of all managers in the management of human resources. Everyone will need to develop people management skills and understand how to manage the programs, practices, and procedures on which good human resource management is built. Managers must become more involved in managing the most valuable resource they have and at the same time personnel professionals must become better able to help develop and implement the practices, programs, and procedures that managers can easily and effectively use to manage human resources to meet business needs.

In this book, we will cover both the skills you will personally need to manage human resources and the practices, programs, and procedures that organizations must develop to help effectively manage human resources. When discussing both, we will adopt a management perspective. By management perspective we simply mean that personnel programs, procedures, skills, and activities are all managed to accomplish organizational and unit objectives. Naturally, then, the objective determines how human resources are managed.

A MODEL OF HUMAN RESOURCE MANAGEMENT

There is a natural flow of human resource management, beginning with the objectives or purpose of the organization or unit, that we can use to organize our thinking and this book. Figure 1–1 presents a model of the flow. The model is not meant to indicate that the activities must follow step by step exactly the sequence presented in the model. Rather, it is presented as a model for organization. The book will follow the flow in the model. As an introduction to the book, let us review the model. The chapters in the book match the topics in the model.

FIGURE 1–1
A Managerial Perspective to Human Resource Management

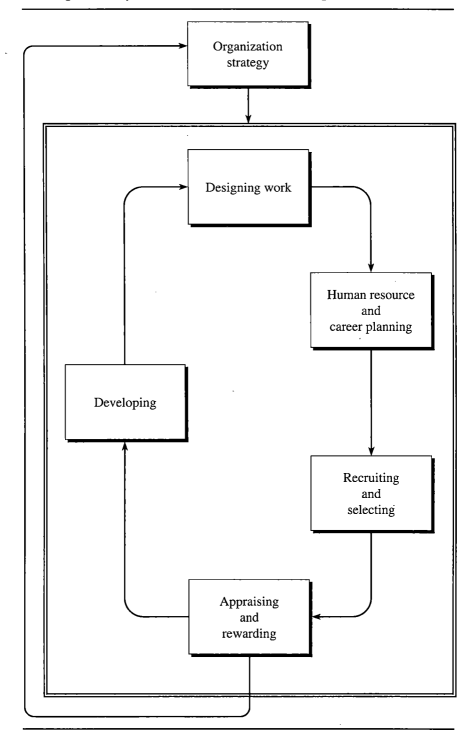

Organization Strategy

To be successful, human resource management must meet the needs of the organization. It is logical, then, for human resource management to start by understanding those needs. Human resource management practices, procedures, and programs are developed, implemented, and managed to help the organization accomplish its purposes and reach its objectives. Organizations that are growing very quickly need help recruiting and training employees to sustain their growth. Organizations that are in stable markets, with products and services well established, need help becoming more efficient by cutting costs and increasing productivity. Organizations that are shrinking need help retraining and reducing the labor force. And as the strategy of the organization shifts dramatically, as it is doing today, it is logical to assume human resource management practices and procedures must also shift. No matter what the strategy, human resource management has a vital role to play, but only managers and personnel professionals who understand the unique needs of the organization created by the organization's objectives and strategy will be effective.

Designing Work

Based on what needs to be done and the results to be accomplished, jobs can be designed to be productive and motivational. Jobs exist to accomplish objectives; therefore, job design should be based on those objectives. How people do their work and whether it is motivational and productive is determined by the activities of the workers, the resources and technology they have to work with, and the relationship the job has with other jobs. Each of these components must be designed so that it contributes to performance on the job. Simultaneously, jobs must be designed considering the unique educational, cultural, and experience background of available workers. As the nature of the work force changes, the nature of jobs must also change.

Human Resource and Career Planning

To implement human resource management, plans must be developed that take into account the jobs to be done and the availability of skilled workers to do them. These plans are the basis for developing, implementing, and evaluating personnel, programs, and procedures. Plans provide a prediction of the future and identify what must be done to prepare for it, both from the organization's perspective (human resource planning) and individual's perspective (career planning).

Recruiting and Selecting

The organization must have people to do the jobs designed. To be productive, the people hired by the organization must have the skills necessary to perform the job or the ability to learn those skills that fit. It will be your responsibility as a manager to find people who can perform the job and convince them to accept employment in your organization. You will base your decisions entirely on performance and not use race, sex, national origin, or religion in recruiting and selecting.

Appraising and Rewarding

What is accomplished is productive if it contributes to the purposes of the organization. Evaluation makes possible adjustments and improvements if employees' efforts are not being directed toward the right results and recognition where performance is good. Evaluation identifies training and development that can increase performance. Only by knowing what has been accomplished in relation to performance goals can future performance be managed.

Appraisal and feedback is the basis of all human resource/personnel activities. Information from appraisals provides managers with an understanding of problems and opportunities. It gives them the data to evaluate how successfully they are managing human resources and what changes need to be made. Appraisals provide employees with explanations of the jobs they have to do and how well they are doing.

Developing

Once deficiencies in skills have been identified, training and development activities and programs can be designed. In modern organizations, development is a continuous activity because the needed skills are constantly changing. Development activities can range from experiences designed into jobs, so that people learn as they do their jobs, to formal training programs held at schools and universities. Which you choose should be determined by what skills and abilities need to be developed. The needed skills and abilities in turn affect how the work should be designed.

THE MANAGEMENT CHALLENGE

How do all these changes affect you, the manager? They mean that now, more than ever before, your ability to manage people will make the difference between success and failure. Human resource management is everyone's job. To the extent that you understand the programs and procedures available to you, the better you will be able to help your people contribute to accomplishing organizational objectives. Human resource management is not a set of independent activities done by some staff group. Human resource management is a set of very integrated practices, procedures, and programs for which you, the manager, are responsible. In the remainder of this book, we will describe programs in each of the areas we have identified: designing work, human resource planning and forecasting, recruiting and selecting, appraising and rewarding, and developing. In each section, we will provide examples of how the programs are designed and give you suggestions on how they can be used and show you how they relate to other human resource management programs and functional activities.

CHAPTER 2

CASE 1   FROST INC.: USING HUMAN RESOURCE MANAGEMENT PRACTICES TO IMPLEMENT ORGANIZATION STRATEGY*

INTRODUCTION

Frost Inc., of Grand Rapids, Michigan, a metalworking company with just under 120 employees, has undertaken what may well be the most ambitious high-tech revitalization program of any smaller, old-line manufacturer in the United States. Very early in the program, Frost recognized that a new approach to human resource management was vital to the implementation of its new high-tech strategy. In implementing its organization objectives, Frost Inc. used each of the program areas of human resource management. They are presented here as an example of how one organization used its human resources to implement a successful organization strategy.

The Organizational Objective

Frost Inc. was founded by C. L. Frost in 1913 as a manufacturer of brass furniture hardware. After World War II, when the furniture industry moved to the South, Frost switched to making overhead conveyor trolleys,

---

*Adapted with permission from Steven P. Galante, ''Frost Inc.: Technological Renewal and Human Resource Management: A Case Study,'' *Human Resource Planning* 10, no. 1, pp. 57–67.

primarily for the auto industry. This business prospered through the 1950s and 60s, but then started to slow down. It was given new impetus after 1969, when Charles C. "Chad" Frost, the great-grandson of the founder, joined the company shortly after graduating with an engineering degree from the University of Michigan. Today, Chad Frost, 42, is president and controlling stockholder of Frost and the prime mover behind the company's revitalization effort.

As Frost explains it, the need to renovate the company grew out of several failed attempts to diversify during the 1970s. Frost initially tried to diversify manufacturing and began making components for lawn mowers, but the parts required greater manufacturing precision than Frost could muster and the company consistently missed delivery dates. The effort was dropped after two years. Then, in 1979, Frost tried to diversify horizontally by applying its ability to manufacture overhead conveyor trolleys to other types of material-handling systems such as roller conveyors, floor conveyors, lift trucks, hoists, and elevators. "It was a total failure," Frost says. "Every time we'd try to make a new product, we screwed up." Production people didn't know how to make a new product and salespeople didn't know how to sell it. "It would just collapse every time," he says. "By 1980, it was a disaster."

Meanwhile, the pressure to diversify was growing more acute. Though the conveyor trolley business was still growing nicely, "we had such a high share of such a small market niche, there was nowhere else to grow," Frost says. By 1981, Frost had record sales of $17.5 million and approximately 55 percent of the market for overhead conveyor trolleys. However, signs of a severe recession were appearing on the horizon. "We were showing huge profits at the bottom," says Frost, "yet we were all standing there knowing we were about to be bludgeoned." The expectation proved to be all too accurate. Frost's sales plunged to $11 million in 1982 and $9.2 in 1983.

Frost and his managers resolved to bring the company out of the recession in a new form. "We determined we had to learn to do business in a different way," Frost states. They first diagnosed the problem that had prevented the company from diversifying as inflexibility. "We had single-purpose machines and single-purpose people," Frost says, adding for emphasis, "including single-purpose managers." Frost decided automating production was the key to flexibility. After studying several options, the company decided the automation project would consist of three parts:

1. Eleven numerically controlled machine tools paired with 18 industrial robots, which would replace 26 old-fashioned screw machines on the factory floor.

2. An automated storage-and-retrieval inventory control system, which Frost would design and build for itself and later sell as a proprietary product.

3. Complete automation of the front office to reduce indirect labor costs.

Human Resources Hold the Key

But what at first glance appeared to be a hardware-oriented strategy in fact turned out to be an exercise in human resource management. Two factors explain this. One, an enormous amount of personnel reorganization and training were required to make the automation project work. And two, Chad Frost had in mind nothing less than completely reshaping the company's culture.

Frost announced the automation project to his employees at an event called ''Benefair'' on October 1, 1983, the beginning of the company's fiscal year. The plant was closed, and employees and spouses were invited to a company party at the local Holiday Inn where Chad announced the revitalization program.

Soon after the 1983 Benefair announcement, employees were brought into the program with the formation of an employee task force to select computerized numerically controlled machine tools. By December, employees were attending classes on how to use advanced machinery. Frost talked about the reasons for getting employees involved quickly:

> The very first time that people begin to understand and realize that things are going to change, and that there are going to be different capability requirements and numbers of people, is during the equipment-selection process. And when people are a part of that, in a task force, that really brings it home fast.

A couple of things were said. Number one, ''We are going to be the most automated small- to medium-sized company in the country.'' Statement. Pow! Number two, ''Each and every individual inside the company today is going to have the opportunity made available to them to become educated and highly skilled in a new way of doing their work. And those new ways will be leading-edge and should carry them for several years within their career and help them." Personal enhancement. And number three, "We will do everything in our power to help those people who elect not to go forward with us by providing as much reasonable outside placement help as possible."

Human Resource and Career Planning

Those remarks hint at several premises that were implicit in the automation project. Perhaps the most emotional one was that, despite Frost's obvious desire to create an atmosphere in which every employee's contribution had an impact, the ranks of Frost Inc. still would shrink. The company's payroll had already declined to around 145 employees by October 1983 from 180 before the recession. Those initial personnel cuts were made the old-fashioned way, through layoffs and attrition. But the business plan Frost prepared in advance of the automation program called for further reductions. Most of the positions to be eliminated, interestingly enough, were not on the factory floor but in the front office and other support areas. Employment at Frost currently stands at about 120 people. The company estimates 35 people opted for outplacement, with the departures partly offset by new hirings.

The employees who took outplacement fell into three categories, according to Frost: people who didn't want to undertake the extensive retraining needed, upper managers who weren't comfortable with the company's new emphasis on a less hierarchical structure, and others who sought elsewhere the advancement they didn't expect to find inside the "new" Frost. "What that implies," Frost says, "is that you've got to get prepared personally as the CEO for a little rejection. Your neat idea isn't going to be neat for everybody. You can't take rejection of the technology or the direction of the company personally. Be prepared to help people who want out to find new jobs. That's critical to the success of the project."

The need for a net reduction in staffing reflects a key premise underlying Frost's remarks: Lean operating levels are an essential part of the culture Frost is creating. "There's an ongoing process here that says "We're going to try to do it with as few people as possible," according to McIntyre. One reason for that is the need to attain financial targets that had been determined at the outset as necessary to justify the project's expense. A key measure is sales per employee, which has jumped to almost $200,000 from $80,000 before the launch.

But a second reason for wanting to attain lean operating levels was to achieve employment stability. Says McIntyre:

> When you go through this in a small company, one of the single greatest assets is something called a person. And what you don't want to have to do is get rid of assets when you have a downturn, and then try and go find other people and make them assets in an upturn. You want to have a core group of people who are highly trained. And when you get through with this at Frost, they are super highly trained, and well educated, and highly motivated. So what you want to have is a company like Frost that is running, for example, seven days a week, 24 hours a day. Comes an economic downturn, you keep the same number of people and you run five days a week, or whatever. You turn the faucet down a little.

Designing Work

To help implement the new organization strategy, Frost hired Gary Weeden as director of human resources. When Weeden arrived in October 1984, he found little in the way of formal job descriptions. So, he says, "one of the things I did when I came on board was to review all of the functions that were being performed in the organization and all the functions that should be or needed to be performed in the organization, and then [I] started to evaluate the individuals that were performing those functions." The task was helpful in two ways. First, it quickly familiarized Weeden with the structure of the company, the jobs that were performed, and who performed them. And second, Weeden was able to begin designing new job descriptions based on the skills, knowledge, and abilities that would be needed as Frost went deeper and deeper into the automation project.

In fact, Weeden wasn't working entirely without a blueprint. Long before he arrived, an outside consultant had carefully modeled exactly what positions and functions were going to be required inside the completely automated company. According to Chad Frost, Weeden's biggest contribution in this area was developing transitional job descriptions as the company evolved.

A complete overhaul of the company hierarchy accompanied the redrafting of job functions. Previously, according to McIntyre, Frost had 11 specific management levels, which expanded to 17 if "implied" management tiers were counted. "How does everything get done quickly or effectively," he asked, "if some poor guy working out in the factory who wants to get a decision made has to go through 17 layers of management, each manager passing the decision up?" Moreover, he says, the people who had the best information at Frost generally were not the ones who made the decisions.

The solution was to "flatten" the management hierarchy to four explicit levels and "maybe six implied" levels. All 12 department heads under the former structure participated in making that decision, though, Frost notes, "not everybody agreed." Four of the ones who disagreed subsequently left Frost, including the heads of the accounting, quality control, and data processing departments.

The four explicit management tiers under the new structure are the chief executive (Chad Frost), four "area managers," 33 office and functional managers, and the approximately 82 employee-shareholders. The four area managers are in charge of external operations (sales, purchasing, etc.), internal operations (production, quality control, telecommunications), finance, and human resources. A functional manager may manage people, as a manager is usually defined, or CNC machines or other equipment.

To ensure that anyone making a decision has sufficient information, Frost made all the company's information available to everyone. Scattered throughout the facility, both in the front office and on the factory floor, are more than 40 computer terminals linked to the company's central mainframe. All employees have access to any information in the mainframe, with the exception of the payroll. "The kind of people you have here, that stayed here, that we're bringing on board, can be trusted to recognize the importance of that data and not tamper with it," says Weeden. "They also recognize and believe that they're entitled to that information. They're all shareholders, remember. If it helps them to do their job better, fantastic."

Recruiting and Selecting

Once job descriptions were prepared for the new positions created by the automation project, a first set of employees was selected to run the equipment. "The first few people out there (on the CNC machines) essentially were drafted," says McIntyre. "But they were drafted because of their ability, because of their knowledge of machine tools, and because of their leadership, the way they were looked on within the company as role models.''

McIntyre explains that the first group was intentionally selected to be diverse, to illustrate to others in the company that change would occur at all levels. Some of the ''draftees'' were operators of the old screw machines. One was a foreman. Another was an employee with 25 years with the company. Two women were moved to the ''autofloor'' at their own request after they scored high on aptitude tests, even though they didn't have prior manufacturing experience.

''All of those were selected as models so individuals could follow that path and they could have someone to talk to who came from a similar background,'' says Randall Nauda of Amprotech. ''That was part of the selection criteria.''

For people hired from outside the company, the selection criteria is more extensive. In addition to technical skills, Frost looks for compatibility with the new company culture. ''Your standard hierarchist doesn't get many interviews at Frost,'' McIntyre says. ''Your standard nonparticipant eight-to-fiver doesn't get very far.'' Instead, he says, Frost looks for ''listeners capable of expressing their ideas clearly. People who want to make a difference. . . . The other thing you look for is small-company orientation. Big-company people who have accomplished many great and wonderful things in their careers but have done it with a cast of thousands aren't going to get along real well with Frost. Because the cast of thousands isn't there.''

Appraising and Rewarding

Management by objectives is practiced at Frost, but that isn't what it's called. In typically irreverent fashion, it's known as ''One-Two-Three, Screw It.'' Each employee, working with a supervisor, develops a set of three priorities to work on during the year. Everyone's priorities ultimately derive from three principal goals spelled out in the company's annual business plan. (The ''screw it'' refers to the belief at Frost that adding a fourth priority only guarantees that none of the priorities would be reached. So, employees settle on three priorities and say ''screw it'' to the fourth.)

The three priorities become the basis for an employee's performance appraisal, which is done informally at least once a month and formally every quarter. In the past, appraisal was strictly an annual event and was done by awarding a number of points to each employee based on such factors as his or her job performance, attendance, cleanliness, and "ability to take direction."

"The appraisal system now tries to tailor the needs of an individual to the job that has to be done and the job they're doing," says Nauda. The factors considered in the evaluation, he says, are not just those mentioned in an employee's job description. Also weighing into the appraisal are such factors as the degree of an employee's participation in company task forces and contributions to helping others advance within the company.

Both the annual appraisals and compensation reviews are conducted around the end of the calendar year. However, they are separated by about one month, with the performance appraisal coming first.

Frost has attempted to redefine notions of compensation and advancement to take the focus off money and hierarchical position. "My objective is to make the compensation issue a nonissue,"Weeden says. "I've always considered it more of a dissatisfier than a motivator."

To accomplish this, and to attract the highly skilled job candidates needed to support the automation program, Frost in recent years has tried to pay wages comparable to those offered by large manufacturing companies in the Midwest. "For the kind of people we want to bring around, it kind of necessitates that you compare yourself with a much larger group," Weeden says.

But the central focus in recognizing accomplishments within Frost is on broadening the scope of an individual's skills and responsibilities, rather than increasing salaries or bestowing titles (of which there are few at Frost).

Developing

Once inside the company, socialization occurs mostly informally. Newcomers view a videotape that describes the Frost culture, then they are largely left to pick up nonverbal cues. Machine operators at Frost, for example, are self-supervised. Left on their own, new machine operators initially feel some anxiety. At previous jobs, "when they've run into a problem, they checked with their supervisors," Weeden says. "We have a situation where they didn't have that supervisor or lead person to check in with. And for the first few weeks, there was this consternation about

'What do I do now?' And a couple of times, they've made some fairly expensive mistakes. But they learned from it. It was much better than saying, 'Oh, we should have a supervisor on the floor that they can check in with that's supposed to know more.'"

An extensive amount of education and training has also accompanied the automation program, both to provide the skills needed to make the project work from a technical viewpoint as well as to support this idea of "redefining" compensation. Most of the training has been in technical areas with immediate application such as mathematics, computer programming, and electrical engineering. However, employees are encouraged to define their own training needs, and broad technical educational experiences are encouraged.

The training hasn't been confined to employee-shareholders operating machines. Others in the company who have expressed interest have been provided with training as well.

THE MANAGEMENT CHALLENGE: USING HUMAN RESOURCE MANAGEMENT PRACTICES TO IMPLEMENT ORGANIZATION STRATEGY

The HRM practice choices Frost has made clearly help implement its strategies and serve as good examples of what other organizations can do. Even before Weeden's arrival, for example, Frost recognized the close link between human resource planning and that of the company overall. The planning was done formally right from the beginning, by indentifying the positions and functions the automated company would require. With Weeden's arrival, the two became even more closely and more effectively linked. In addition, job descriptions have tended to be broad, or at least to allow for the broadening of responsibility if employee-shareholders are so inclined.

This broadening aspect turns up as well in the career paths encouraged in the staffing practice area. Says Weeden: "I think a person with broader responsibilities ends up having more of an impact and more decision-making authority and more compensation." Criteria for staffing are implicit in the technological thrust Frost has made. They become explicit through the job analysis Weeden performs and in the regular performance planning sessions held with shareholder-employees. There is open posting of jobs at Frost, and Weeden is available to discuss with shareholder-employees positions that are not yet open but that interest them. The socialization experience is extensive at Frost and essential to learning the culture.

Frost's appraisal process is results-oriented, based on the performance plan drawn up annually between a shareholder-employee and his or her supervisor. The process actually attempts to achieve two sets of results simultaneously: the goals set for the employee-shareholder's personal enhancement and, indirectly, the goals presented in the company's annual business plan. A high degree of employee participation is incorporated into the appraisal process. An employee not only participates in drawing up a personal performance plan, but is also responsible for seeking feedback from a supervisor on a regular basis.

Employee-shareholders participate to a large degree in establishing their incentives. In addition to the salary, the short-term incentives include a quarterly bonus based on companywide productivity and a "celebration fund" that managers can tap at their discretion to reward significant employee contributions. The reward may be as simple as lunch with Chad Frost, or as lavish as a weekend for an employee-shareholder and spouse at the Grand Rapids Marriott Hotel. (They can also be refreshingly irreverent. When one employee succeeded in lowering the level of outstanding receivables, Frost granted his unusual request to have a belly dancer give a performance in the office.) The long-term incentives consist of a standard profit-sharing plan and a discretionary profit-sharing plan administered by Chad Frost.

The training choices Frost has made also match with those of the entrepreneurial and dynamic growth strategies; they stress a high degree of employee participation and a broad focus. The emphasis emphatically is on productivity, a hallmark of the dynamic growth strategy.

Each of the human resource management practices and programs Frost implemented contributed to its business success. In succeeding chapters, detailed explanations are provided for each area of human resource management so you can do likewise.

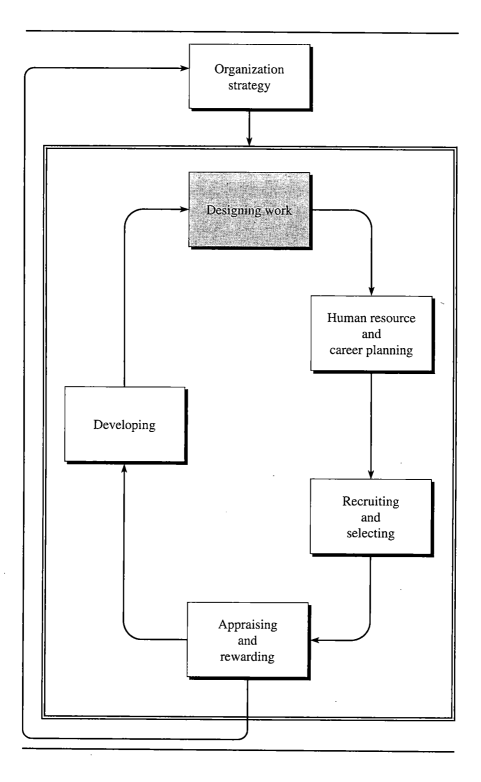

Organization
strategy

Designing work

Human resource
and
career planning

Developing

Recruiting
and
selecting

Appraising
and
rewarding

CHAPTER 3

DESIGNING WORK

INTRODUCTION

Work is done to accomplish organizational results. Naturally, then, the nature and focus of the work should be determined by the purpose and strategy set to accomplish it. The purpose and direction of an organization or unit is set in its mission, objectives, and strategy. The mission is the general reason for the existence of the organization; what it is all about. The mission statement specifies the general thrust of the organization and what are acceptable and unacceptable actions to accomplish the organization's purpose. From the mission statement are developed more specific objectives that serve as a guide to management decision making. The strategy will include objectives—which are desired results in the future—and the actions necessary to accomplish them. Using the objectives as the basis for structuring jobs people do and what they are expected to accomplish is the beginning of good human resource management practices. Once the purpose is defined in a mission, objective, and/or goal, work can be designed to be motivational and accomplish organizational objectives. Then job descriptions and performance standards are set so employees know what they are expected to accomplish and given some guidelines on how to meet these expectations.

Organizational Objectives

Organizational objectives are descriptions of desired future results. They identify what the organization wants to accomplish. Organizations exist to accomplish something—the objectives identify what that something is. Once identified, the objectives communicate to organization members and the environment in general the purpose of the organization.

In addition, organizational objectives provide a focus around which managers and employees can coordinate their activities—organizations exist because people have a common purpose. How they work together is determined by how they can best contribute to accomplishing the common purpose.

Organizational objectives also serve as the basis of performance standards against which actual performance can be checked—how an organization is doing is determined by comparing the actual results with what was desired. Maybe what was desired as expressed in the objectives is a good target and if the actual results do not reach the target, renewed efforts need to be made. Maybe what was desired was a bad target and different objectives need to be set. Either way, the objectives provide the benchmark against which actual performance can be compared.

Organizational objectives are set after considering the competition, the organization itself, and the environment. Let us consider each: first, the competition. The manager must understand the nature of the products or services that the organization provides to customers and the actual and potential rivals to whom customers can turn. Organizational objectives are not set in a vacuum. The organization cannot do everything it wants. Some products and services are better produced by competitors, which leads to the second factor to consider when setting organizational objectives, the organization. The strengths, weaknesses, and values of the organization determine what objectives can be reached. The organization may not want to produce some products and services because of its values and beliefs. It may not be able to produce others because employees do not have the needed skills.

Lastly, organizational objectives are set to be consistent with the environment. The environment includes the labor force, government regulations, and economic conditions in general. For example, maybe the organization has identified a product customers want, and no competitors are supplying it, but the organization cannot recruit and hire people with the necessary skills or buy the material needed to produce the product.

Within the constraints and opportunities set by competition, the environment, and the organization, managers establish objectives to guide their actions. Objectives set by one level of management become the guides for the next level to set their objectives. This hierarchy of objectives is referred to as a cascade of goals. Objectives of each level in the organization are supportive of objectives on the levels above them and, thus, the efforts of employees are woven together to accomplish common goals. How jobs fit together to accomplish organizational objectives is referred to as the organization structure. It is the organization's structure that determines the nature of employees' jobs. Let us consider first how organization structure creates employees' jobs and then how work on those jobs can be designed to be productive and motivational.

DESIGNING ORGANIZATION STRUCTURE

The work of an organization is divided into small tasks an employee can do to contribute to achievement of the organization goal. Once the work has been divided into jobs, the work of each individual and unit must be coordinated so that all employees are working toward common objectives. The method used to divide the work into jobs and then coordinate the employees' work to accomplish goals creates the organizational structure. Let us look at different ways of dividing up work (differentiating) and then coordinating (integrating) the jobs. Together, the division of work and coordinating mechanisms determine what each individual does and how it relates to what others are doing.

How the Work Is Divided—Differentiation

We can divide work several ways, most commonly by products, customers, market channels, locations, and business function.

- *Product.* Differentiation by product is illustrated in Figure 3–1a. One department is responsible for each product.
- *Customer.* Differentiation by customer is illustrated in Figure 3–1b. Each unit handles several products but is organized to service the needs of a particular customer.

FIGURE 3–1a
Product Organization

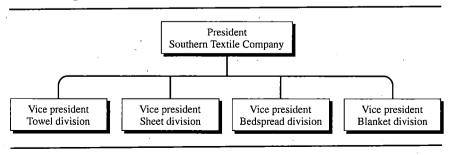

FIGURE 3–1b
Customer Organization

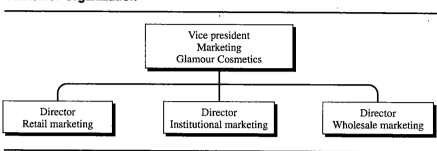

- *Market channel.* Differentiation by market channel is illustrated in Figure 3–1c. A market channel is the distribution network the product moves through between production and customer.
- *Location or area.* Differentiation by location or area is illustrated in Figure 3–1d. Work is organized according to geographic area served.
- *Business function.* Differentiation by business function is illustrated in Figure 3–1e. The work is organized according to the function the job performs rather than according to some national customer or product division.

All of these methods of differentiation are based on either purpose or process. Those based on purpose include division by product, customer, market, channel, or location. The advantage of organizing by purpose is that each unit will have all the necessary skills and

FIGURE 3–1c
Market Channel Organization

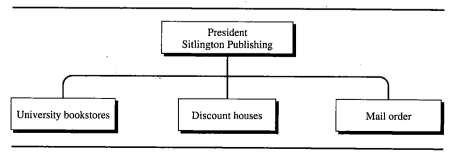

FIGURE 3–1d
Area Organization

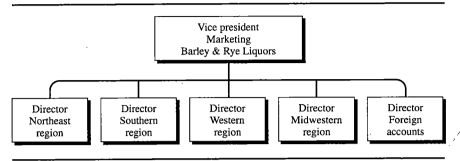

FIGURE 3–1e
Functional Organization

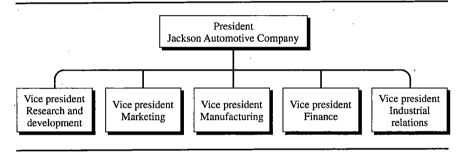

facilities necessary to service the purpose. A customer-oriented organization provides all the services needed for a particular customer within each unit. A product organization has all of the necessary facilities and functions necessary to produce the product or service in each unit. The disadvantage of these types of organizations is that they duplicate services and functions. For example, each unit will have a self-contained personnel and financial service. This duplication across business units becomes expensive.

Organizations that divide their work according to process focus on specialized functions such as production, finance, accounting, and personnel (Figure 3–1e). Because they are grouped according to function, the jobs tend to become specialized and can be done more efficiently within that function. However, because of this specialization, work will not be focused on the needs of the customer or the product. The accounting department may keep meticulous records, but that may not be what will help the organization be productive and profitable because what is needed is aggressive financing campaigns. The personnel department may run training programs that employees enjoy but that do not necessarily help them perform on the job. The manager's job is to integrate the separate specialized units and keep them focused on the overall purpose of the organization.

In an attempt to overcome some of the problems associated with both of these types of organizations, a third general method of work division has been introduced in the recent years: the matrix. The matrix organization is based on the premise that because differentiation by purpose and process each have limitations, work should be organized by both, simultaneously (see Figure 3–2). In a matrix organization, each worker and unit has a dual reporting relationship and responsibility. Take, for example, the professors of a typical school of business administration. On the one hand, they work within a department such as accounting, finance, or organizational behavior, and report to a department chairperson. On the other hand, they also teach in an undergraduate, graduate, or doctoral degree program, and in that capacity they report to a program director—for example, an associate dean. The program director is responsible for weaving the departments together so that a coherent, focused program is offered that meets the needs of the students.

Professors thus have two bosses to whom they are responsible: the department chair and the program director. The power and control of these two bosses will vary according to the school. In some institutions, the department chair will control class assignments, salary recommendations, and hiring decisions. In others, the program director performs these functions.

The advantage of the matrix organization is that there is someone responsible for both process and purpose. The disadvantage is that it can be confusing and thus cause increased conflict. There are bound to be disagreements and conflicts because of the natural tension between process and purpose. Is a person a professor of marketing or a professor in the undergraduate program? Is the purpose of the school to further finance research and practice or to teach undergraduates? In the matrix organization, these conflicts must be resolved if the organization is to be successful.

In sum, the way in which work is divided determines the responsibilities of employees and will vary substantially in different types of or-

FIGURE 3–2
Differentiation by Purpose and Function Simultaneously (The Matrix
Organization)

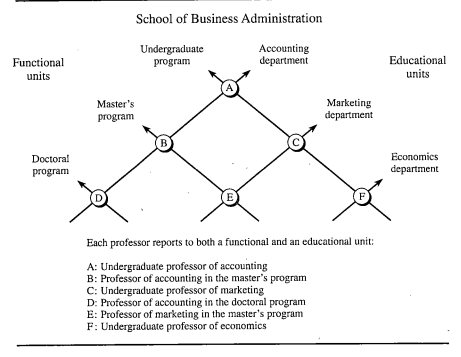

School of Business Administration

Each professor reports to both a functional and an educational unit:

A: Undergraduate professor of accounting
B: Professor of accounting in the master's program
C: Undergraduate professor of marketing
D: Professor of accounting in the doctoral program
E: Professor of marketing in the master's program
F: Undergraduate professor of economics

Source: Lloyd S. Baird, James E. Post, and John F. Mahon, "Differentiation by Purpose and Function
Simultaneously—The Matrix Organization," *Management: Functions and Responsibilities* (New York:
Harper & Row, 1990), p. 204.

ganizations. When work is organized by purpose, such as by product or
customer, work will most likely focus on the product or customer and
employees will likely work with others with different specializations.
When work is organized by process, those with common specializations
work together and the focus is to be as efficient and productive as possible within that specialization.

How Work from the Various Units Is Coordinated—Integration

After the work has been divided into jobs, it must be coordinated and
focused on the objectives of the organization. This process is referred to
as integration. Just as there are various ways of dividing work into jobs,

there are many ways of coordinating the jobs once they have been created. Jobs are usually integrated through hierarchical procedures or through informal or formal contacts.

Hierarchical Procedures.   One way of integrating jobs is to rely on formally established plans, rules, and procedures. Each unit is given a goal and a plan for achieving it. The goals and plans are developed so that if each unit accomplishes its objective, the overall objectives of the organization are accomplished. In any job, coordination necessary beyond the plans is done by the manager of the unit. The manager becomes responsible for ensuring that the work of the various departments fits together.

Coordination through hierarchical procedures works well as long as the work is not too complex and there are not too many changes to the formally established plans. If quick responses and many adjustments are necessary, formal procedures become too cumbersome. Assume that one unit must coordinate with another in a different area. For example, those in the marketing department have to coordinate their advertising and product introduction with the production department. If changes in the product can be planned in advance and there are only a few such changes, the regular plans and working through the managers should be fine. If there are special orders requiring many rapid changes, the formal plans and normal reporting channels will not work—they cannot adjust and change quickly enough. Coordination will have to be done more quickly through informal contacts using the formal plans and procedures as general guidelines.

Informal Contacts.   If some units need more frequent contact with others than can be provided by the formal organizational structure, one option is to develop informal coordinating mechanisms. For example, someone from the production department can make contact on an informal basis with the marketing department to work on mutual problems. The relationship may be sporadic and exist only when problems arise, or it may be ongoing. Either way, personal contacts are invaluable coordinating mechanisms.

Formal Contacts.   If contacts between units must occur more often and/or be more standardized, various other formal coordinating mechanisms such as formal liaisons, third parties, task forces, and permanent committees are available.

1. *Liaison.* Someone from one department can be assigned to work with another department. This person becomes a member of the second group responsible for coordinating the work of both groups.

2. *Third party.* The unbiased perspective of a third party who is not a member of any group may sometimes be desirable. In this case, the third party adopts the role of mediator between two groups.

3. *Task force.* When more interaction than can be provided by one person between units is desirable, a task force may be the answer. Task forces are formed to address a specific issue or problem, and their members should be selected on the basis of the experience, ability, or perspective they will bring to bear on the problem.

4. *Permanent committees.* When complex forms of coordination and continuing relationships among units are necessary, a permanent coordinating committee may be formed. Representatives from each unit should be assigned to the committee and given the responsibility of coordinating two units. These committees should be given formal recognition and should become part of the organizational structure.

The coordinating mechanism you choose will depend on the nature of the organization and its competitive environment. In complex, fast-paced organizations that face rapidly changing environments, more formal forms of coordination will be required. When employees must look beyond their own job to determine how their work fits into the work of others, continuous coordinating activities will be necessary. Permanent committees or task forces will probably work best in this situation. In a more stable, predictable environment, employees can do their job and leave the coordinating to others. Relationships among workers and departments will not change rapidly and coordinating requirements will be stable enough to be handled by the normal organizational structure.

The coordinating mechanism chosen will affect the nature of the job because it determines with whom the person on the job interacts and how. It will also affect the responsibilities of the job. For those employees whose jobs greatly depend on the work done by other workers in different departments, coordination will become a major responsibility. They may serve on task forces, permanent committees, or as liaisons with other units. Those workers with whom they must coordinate will have a definite impact on their jobs.

DESIGNING THE JOB: FITTING THE JOB AND THE EMPLOYEE TOGETHER

The organizational structure determines the general characteristics of jobs. The jobs are then designed so that they engage and involve the skills and energy of individuals. To be motivational and productive, jobs must be designed to fit the needs of both the organization and the individual. Scientific management, the sociotechnical systems, and job enrichment are three approaches to job design that you might use to change the job. Each of these makes different assumptions about the nature of work and people and offers different methods of solving productivity problems.

Scientific Management

Scientific management had its beginnings with Frederick Taylor. His methods were based on two assumptions: first, that the single best way to do a job can be identified through proper analysis (usually watching those who are performing the job correctly) and taught to others; and second, that people can be motivated to perform their jobs correctly through the use of rewards and punishments.

Scientific management standardizes and simplifies jobs so that all employees can do them properly. It eliminates unnecessary work and teaches employees the fastest, most efficient work methods. The principles of job design based on scientific management are:

1. Work should be studied scientifically in order to break it down into small, easily mastered tasks.
2. Each small task should be studied to determine how it can best be done. Once this is determined, every worker is expected to adopt the standardized approach.
3. Employees selected for the work should be as perfectly matched to the demands of the job as possible. Workers must, of course,

be physically and mentally capable of the work, but care should be taken as well to ensure that they are not overqualified for the job.

4. Employees should be trained very carefully by managers to ensure that they perform the work exactly as specified by the scientific analysis of the work. In addition, many planners and managers are kept near the work to make certain that the person is, in fact, performing the work exactly as expected, and that there are no distractions or activities the worker must attend to other than productive work itself.

5. Finally, to provide motivation for the employee to follow the detailed procedures and work practices that are laid out and constantly enforced by managers, a substantial monetary bonus should be established to be paid on successful completion of each day's work.

Since Taylor, scientific management has been refined and improved to produce more accurate job analyses and more efficient job designs. Presently, the most technologically sophisticated practices of scientific management use closed-circuit television and videotapes to determine the most efficient way of doing jobs. This is still the approach to job design used by many manufacturing companies in which jobs are specialized and repetitive and employees need only simple skills. As work becomes more complicated, however, more and more organizations are adapting sociotechnical systems, other work group approaches, and job enrichment to designing jobs.

Sociotechnical Systems and Work Group Approaches

Sociotechnical systems and work group approaches provide a second approach because they consider the social and technical components of the job as a system that must be integrated. We consider them together because the way they are implemented is very similar. Sociotechnical approaches ''jointly optimize'' the social and technical aspects of a job so that together they are productive and motivational. Group approaches organize both the production process and social interaction in teams.

The sociotechnical systems and group approaches are methods that encompass many orientations. Some who use this approach may focus on building work group relationships, while others focus on technological adjustments. Despite these variations, three characteristics define the sociotechnical and group approaches. First, they are multifaceted— rewards, physical facilities, and production are all considered. These approaches focus on the interaction of all of these components, not on any one in isolation.

Second, they involve the creation of autonomous work groups— employees who share production responsibilities will be grouped together to share decisions about how the work will be done. These autonomous work groups will be given many of the responsibilities usually performed by management, including working with and varying the technology. They will cope with manufacturing problems, participate in organizational decision making, and suggest production improvements.

Third, they include techniques for managing both technological and human resources. Compensation programs, definition of job responsibilities, and organizational structure are all organized to facilitate work being done by a group.

Job Enrichment

Job enrichment makes different assumptions about people and the nature of work than does scientific management. Job enrichment assumes that by expanding job responsibilities, workers can be motivated to perform well, will produce high quality work, and will be highly satisfied with the work that they do. The key to successful job enrichment is expanding jobs properly so that the employees obtain their satisfaction from performing well. Three components are critical to job satisfaction.[1]

The first component is the *meaningfulness of work:* People have to see their work as useful and valuable. Employees consider their jobs meaningful if they can see that what they are doing has an impact on others and if they are required to use skills that they value. We all like to do what we do well, and if the job offers us some variety in the skills that we use, we tend to enjoy it even more. The job is also meaningful if we can identify results for which we are responsible.

Second is the *knowledge of actual results of work activities:* Before we can derive any satisfaction from what we have accomplished, we need

---

[1]For a full explanation of these concepts see J. R. Hackman and G. R. Oldham, "Development of the Job Diagnostic Survey," *Journal of Applied Psychology* 60 (1975), pp. 159–70.

information on the results we have produced and feedback on the quality of our work.

The third component is *responsibility for work results:* We need to feel responsible for what we have accomplished before we can get any sense of satisfaction from it. That is why we like to see a job through from beginning to end. We will feel responsible for the results we produce when we are given the freedom, independence, and discretion to complete the job. This is referred to as job autonomy.

To the extent that these factors are present, the job is motivating and satisfying. The following are some guidelines that create these factors and enrich jobs. To the extent that the production process limits the use of these principles, jobs will be unmotivating. For example, the continuously repetitive work required by many production lines will continue to be unmotivating until the production process is changed. Those implementing job enrichment generally use the following principles.

Principle 1: Form Natural Work Units.   Fragmenting tasks and then coordinating them to produce finished products takes its toll in human productivity. Employees who repeatedly perform the same task over and over again become bored and unproductive. Often, they cope with the boredom through absenteeism. By combining tasks so that the job involves many activities, employees can use a wider range of skills and thus avoid boredom. Combining the tasks employees perform will also increase the degree of responsibility they feel for the finished product and thus enhance the satisfaction they take in their own accomplishment.

Principle 2: Establish Client Relationships.   Workers find it difficult to be committed to a product if they do not see it in use. If workers can be brought into contact with their customers, their jobs will be enriched in three ways. First, they will be able to receive direct feedback from the customer; second, their jobs will become more varied as they use their interpersonal skills to work with the clients; third, they will have greater autonomy as a result of having managed relationships with others.

If it is impossible for the worker to have direct relationships with the client, some form of contact between them can still be established. For example, quality control inspectors who identify their work with the serial number on the machinery they inspect and hotel maids who identify themselves with notes to the guests they serve both maintain this kind of indirect contact. If there is praise or blame to be meted out, the customer will know who to get in touch with. This helps build the same sense of responsibility in the employee as direct contact with the customer.

Principle 3: Include Planning and Evaluation Responsibilities in the Job. Management is usually thought to be responsible for planning and evaluating jobs, but if employees are to feel responsible for the work they do, they need to become more involved in these aspects of their jobs. You can encourage employees to do this by:

1. Letting them decide how they will do their jobs; that is, the work methods they will use.
2. Giving them increased freedom to manage their own time.
3. Providing them with as much information as possible about their work and involving them in evaluating the results they produce.

Principle 4: Create Feedback Channels. Employees need to know how they are doing. Only by knowing what they have accomplished can they improve what they have done and gain the satisfaction that goes with doing well.

COMMON PROBLEMS IN IMPLEMENTING JOB DESIGN

Several problems may arise in your effort to design the job no matter which approach you have used (i.e., scientific management, sociotechnical systems, or job enrichment). Let us consider these problems and some possible solutions to them.

Inadequate Analysis

Certain job design techniques are more appropriate for some jobs than for others. Job enrichment, for example, is appropriate when employees are willing and able to devote more time and energy to their jobs and when they can be allowed increased responsibility and autonomy. Scientific management is appropriate when technology dominates the production process and when the work is fragmented, very specialized, and must be tightly controlled. Before jobs can be properly designed, therefore, you should conduct a thorough analysis of the work to be done.

Failure to Understand and Prepare for the Changes that Come with the Implementation of New Job Design

Those who will be affected by the new job design (e.g., managers, employees, and unions) need to understand and prepare for the changes that will result. Union leaders, for example, may support the concept of job enrichment until they discover, after implementation, that their members are now doing jobs with more responsibility for the same wages. When implementing changes, you should anticipate and prepare for all possible consequences.

Unwillingness to Devote the Necessary Resources to Implement the Job Design

Implementing a new job design requires time, energy, and money. Employees have to learn new skills, and new relationships among jobs have to be established. This will probably result in temporarily decreased productivity, which should be considered part of the startup cost of the program. To implement a new job design successfully, the organization must be willing to devote time, energy, and money to the endeavor.

Inadequate Attention Given Technology

If technology is a locked-in feature of the organization, it must be considered in the job design. For example, any change made to one job in an assembly line will, of course, affect others. These limitations must be recognized before any changes in job design can be attempted.

Poor Management of Implementation

Any job change is difficult to implement. Employees may resist the proposed changes because they feel threatened by the necessity of learning new skills and interacting with new people. This resistance needs to be recognized and managed.

Failure to Consider the Organizational Structure and Culture

Sometimes new jobs do not fit old management and organizational practices. For example, enriched jobs usually require flexibility and openness on the part of management. If the organization is structured as a strict hierarchy, with decision-making power concentrated at the top and all the personnel practices and systems oriented towards control, job enrichment will not work. If the organization is open, employee-centered, and places a high premium on flexibility and group process, scientific management will not work. The new job has to fit within the existing organizational structure. If this is not the case, either the job or the structure will have to be changed.

Failure to Address Related Personnel Issues

New job designs must take existing personnel practices and policies into consideration. When a job is changed, changes must be made in these practices, too. Job changes will affect superior-employee relationships as well as selection and training, performance appraisal, and pay policies. Each of these must be adjusted so that they support the new job design. For example, if a job changes, it means that the managers will be responsible for supervising new work procedures and helping employees develop new skills. If they do not anticipate these changes and develop the skills and systems they need to manage them, the new job design will fail.

Lack of Job Design Evaluation

Implementing job design is an art that will vary from one organization to another. The best way to learn how to do it is by evaluating past job design efforts; what we learn from one job design project can be applied to the next. Without evaluation, there is no way to know what effect the new job design has had on your organization. Remember that your evaluation must begin before you implement your job design. You will have to measure such factors as employee satisfaction, turnover, and production beforehand in order to create a baseline from which you can then assess your job design.

CURRENT TRENDS IN JOB DESIGN:
MATCHING THE JOB TO THE EMPLOYEE

In today's modern organizations, the three approaches to job design we have discussed are not mutually exclusive; in fact, they can be integrated to achieve maximum motivation and productivity. Let us look briefly at four trends emerging in job design that use combinations of these approaches: robotics and flexible manufacturing systems, ergonomics, quality of work life projects, and quality programs.

Robotics and Flexible Manufacturing Systems

One way of fighting the boredom created by scientific management and production lines is to automate them out of existence. New advances in technology make it possible to create flexible manufacturing systems that are built to make a wide variety of parts or products through instant reprogramming. One flexible manufacturing system can replace several conventional systems and reduce the costs of new plants and equipment when production shifts to new products.

At the heart of flexible manufacturing systems are robots: flexible machines that can be programmed to do numerous tasks. A company that already takes full advantage of robotics is GMFanuc, which makes robot parts and machine tools. This firm has a production operation that occupies 54,000 square feet, but at night is supervised by just one controller who monitors the production process through closed circuit TV. During the day, others come to repair and reprogram robots and assemble parts. The plant has 100 employees where 1,000 would be needed to maintain the level of production in a conventional plant. The employees of GMFanuc do computer operations, monitoring, and repair work; robots do the production and assembly work. Employees' jobs require skills in computer operation and design, whereas the assembly-line jobs at a conventional factory would require skills in dexterity and eye-hand coordination. Some industrial engineers predict that flexible manufacturing systems and robots will have a greater impact on the jobs that people do than anything in the history of manufacturing.

Ergonomics

Ergonomics is the study of the physical relationship of human beings to the environment, most importantly to the machines with which they work. Ergonomics attempts to optimize a worker's interactions with his or her environment to make the worker more comfortable . . . and ultimately more productive. Machines can work at a set pace in a set way; people cannot. Through measurement and observation, ergonomics takes into account the differences among people and finds the size and shape of furniture, tools, and equipment that will meet physical needs of each worker. As an example, the following are taken from the IBM *Ergonomics Handbook*:[2]

• *Why ergonomics?* Ergonomics, the European word synonymous with human factors, was invented in the early 1950s by a group of scientists and engineers interested in the relationship between people and machines. The word is derived from the Greek *ergon,* ''work,'' and *nomos,* ''natural laws of.'' A properly designed workstation can contribute to an employee's comfort, job satisfaction, motivation, and sense of well-being and accomplishment.

• *Job design and the back.* The best way to reduce back injuries is to design out the lifting tasks. This statement should be taken seriously and IBM Corporation strives to limit the weight of components in both manufacturing and service. Intelligent job design will reduce problems. For example, when you bend over and twist, the load is much heavier than when you simply bend over forward. (In the United States, the action of bending and twisting is the most common cause of back injuries.) Changing the layout of common lifting tasks, for example, moving boxes from the end of a roller conveyor onto a pallet, eliminates twisting actions at no cost.

• *The hand: Techniques for reducing repetitive-task injuries.* The basic technique for reducing hand and wrist injuries is to reduce the exposure of the hand to repetitive motion. This can be accomplished through good work practices, training procedures, and hand tool design.

• *Noise.* Noise can be very distracting and prevent concentrated mental work. In extreme cases, it can also result in physical disorders. Direct noise should be suppressed by placing covers over impact printers or by isolating sources of noise from the rest of the work area. Reflected noise can be reduced by introducing sound-absorbing materials into the environment.

• *Lighting.* Different tasks require different lighting levels. Intricate assembly tasks require more lights than warehouse areas. Putting light where it is needed on the working plane and reducing general light levels can often improve lighting significantly.

Care should be taken to avoid glare. Dials, instruments panels, and visual display terminals (VDTs) should be very carefully positioned in

---

[2]Source: Adapted from *Ergonomics Handbook,* IBM Corporation.

relation to light sources so that the latter cannot produce glare from reflection in the glass fronts of the equipment, which makes them difficult
to read.

Quality of Work Life—Productivity Improvement Programs

Quality of work life (QWL) is the general name given to many approaches focusing on improving the motivation and productivity of
workers. Those who advocate such projects argue that when employees
become more responsible for managing themselves, and their jobs are expanded to include more responsibilities, they will be more motivated
and productive. Figure 3–3 presents a brief description of eight quality
of work life projects illustrating the diversity of approaches used. Each
was designed to meet the unique needs of a specific group of employees

FIGURE 3–3
Quality of Work Life Projects

Type of Organization	Some Productivity-Related Changes Attempted in Project
1. Coal mine	Autonomous work groups job training; super-visor training; pay changes; intershift communication
2. Auto parts factory	Time-off bonus incentives; training; union-management cost reduction to retain business; safety program; plant newsletter
3. Wood products plants	Survey feedback and other communication activities
4. Bakery	Survey feedback; newsletter; new equipment; job training; interdepartmental coordination
5. Federal utility company (engineering division)	Merit pay; performance appraisal; four-day work-week; survey feedback; other communication activities
6. Hospital	Survey feedback; staff meetings and training; management development; attempts to increase interdepartmental coordination
7. Municipal transit system	Survey feedback; management development; work team system; communication efforts
8. Municipal government	Better equipment; increased communication

Source: Edward E. Lawler III and Gerald E. Ledford, Jr., "Productivity and the Quality of Work Life,"
National Productivity Review, Winter 1981–1982, p. 34.

and the organizations in which they worked. No matter what approach was adopted:

1. The current levels of productivity and the needs of employees were analyzed.
2. Employees helped identify productivity problems and design the programs to solve them.
3. It was determined what programs or combinations of programs would increase productivity by improving the quality of work life.
4. The programs were implemented with the aid of employees.
5. Results were evaluated and adjustments made.

Quality Circles

A quality circle is a small group of workers who volunteer to meet regularly to discuss productivity and quality problems within their organization. Members identify problems and after studying the problem in depth, recommend solutions and then take appropriate action. Often the problem can be solved by the group, but when outside approval or expertise is needed, a formal proposal is made to management.

Quality circles have proven to be highly effective in improving workers' commitment to quality as well as for taking advantage of often unrecognized employee expertise in solving problems related to work. Circles have helped numerous organizations by improving costs, reducing rejects, cutting processing times, and reducing absenteeism.

Autonomous Work Groups

Autonomous work groups are becoming increasingly popular as organizations form more and more teams focused on quality, product development, and customer satisfaction. Autonomous work groups are often given almost total responsibility for creating a product. The autonomous work group is involved in all the production decisions such as assigning work, scheduling, choosing methods, and selecting new members. Management's involvement is providing any information the group may need to accomplish its task.

Many companies have found autonomous work groups to increase productivity up to 50 percent. But in order to achieve this kind of success, the group must have freedom to function. And unless a company

removes strict bureaucratic procedures and loosens its control systems,
the group will not produce positive results. Union restrictions can also
hamper the effectiveness of the group and the union must be convinced
to relax its restrictive demands.

Total Quality Management

When the quality effort extends to all facets of the organization, it is referred to as total quality management (TQM). Total quality management
involves every employee in the organization in taking responsibility for
improving quality daily. A successful total quality management program
usually means a significant change in organization culture. Four principles serve as the basis of total quality management programs:

1. *Meet the customer's requirements on time, the first time, and 100
   percent of the time.* In TQM, each employee meets with his or
   her customer to clarify what the customer needs from the employee and then proceeds to try to satisfy customer expectations
   at all times.
2. *Strive to do error-free work.* TQM strives to reduce defects to
   zero, not merely 95 percent correct.
3. *Manage by prevention.* Every case of poor quality is investigated and its source found. Changes are then made to prevent the
   defect from happening again.
4. *Measure the cost of quality.* Whereas quality used to be thought
   of as free, TQM involves assessing the costs of quality, in
   order to show that prevention is the least costly way to achieve
   high quality.

The basis of TQM is making employees aware of quality as an organizational priority. To do this, a great deal of training is involved. The
emphasis in this training is to get every employee to fully understand and
effectively use the four principles of total quality management.

There are many variations of total quality management systems, as
different concepts work for different companies. Some implement suggestion systems and quality task forces. Most involve extensive collaboration and communication between different departments to produce a
product. Organizations who use TQM have found it to be very successful
in improving quality and productivity. We will discuss TQM procedures
more fully in Chapters 9 and 10.

Current Issues in Job Design

Several trends are having a significant impact on how jobs are designed. Organizations are flattening, reducing levels from the top to the bottom. This increases the responsibility and broadens the scope of most jobs in the organization. Unfortunately, many organization do not recognize the need to increase the authority, skills, and areas of discretion a person needs to deal with these increased responsibilities.

Organizations are forming more and more teams at all levels; product development teams, process improvement teams, production teams, and so on. Indeed, teams are the basis of most participative management approaches now in use. The team rather than any one individual, is given as set of responsibilities. The job must be designed for the team. This has significant implications for how people are managed. Job assignments must be given to the team and then the team organizes itself to accomplish the objectives. People are selected onto the team based on how they fill the needs of the team. Rewards must be restructured to recognize team performance. All the principles of job design we have discussed are still valid, but the unit of application shifts from the individual to the team.

In addition to these general trends, which are affecting most organizations, some are experimenting with even more radical changes in the nature of jobs. Some organizations are experimenting with structures that uniquely combine the principles of both centralization and decentralization.

- *Network structures.* A network structure is a decentralized structure where higher levels are dependent on lower levels in the organization. Unlike traditional hierarchical structures, centralization occurs at the discretion of lower level managers. Members delegate authority to coordinate their activities to a central body of representatives.
- *Collegial or collective structures.* In a collegial structure, members assist each other in achieving their individual goals. The only common goal they share is a goal to preserve the system. They do not necessarily share visions, aspirations, or intentions. Collegial structures are dependent on mutual interdependence. Members must need each other's skills to accomplish their own goals.
- *Loosely coupled structures.* This type of decentralized structure is composed of two systems that are weakly related. Each system

has its own goals and is influenced by independent factors, but each system benefits from the allegiance.

Each of these new methods for structuring organizations has significant implications for the jobs managers are asked to do. Jobs become much more flexible and ambiguous. More is left to the initiative, creativity, and motivation of the individual and the group.

ANALYZING AND DESCRIBING JOBS

After jobs have been designed, job analysis and job descriptions are used to establish and communicate to employees their responsibilities in performing the jobs established. *Job analysis* is a systematic investigation of jobs using observations, interviews, or questionnaires to determine what an employee should do and accomplish on the job. *Job descriptions* are one- or two-page summaries developed from the job analysis of the tasks to be performed on a job and a general explanation of the results expected from the employee doing the job.

Good job descriptions are the basis of many human resource management practices, procedures, and programs. Job standards that explain what is to be accomplished on the job can be written from the descriptions. From the job description, *job specifications*, which are explanations of the skills necessary to perform the job, can be identified. The skills identified then become the basis for training and recruiting programs. Compensation specialists can determine the salary and benefits a job should receive based on how its responsibilities compare with other jobs. Managers can develop performance appraisal forms and procedures that correctly evaluate an employee's performance on the job. Because job descriptions are the basis of so much of what managers do to work with people, they must be accurate representations of the job. Let us look first at how job analyses are used to construct accurate job descriptions and then how they are used to develop job specifications and performance standards.

Job Analysis

The skills, activities, and results that are important to competent performance on a job can be determined by analyzing the work included. There are six currently popular ways to analyze jobs: observation, interviewing, managerial conferences, notation of critical incidents, work sampling, and questionnaires. Let us review each briefly.

Observations. Observation techniques gather information by directly studying what the employee does on the job. By watching and recording the behavior of those who do the job particularly well, we can identify those activities that contribute most to good performance and use them as a basis for selecting and training others to do the job.

This approach is best for jobs that have repetitive and easily observable activities. The observation method is not suited to jobs that involve less observable behavior such as interpersonal interactions. For that reason, it would be hard to develop a description of what a manager does based solely on observation.

Interviewing. Interviewing as a method of analyzing jobs assumes that the employee can accurately describe his or her job. The interview should be structured to identify the activities, skills, and results that are characteristic of the job. It is a good idea to interview more than one person holding the job in order to obtain a more general description of what the job holder does.

Managerial Conferences. The job holder's manager will often have a good idea of what the job entails and how it fits into the organization as a whole. The managerial conference should be conducted in much the same way as the interview. The objective of both is to develop an accurate description of the activities and goals of the job.

Critical Incidents. The purpose of the critical incident method is to identify behaviors that are critical to good job performance. The manager keeps a record of the job holder's activities and at the end of the observation period, behaviors that are most critical to good performance will have been repeatedly observed and documented; these are the critical behaviors for the job. The manager can easily develop job descriptions based on these critical behaviors. This approach works best for jobs that extend over long periods of time.

Work Sampling. This technique samples portions of the work at random intervals and develops a picture of the job from these snapshots. The samples may be observations of the same person at different points in time or they may be samples of the work of different people doing the same job. In either case, the observations are combined to develop an overall description of the job. The information may be collected by observing the work, conducting interviews, or using questionnaires and checklists.

Questionnaires and Checklists. Questionnaires and checklists are structured lists of job characteristics. The manager uses them to identify which behaviors, skills, and results apply to the job being analyzed. Questionnaires provide general categories of activities and ask the job holder to indicate which activities are important in performing the job.

Checklists provide a detailed list of activities and are highly structured and carefully developed to include a wide range of activities. Figure 3–4 describes the categories that are analyzed using one such checklist, the Position Analysis Questionnaire. Figure 3–5 describes another checklist used to analyze management position, the Management Position Description Questionnaire (MPDQ).

Which Approach Should You Use?

Which of these approaches you use will be determined by the types of information you need and how much general information you already have. The key to job analysis is to collect enough information so you can accurately describe the job to be done. The purpose is to communicate to employees as clearly as possible what their responsibilities are.

Job Descriptions

From the job analysis, job descriptions, performance standards, and job specifications can be developed to direct employees' efforts toward performing well on the job. There are no set rules for what a job description should include or how it should be written. Remember that its purpose is to accurately describe the job in such a way that the proper people will be hired, competitive and equitable salaries paid, employees on the job know what they are to do, and training programs focus on the proper skills. The job analysis provides the information for writing the job description. Following are some hints for writing clear and useful job descriptions (see Figure 3–6 for an example that is written following these guidelines).

FIGURE 3–4
Position Analysis Questionnaire—Job Divisions

1. Information input:
   a. Sources of job information.
   b. Discrimination and perceptual activities.
2. Mediation processes:
   a. Decision making and reasoning.
   b. Information processing.
   c. Use of stored information.
3. Work output:
   a. Use of physical devices.
   b. Integrative manual activities.
   c. General body activities.
   d. Manipulation/coordination activities.
4. Interpersonal activities:
   a. Communications.
   b. Interpersonal relationships.
   c. Personal contact.
   d. Supervision and coordination.
5. Work situation and job context:
   a. Physical working conditions.
   b. Psychological and sociological aspects.
6. Miscellaneous aspects:
   a. Work schedule, method of pay, apparel.
   b. Job demands.
   c. Responsibility.

Source: Adapted from E. J. McCormick, P. R. Jeanneret, and R. C. Mecham, "A Study of Job Characteristics and Job Dimensions as Based on the Position Analysis Questionnaire (PAQ)," *Journal of Applied Psychology*, 1972, Vol. 56, p. 349. Copyright 1972 by the American Psychological Association. Reprinted by permission.

1. *Be clear.* The job description should portray the work of the position so well that the duties are clear without reference to other job descriptions.

2. *Describe the scope of job responsibilities.* In defining the position, be sure to indicate the scope and nature of the work by using phrases such as "for the department," or "as requested by the manager." Include all important relationships.

3. *Be specific.* Specify (*a*) the kind of work involved in the job, (*b*) its degree of complexity, (*c*) the skills required, (*d*) the extent to which problems are predictable, (*e*) the extent of the worker's responsibility for each portion of the work, and (*f*) the degree

FIGURE 3–5
Development and Use of the MPDQ

About 1,000 items were initially written describing managerial job behavior. From these, 505 nonoverlapping items were given to a test sample of 41 managers from diverse functions, levels, and companies (within one large organization). Following are examples of items used and the format to be used in answering each item:

Makes final and, for the most part, irreversible decisions.
Uses accounting procedures in analyzing financial information.
Decides what business activities the company is to be engaged in.
Phases out unprofitable products/services.
Develops high-level management talent.
Touches base with many different people before making major decisions.

0—Definitely not a part of the position, does not apply, or is not true.
1—Under unusual circumstances may be a minor part of the position.
2—A small part of the position.
3—A somewhat substantial part of the position.
4—A major part of the position.
5—Definitely a most significant part of the position.

A total of 204 of the items were responded to differently by managers in different functions, levels, or companies. The final version contained these and four other items. The 208 items related to position concerns and responsibilities, demands and restrictions, and miscellaneous characteristics. The 208 items were given next to 489 managers (212 executives, 172 middle-, and 105 first-line) in manufacturing, service, education, finance, and marketing organizations. The responses of these managers were statistically analyzed to determine which items were most strongly related to each other. The following figure gives the resulting job description factors and their interpretation.

1. *Product, Marketing, and Financial Strategy Planning.* This factor indicates long-range thinking and planning. The concerns of the incumbent are broad and are oriented toward the future of the company. They may include such areas as long-range business potential, objectives of the organization, solvency of the company, what business activities the company should engage in, and the evaluation of new ideas.

2. *Coordination of Other Organizational Units & Personnel.* The incumbent coordinates the efforts of others over whom he/she exercises no direct control, handles conflicts or disagreements when necessary, and works in an environment where he/she must cut across existing organizational boundaries.

3. *Internal Business Control.* The incumbent exercises business controls; that is, reviews and controls the allocation of manpower and other resources. Activities and concerns are in the areas of assignments of supervisory responsibility, expense control, cost reduction, setting performance goals, preparation and review of budgets, protection of the company's monies and properties, and employee relations practices.

4. *Products and Services Responsibility.* Activities and concerns of the incumbent in technical areas related to products, services, and their marketability. Specifically included are the planning, scheduling, and monitoring of products and services delivery along with keeping track of their quality and costs. The incumbent is concerned with promises of delivery that are difficult to meet, anticipates new or changed demands for the products and services, and closely maintains the progress of specific projects.

5. *Public and Customer Relations.* A general responsibility for the reputation of the company's products and services. The incumbent is concerned with promoting the company's

FIGURE 3–5 (concluded)

products and services. The incumbent is concerned with promoting the company's products and services, the goodwill of the company in the community, and general public relations. The position involves first-hand contact with the customer, frequent contact and negotiation with representatives from other organizations, and understanding the needs of customers.

6. *Advanced Consulting.* The incumbent is asked to apply technical expertise to special problems, issues, questions, or policies. The incumbent should have an understanding of advanced principles, theories, and concepts in more than one required field. He/she is often asked to apply highly advanced techniques and methods to address issues and questions which very few people in the company can do.

7. *Autonomy of Action.* The incumbent has a considerable amount of discretion in the handling of the job, engages in activities which are not closely supervised or controlled, and makes decisions which are often not subject to review. The incumbent may have to handle unique problems, know how to ask key questions even on subject matters with which he/she is not intimately familiar, engage in free-wheeling or unstructured thinking to deal with problems which are themselves abstract or unstructured.

8. *Approval of Financial Commitments.* The incumbent has the authority to approve large financial commitments and obligate the company. The incumbent may make final and, for the most part, irreversible decisions, negotiate with representatives from other organizations, and make many important decisions on almost a daily basis.

9. *Staff Service.* The incumbent renders various staff services to supervisors. Such activities can include fact-gathering, data acquisition and compilation, and record keeping.

10. *Supervision.* The incumbent plans, organizes, and controls the work of others. The activities are such that they require face-to-face contact with subordinates on almost a daily basis. The concerns covered by this factor revolve around getting work done efficiently through the effective utilization of people.

11. *Complexity and Stress.* The incumbent has to operate under pressure. This may include activities of handling information under time pressure to meet deadlines, frequently taking risks, and interfering with personal or family life.

12. *Advanced Financial Responsibility.* Activities and responsibilities concerned with the preservation of assets, making investment decisions and other large-scale financial decisions which affect the company's performance.

13. *Broad Personnel Responsibility.* The incumbent has broad responsibility for the management of human resources and the policies affecting it.

Since its development, the MPDQ has primarily been used as a tool for analyzing and evaluating new jobs for compensation purposes. For example, if a new management position were created, an appropriate salary level could be determined by examining the prevalence of certain tasks in that job and relating them to the level and function factors previously determined.

Source: Adapted from W. W. Tornow and P. R. Pinto, "The Development of a Managerial Job Taxonomy: A System for Describing, Classifying, and Evaluating Executive Positions," *Journal of Applied Psychology*, 1976, pp. 61, 410–418. © 1976 by the American Psychological Association, Reprinted by permission.

FIGURE 3–6
Job Description and Specifications

JOB TITLE: Compensation Manager	**NO.** _____
INCUMBENT:	**GRADE** _____
SUPERVISOR'S TITLE: Senior Vice President—	**STATUS** Exempt_____
Human Resources	**CLASS** O/M_____

GENERAL SUMMARY: Responsible for the design and administration of all cash compensation programs; insures proper consideration of the relationship of sales to performance of each employee and provides consultation on salary administration to Managers and Supervisors.

PRINCIPAL DUTIES & RESPONSIBILITIES:

1. Insures the preparation and maintenance of job descriptions for each present and proposed position. Prepares all job descriptions, authorizing final drafts. Coordinates periodic review of all job descriptions making revisions as necessary; educates employees and supervisors on job description use and their intent by participation in formal training programs and by responding to questions from employees and supervisors; maintains accurate file of all current job descriptions, distributing revised job descriptions to appropriate individuals.

2. Insures the proper evaluation of job descriptions. Serves as chair of Job Evaluation Committee, coordinating its activities. Resolves disputes over proper evaluation of jobs; assigns jobs to pay ranges; re-evaluates job periodically through the Committee process; conducts initial evaluation of new positions prior to hiring; insures integrity of job evaluation process.

3. Insures that Company compensation rates are in accordance with the Company philosophy. Maintains current information concerning applicable salary movements taking place in comparable organizations; obtains or conducts salary surveys as necessary; conducts analysis of salary movements among competitors and presents recommendations on salary movements on an annual basis.

4. Insures proper consideration of the relationship of salary to the performance of each employee. Reviews all performance appraisals and salary reviews, authorizing all pay adjustments.

5. Develops and administers the performance appraisal program. Develops and updates performance appraisal instruments; assists in the development of training programs designed to educate supervisors on appropriate use of performance appraisal—may assist in its delivery; monitors the use of the performance appraisal instruments to insure the integrity of the system and its proper use.

6. Assists in the development and oversees the administration of all bonus payments up through the Officer level.

7. Researches and provides recommendations on executive compensation issues.

FIGURE 3–6 (*concluded*)

8. Coordinates the development of an integrated Human Resource Information system. Assists in identifying needs; interfaces with the Management Information Systems Department to achieve departmental goals for information needs.
9. Performs related duties as assigned or as the situation dictates.

REQUIRED KNOWLEDGE, SKILLS & ABILITIES

1. Knowledge of compensation and personnel management practices and principles.
2. Knowledge of effective job analysis procedures.
3. Knowledge of survey development and interpretation practices and principles.
4. Knowledge of modern principles and practices of performance appraisal design and administration.
5. Skill in conducting job analysis interviews.
6. Skill in writing job descriptions, memorandums, letters and proposals.
7. Skill in making presentations to groups, in conducting job analysis interviews, and in explaining divisional policies and practices to employees and supervisors.
8. Skill in performing statistical computations including regression, correlation, and basic descriptive statistics.
9. Ability to conduct effective meetings.
10. Ability to plan and prioritize work.

EDUCATION & EXPERIENCE:

This position requires the equivalent of a college degree in Business Administration, Psychology or a related degree plus 3–5 years experience in Personnel Administration, 2–3 of which should include compensation administration experience. An advanced degree in Industrial Psychology, Business Administration, or Personnel Management is preferred, but not required.

COMMENTS:

This position may require up to 15 percent travel.

---

and type of accountability. Use action words such as *analyze, gather, assemble, plan, devise, confer, deliver, transmit, maintain, supervise,* and *recommend.*

4. *Be brief.* Remember that brief, accurate statements will best accomplish your purpose.

5. *Recheck.* Finally, to check whether the description fulfills the basic requirements, ask yourself: Will new employees understand the job when they read this job description?

Performance Standards

The job description describes what the job holder does and how. Performance standards define what the job holder should achieve. The concepts of management by objectives, results management, goals, target, and desired results, all refer to performance standards. The purpose of all of them is to describe the results expected from employees on the job. What performance standards should be is limited only by the imagination of the people involved and the environment in which they work. They can range from standards that focus on the task, such as the number and type of tangible products that should be produced, to standards that focus more on the person, such as standards of development, learning, attitudes, morale, and cohesiveness.

When managers think of performance standards, they usually focus on amounts and quality of products or service. As well they should, because managers are responsible for accomplishing results. Those desired results should be described as accurately as possible in the performance standards. At the same time, however, managers cannot ignore human resource results such as development, morale, cohesiveness, and positive attitudes for which they are also responsible. These desired results should also be specified in the future. For example, assume cohesion and morale in a group decline because it has been assigned the impossible task of producing 90 units per day. When the group fails to accomplish this task, each member blames the others, and the group falls apart. Management does not notice that the group has disintegrated because it is too busy concentrating on their failure to produce 90 units a day. An easier goal is set for the group with the expectation that they certainly should be able to handle it. By this time, however, the group has disintegrated so far that it cannot do anything productive.

Because the results of the present become the basis of performance in the future, the full range of results must be included in the performance standards. Management and workers cannot be solely concerned with quantity and quality of products and services. They have to be aware of what has happened to the materials and human resources in the production process. A high quality and quantity of goods produced may have been done at the expense of an exhausted and very discouraged group who will not be able to perform in the future. An individual may focus all his or her energy on accomplishing the task because that is the performance standard. The person accomplishes the task but learns nothing, develops no new skills or insights, and feels terrible about the experience. Employees, too, need job standards covering development, skills, and attitudes.

The advantage of having clear performance standards is that prospective employees will know what will be expected of them. They can then focus their time and energy in such a way as to contribute to the productivity of the organization. Performance standards for a particular job are usually established through negotiation. The final standard is a combination of what needs to be done on the job and what the employee can do. Why negotiation? Many people think negotiation means that both parties have to make concessions and lose something; but is that really necessary? The discussion is necessary, and the blending of perspectives is necessary; but it is not necessary for both parties to lose anything. Both can gain simply by agreeing on performance expectations so that the employee's time and effort can be focused on the desired result.

Negotiating increases the commitment of both manager and worker to improve performance because each is actively involved in defining the goals of the job and in developing realistic expectations. Let us discuss the steps involved in determining performance standards for a particular job.[3]

Step 1: Preliminary Planning

Before the manager and employee discuss performance standards, initial standards should be developed. At this stage, both the manager and the employee should develop preliminary performance standards based on the job description that are stated as clearly and concretely as possible. These should be exchanged so that each party has an understanding of what the other expects. By comparing the two lists, both participants should be able to develop a list of problems and questions to be discussed.

The manager should be specific about the purpose of the discussion and define what needs to be accomplished. He or she should then develop a plan for accomplishing this purpose. The two main questions the manager will have to answer previous to the discussion are: (1) To what extent should the interview be planned and controlled and to what extent should it be free flowing? and (2) What type of questions should he or she ask?

---

[3]Adapted from Lloyd Baird, *Managing Performance* (New York; John Wiley & Sons, 1986), pp. 89–92.

The manager will want to provide a high degree of planning and control if the job involves very specific responsibilities. In this case, most of the performance standards can be clearly identified in advance, and there will be limited flexibility. The discussion is then a chance to communicate the expectations that have already been established and make sure they are understood by both parties. If the responsibilities of the job are unclear, the discussion will be less structured, and the flow of the discussion will be determined by the problems that arise in setting realistic performance standards.

Step 2: Clarifying the Purpose of the Interview

Even though the interview's purpose is to establish or communicate specific performance standards, this purpose needs to be reviewed at the beginning of the interview. Both parties usually assume that they understand the purpose of the discussion, but after 30 minutes of talking together, they may discover that they are not in agreement at all. It is better to repeat the obvious and make sure that both parties agree, rather than assume that this is the case until you find out differently.

Step 3: Discussing How the Interview Will Proceed

After the purpose of the meeting has been clarified, the next step is to determine what the participants should talk about and how the discussion should proceed. The types of information needed for the discussion will have been previously decided on in your preliminary planning. This is a chance to make sure the necessary information is available and to decide how it should be used in the discussion. The two parties should also decide how they will relate during the discussion. The person being interviewed needs to know what level of involvement is expected; for instance, is he or she to help define the performance standards or merely to understand the performance standards that have already been developed?

This is also the time to lay out the sequence of the interview. If more information is needed, it should be collected before proceeding with the discussion. If performance standards are to be defined, that must be done before activities for accomplishing them are specified. The natural tendency of both participants will be to jump immediately to the activities unless it is made clear at the beginning that the initial focus will be on defining the standards, followed by a discussion of how to achieve them.

Step 4: Motivating and Involving the Employee

In order to define and communicate performance standards effectively, employees have to be involved. They need to help define the performance standards of their jobs so that they will be committed to accomplishing the objectives to which they have agreed.

Most employees will approach this kind of discussion with some apprehension. They will be unsure of what is to happen during the discussion and assume that since the superior is in a dominant position, he or she should lead the discussion. However, if the employee is to understand and be committed to performance standards, he or she must be involved.

Two ratios can be used to analyze whether or not an interview has given the employee a chance to become involved; the ratio of questions to answers, and the ratio of listening to talking. Asking questions is the best way to involve an employee in a discussion. If the manager is continually asking questions, the employee will naturally be involved. If the manager spends most of the time giving answers, the employee has no opportunity to become involved. If the employee wants to become involved, his or her only option is to challenge the answers the manager is providing.

Another way to involve the employee in an interview is by listening. While a question is an invitation to the employee to become involved, listening makes it possible for the employee to do so. If the manager wants the employee to become involved, he or she must make a conscious effort to listen.

Step 5: The Body of the Discussion

Specific performance standards should be developed and misunderstandings cleared up in the body of the discussion. Although the sequence of the discussion will be determined by the problems to be discussed, it is important not to let the discussion move to solving the performance problems and defining expectations until both participants have agreed on what the problems are. Each needs to understand each other's perception of the job and how they are going to work together in the future. They can then specify concrete, realistic performance expectations.

Step 6: Summary of the Conclusions

By the end of the discussion, a great deal of information will have been exchanged. Much of the discussion will have centered on defining performance expectations, but a large proportion of it may have been irrelevant.

For this reason, the conclusions of the discussion may be unclear. The interview should therefore end with a summary and a restatement of the specific performance standards that have been established.

Since the employee and the manager may perceive the conclusions somewhat differently, this is a chance for them to rectify any misunderstandings and resolve any differences they may have. Too often, if the summary and conclusions are not stated, differences remain that affect the work done afterward. The manager assumes the employee will be doing one thing while the employee expects to be doing something completely different.

The summary should not be a one-sided affair. Whenever performance standards are defined, both parties have responsibilities. The employee's job is to meet the standards and the manager's job is to make it possible for the employee to meet them; both sets of responsibilities should be summarized.

Differences carried into the work situation result in conflict and worsened performance. It is far better to uncover differences and reconcile them during the discussion rather than to wait until they surface as real problems in the work itself.

Job Specifications

Job specifications are explanations of skills employees need to master well enough to accomplish the standards. The skills, as described in the job specifications, are used to recruit, select, and train employees to perform well on the job. The assumption, of course, is that the skills identified are, in fact, needed for good performance. If the skills listed are not needed for good performance on the job, the wrong people will be recruited and selected and the wrong skills will be trained. For example, a common qualification sought in new recruits is a high school education. Many jobs, however, do not require a high school education for the employee to perform well and that specification should not be used. One of the first court cases addressing this issue was *Griggs* v. *Duke Power*

Company. The Duke Power Company used high school education as a specification for recruiting and selecting people into the organization. The defendant, Griggs, successfully argued that a high school education was not related to performance on the job. Those with a high school education were no more able to perform the jobs than those without a high school education. By using high school education as a specification, the company was systematically excluding a protected minority, African-Americans, from employment and promotion in the company. They were using a specification unrelated to performance on the job as the basis for management decisions.

The best way to develop accurate job specifications that list the right skills is to develop them using the job description and observing the job itself.

VALIDITY OF JOB DESCRIPTIONS, STANDARDS, AND SPECIFICATIONS

Validity refers to accuracy. A job description is valid if it accurately reflects the job content. A performance standard is valid if it accurately describes the results employees are expected to produce. A job specification is valid if it accurately explains skills needed to do the job. The importance of having valid descriptions, standards, and specifications is clear when you consider what would happen if they were not valid.

If the job descriptions are inaccurate, the wrong people are hired and trained. For example, an electronics firm hired a recruiting agency to locate a senior engineer. The job description listed the job responsibilities as product development, coordination with other engineers to develop new products, and training of junior engineers. Based on the job description, the recruiting firm located, and the firm hired, a senior engineer from a competing firm who had many of the same responsibilities. Two weeks into the job, he resigned because the job was very different than he had been led to believe. The job actually required coordination with the production and inventory departments in the organization, numerous management meetings to plan and evaluate projects, and management of a team of junior engineers working on the projects, none of which the newly hired senior engineer expected or wanted.

If the wrong performance standards are written, employees will devote their time and energy trying to accomplish the wrong results. For example, the sales force of a computer manufacturer is on an incentive program in which they are paid according to the number of computers they sell. Performance standards are written in terms of numbers of computers sold each month. The company wants employees to sell computers and service customers to install the computers and get them into operation. The sales force naturally is not too interested in servicing customers because that is not one of the standards that has been communicated to them, nor is it one on which they are rewarded.

If the job specifications do not identify the right skills employees need to perform well on the job, the wrong people will be recruited and the wrong training programs established. For example, the civilian employees on a Navy base were recruited to handle the purchasing of supplies and materials for the base. The job specification listed accounting and writing skills but made no mention of familiarity with government purchasing procedures or computer skills that were in fact the most important skills a person could have to do the job. The training programs established focused on accounting and writing, which did not relate much to performance.

One note of caution; analyzing and describing jobs can become very cumbersome. What has been presented is the idealized approach. Often jobs change so fast and people rotate so quickly that you will have to develop general descriptions from quickly done analyses. However, even with a quicker, more general approach the objective is still the same: provide the workers with a good understanding of their jobs, what they are expected to accomplish, and how they should work.

APPLICATIONS

1. Work is done to accomplish organizational objectives. Naturally then, the nature and focus of work should be determined by those objectives. First, define the objectives. Second, design the work to be motivational and productive. Third, develop job descriptions and performance standards so employees know what they are expected to accomplish and have some guidelines on how they should work.

2. Do not set organization objectives in a vacuum. Recognize the constraints and opportunities set by competition, the

environment, and the organization's strengths and weaknesses. Set objectives for each level in the organization that are supportive of and fit with objectives of higher levels.

3. Based on the responsibilities assigned, divide the work to be done into small tasks a group or individual can do. Once the work is divided into jobs, establish coordinating mechanisms so all employees are working towards common objectives.

4. Choose the way of dividing work (differentiation), based on what would be most productive, by product, customer, market channels, locations, or business function.

5. Choose the way of coordinating work (integration); hierarchy, informal contacts, or formal contacts based on what relationships best accomplish the organizational objectives.

6. Design work to be motivational and productive by:
   a. Forming natural work units.
   b. Establishing direct relationships between the workers and their customers or clients.
   c. Including planning and evaluation responsibilities in the job.
   d. Creating feedback to employees so they know how well they are doing.

7. Whenever you use any of the current approaches to job design—robotics and flexible manufacturing systems, ergonomics, quality of work life projects, quality circles or other total quality management programs, or autonomous work groups—remember that the same principles for designing motivational and productive work must be used.

8. After jobs have been designed, do a job analysis and develop a job description so you can establish and communicate to employees the responsibilities they have. Be clear, specific, brief, and make sure the job descriptions are understood.

9. Based on the job to be done, establish performance standards that establish goals, objectives, and targets for people toward which they can direct their efforts.

CHAPTER 4

CASE 2 DESIGNING WORK: A COLLABORATIVE EFFORT BETWEEN XEROX AND THE AMALGAMATED CLOTHING AND TEXTILE WORKERS UNION (ACTWU)*

An excellent example of the principles of application for designing jobs explained at the end of Chapter 3 is the establishment of autonomus work groups at Xerox. This case example begins in 1980, a time when traditional forms of dispute resolution—collective bargaining and the grievance procedure—were well developed between Xerox and ACTWU. The parties' capacity to identify and pursue common concerns, however, was limited to informal arrangements on the shop floor and regular, but informal, briefings by top management with union leaders. The case traces the development of this capacity to pursue common concerns without the abandonment of traditional collective bargaining responsibilities.

When Local 14A of ACTWU and Xerox entered into collective bargaining negotiations in 1980, the company had already begun to experience shrinking market share, but had not shifted its business strategy in response. Though similar in most respects to previous negotiations, the parties did agree to experiment with what was then termed a quality of work life (QWL) effort. The focus was on creating shop floor

*Adapted with permission from: Cutcher-Gersehnfeld, Joel, "Tracing a Transformation in Industrial Relations: The Case of Xerox Corporation and the Amalgamated Clothing and Textile Workers Union." (Washington, D.C.: U.S. Department of Labor, BLMR 123, 1988).

problem-solving groups comparable to quality circles. Oversight would be handled jointly through union-management plant advisory committees (PACs) in each of the four main manufacturing plants in the Webster complex, along with a network of department-level steering committees. Union and company officials each designated ''trainer/coordinators'' who received extensive training in facilitating the work of the problem-solving groups (PSGs). Membership on a PSG was voluntary and accompanied by about 40 hours of training in problem solving, statistical methods, and group dynamics.

Within the first year and a half, over 90 problem-solving groups were established in the four main plants. After two years, about 25 percent of the 4,000 employees in the bargaining unit had volunteered for QWL training and participated in a problem-solving group. By two and a half years, the collaborative efforts had spread throughout the four manufacturing plants and into other facilities in the Webster complex, accounting for a total of over 150 problem-solving groups.

The range of problems successfully solved by these groups included: improving the quality of manufactured parts, developing training for new technology, eliminating chemical fumes, reducing paperwork, upgrading machines, reducing downtime, eliminating oil spills, organizing tool storage, improving communications across departments, developing orientation for new employees, and redesigning floor layout to be more efficient. About 20 percent of the successful proposals included estimates of cost savings, which totaled close to a half a million dollars. The initial QWL structure is depicted on Figure 4–1.

Despite the successful problem-solving experiences, there were clear limitations on the QWL effort. Some of the barriers derived from the traditional structure of collective bargaining and labor-management relations. For example, as a result of the extensive bumping and bidding rights guaranteed by the contract, there was high turnover in many of the groups. These job moves occurred almost every two months. Layoffs of over 5,000 Rochester area employees during 1981 and 1982—approximately 1,200 of whom were union members—brought additional turnover on the teams. Moreover, while the layoffs were an accepted part of a traditional collective bargaining relationship, they directly undercut attempts to emphasize the commonality of interests between labor and management.

Some of the barriers derived from the QWL process itself. For example, there was dissatisfaction with the time required to solve major problems and, more frequently, dissatisfaction with the time required

FIGURE 4–1

Initial Labor-Management Monitoring and Support Structure for Problem-Solving Teams

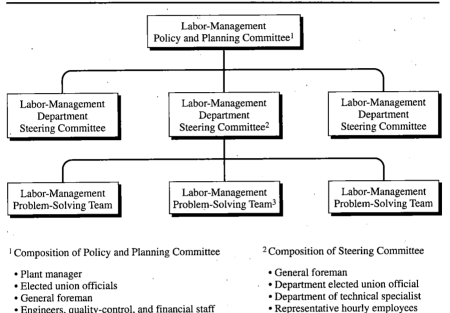

[1] Composition of Policy and Planning Committee

- Plant manager
- Elected union officials
- General foreman
- Engineers, quality-control, and financial staff
- Representatives of hourly employees

[2] Composition of Steering Committee

- General foreman
- Department elected union official
- Department of technical specialist
- Representative hourly employees

[3] Composition of Problem-Solving Teams

- Foreman
- Hourly employees

to implement the solutions. During the three years, the average time required just to generate a solution to a problem was between three and four months. A handful of problems took a year or more before solutions were proposed for implementation.[1] These perceived delays resulted in part from workers tackling problems not amenable to quick solutions, but they also reflected the need to develop procedures (and overcome

---

[1] In fact, this experience is quite consistent with the time period required for problem-solving in other locations studied in the course of the larger U.S. Department of Labor Study of which this case is a part. This issue, however, is that the workers' expectations were apparently for a much speedier process.

internal politics) associated with workers being given access to people and information not previously available to them.

The constraints on the QWL effort—seniority, job movement, lay-offs, and delays—involved issues that were either at the core of the collective bargaining contract or that directly involved issues traditionally considered managerial rights. Addressing these barriers was well beyond the scope of QWL efforts, which were intended to serve as adjuncts to bargaining. The barriers were choice points in which the choice was made in favor of the status quo. Yet in the second year of the QWL efforts, a crisis led to direct union and management consideration of all these core issues.

EXTENDING THE PRINCIPLE OF JOINT DECISION MAKING

Early in 1981, the union learned that management was in the process of vending out certain work in the sheet metal area of the components manufacturing plant. Originally, it had been both parties' intention to keep QWL separated from the adversarial side of the labor-management relationship. However, the potential loss of jobs was so divisive an issue that the union informed management that it could not continue to cooperate on the joint QWL effort while seeing work vended out without joint consideration. Thus, the union's threat to pull out of the QWL effort was a pivotal event.

If QWL was to persist as a joint effort, the union, in effect, was demanding that the principles of joint decision making would have to extend to other aspects of the employment relationship. In response, management agreed to halt the subcontracting in the sheet metal area. Further, there was an understanding that future decisions on subcontracting would not take place on a unilateral basis.[2] That this first challenge to the cooperative efforts emerged in the components portion of the manufacturing organization should come as no surprise, since this is the portion of the business most subject to external market pressures and hence most likely to encounter conflicts of interest.

---

[2]Legally, of course, the union could only insist on its right to bargain over the effects of such a decision, not over the decision itself.

The Wire Harness Study Team

The first test of the new understanding about subcontracting also arose in the components plant in October 1981. At that time, the company announced the possibility of a $3.2 million savings from subcontracting the assembly of wire harnesses used in Xerox machines. This raised the specter of an entire department—around 180 people—being laid off. Not only would this have been devastating for the individuals involved, but the handling of this issue would now have clear consequences for the joint QWL efforts. Tony Costanza, now an international vice president and director of ACTWU, was chief shop steward at the time. He recalls that this was an issue clearly outside the purview of QWL, yet it so deeply affected the quality of so many people's work lives that any unilateral decision would have been inconsistent with the principle of joint decision making about QWL issues.

A series of top-level union-management meetings led to management's suspending outsourcing plans for the wire harness area pending the establishment of a joint study team to be composed of six workers from the affected area, an engineer, and a manager. In essence, the parties saw themselves as applying the QWL problem-solving model to a new set of issues. Many in management privately protested the establishment of a study team, feeling that all reasonable possibilities for saving the work had been investigated. Nevertheless, six months was allowed for a team to fulfill the following mission: Find ways to be competitive, improve quality and cost, and deliver performance of the business to levels that will ensure a positive competitive position and, ultimately, secure jobs. Over 180 hourly employees volunteered for the team—practically all the employees in the affected area of the plant. The union shop chairmen and top union officers made the selection. Management picked the engineer and manager who were to serve on the team and both sides conferred to ensure that the final work group would be compatible.

The study team's task would not be easy. Xerox had recently established a competitive benchmarking program to evaluate its operations and products against the competition along the following dimensions: customer satisfaction, product reliability, design effectiveness, service cost, installation quality, and manufacturing cost.[3] Over $3 million in

---

[3]This competitive benchmarking represented one of the most significant early responses of Xerox to increasing world competition. For some operations, parts, and products, Xerox has concluded

savings had to be achieved while meeting all of the benchmarks that had been set.

At the outset, the team was trained in group problem-solving skills, communications techniques, and Xerox's accounting and financial methods. They were given office space, telephones, and a promise of complete access to anyone in the corporation. A plant labor-management steering committee, with its own executive committee, was established to meet regularly with the team in the expectation that some of the team's work would need approval beyond the authority of the plant and divisional union and management officials.

Initially, it was not only the scope of their task that frustrated the team—the rest of the management organization was not prepared to deal with such a group. Financial information was not always available when it was needed. Policy decisions had to be made about access to confidential information such as supervisors' salaries. At times, projects or progress were undermined by operations managers or general supervisors who "took independent action to implement the changes before the team had presented its ideas to appropriate managers or union officials."[4] Pete Lazes, an external consultant to the QWL initiatives, assisted the study team in surfacing these issues, channeling support from top labor and management leaders, and sorting out the internal frictions that initially emerged between hourly and salaried team members. The study team also succeeded in building the trust of other hourly workers through a request for suggestions (over 200 suggestions were generated) and via weekly "walk around" visits within all parts of the department.

At the conclusion of six months of study, the team proposed changes ranging from physically redesigning the department, to expanding employee responsibilities, to upgrading equipment, to changing the calculation of certain overhead expenses. The biggest concentration of anticipated savings (over 38 percent) involved changes in the organizational structure and procedures such as limiting job movement, redesign-

---

that its own work represents the world benchmark; in other cases, the benchmark is held by one of Xerox's competitors; and, sometimes, the benchmark is in an unrelated industry. For example, after studying automated warehouse procedures in a variety of firms, Xerox identified the L.L. Bean mail-order company as the benchmark in this area.

[4]Peter Lazes, and Tony Costanzo, "Xerox Cuts Costs Without Layoffs Through Union-Management Collaboration" (Washington, D.C.: U.S. Department of Labor, 1984).

ing work, and consolidating jobs. In all, the estimated value of the savings significantly exceeded the team's target of $3.2 million.

Some of the proposals, however, were directly contrary to provisions in the collective bargaining agreement. For example, the reduction of job movement directly contravened the seniority bumping and bidding rights specified in the contract. (At the time, these contractual provisions might account for as many as two or three job changes a year for a low-seniority worker.) As well, the team recommended a reduction of 10 minutes in the personal fatigue and delay allowance. Changes in the organization or work required changes in contractual work rules regarding lines of demarcation. Further, proposed reductions in the amount of supervision and in the calculation of overhead went directly to issues usually considered the province of management. After considerable discussion, the parties agreed to implement the suggestions that involved no contractual changes, keep the outsourcing decision on hold, and grapple with the balance of the issues in the upcoming 1983 negotiations.

Placing the study team issues on the bargaining table was a pivotal decision. It suggests that broadening the concept of joint decision making could not occur without having implications for other aspects of the relationship—especially collective bargaining. During the 1983 negotiations, the parties agreed to implement the remaining recommendations (concurrent with a three-year guarantee of no layoffs for those ACTWU employees in Webster on the March 1983 payroll). Moreover, the parties agreed to institutionalize the study team concept by stating that subcontracting decisions would have to be subject to the establishment of such a team. In the years since 1983, four additional study teams have completed similar analyses. In addition to the wire harness study team, these teams have been in the following areas: turnings, castings, extrusions, and sheet metal. In four out of the five efforts, the recommendations have led to the continued in-house operation of these activities (rather than the anticipated subcontracting).

TRANSFORMATION IN THE ORGANIZATION OF WORK

With neither advance planning nor fanfare, a handful of work groups at Xerox have continued to function for over five years as semiautonomous work groups. This form of work organization, in which work groups operate without direct supervision, typically emerged in selected areas where workers were used to operating independently and either a supervisor retired or was overextended.

The first such group was established in the components manufacturing organization in 1982 under a proviso from the plant manager that (1) all work would be completed on time and (2) that there would be no defects. Twelve people were in the initial group, which split a year later into two groups due to product changes. Over the last six years, these two groups have fulfilled their initial commitment to the plant manager. In this, an area that reportedly had a reputation for poor quality, these groups have managed for over four years to complete their complex sub-assembly routines without a single defect reported from the field.

While there have been a number of studies of such semiautonomous work groups in new manufacturing facilities, little has been written about the emergence of such groups in established facilities. As such, it will be instructive to review the way these groups allocate work, handle membership, conduct training, and interact with both the union and management.

AUTONOMOUS WORK GROUP OPERATIONS

In describing the functioning of one of the groups, a member observed:

> It used to be that you were assigned to a job and that was it. Now we get together as a group and decide which jobs should be run, and how they should be run. Also, we do our own inspection and our own material handling. The people at quality assurance and material handling are not crazy about this, but there hasn't been enough hollering for us to stop. We report directly to the plant manager and do our own attendance and lateness sheets. We order our own material. Production control gives us orders 30 days in advance.

An engineer works directly with each group, sometimes providing information across shifts. One such engineer expressed enthusiasm for the arrangement, stating "these people break their backs for you. This is beautiful; this is perfect; I've never worked anywhere like this."

Apparently, however, there is some variability in group relations with engineers, including some instances of sharp disagreement. In this sense, the increased worker autonomy can be thought of as elevating the importance of relations between engineers and workers. Thus, it poses a pivotal choice in which the outcome is either much deeper collaboration between workers and engineers or more contentious relations.

Although group members still tend to specialize in certain jobs, they note that they always make sure at least two people know how to do each job to fill in for one another. This holds true for paperwork as well. According to group members, once people join, their attendance improves along with the quality of their work. One member explains:

> It's because the company gives us responsibility. When you're in the main subassembly area, you figure that if you build it wrong, they'll be inspecting it. In our area, your number is on your ticket. There is no blaming anyone else but you. It used to be that you would get up in the morning and only think about having to go to a bench, but now you want to see your buddies. I look forward to days off as much as anyone, it's just that I also look forward to being in.

The groups often deal with vendors and sales representatives on their own. Most of the training of new members is on the job. At most, three hours may be spent initially to show a new member how the system works and the rest is learned over time.

In discussing relations with the union, group members indicated that they had first approached the union representatives at the same time that they initially approached the plant manager. It was particularly these union officials that urged that the groups be established on a voluntary basis. Still, there is some ambiguity in the situation since some of what the groups are doing does not precisely fit within the contract. For example, the employees in this area are technically working out of classification with respect to certain quality inspection and materials handling activities. As a result, as one group member noted, "the floor union representatives are behind us. They back us behind the scenes, but they can't do it publicly."

Given their initial quasi-official status, it was critical for the groups to remain voluntary. That created tension, however, with the seniority-based system for job bumping and bidding. Job moves happen on approximately a quarterly basis and as many as four of the six members of the group have been bumped in a single move. This turnover makes the record of continuous, high-quality performance all the more striking, though it does not make the job moves any more popular with the group members. Commenting on the impact of these job moves, one group member stated: ''When you have a group, you all work together and socialize together. The promotions and transfers break that up. It's two steps forward and one back. This is the fourth full turnover in two years.''

Within the past year, there have even been involuntary bumps into the autonomous work groups, with the consequent disruption of additional training and a greater degree of specialization. Former autonomous work group members who have been bumped into other areas have contributed to a diffusion of the general concept of semiautonomous operations. Still, the overall experience raises an important institutional issue: the direct tension between the seniority job rights of individuals and the continuity needs of groups.

In comparing this experience to that in facilities designed from the outset to be team oriented, what is most striking is that the daily work operations are quite similar. However, two distinctions are notable. First, the tensions with the existing system of rules are more salient here (though these issues do emerge over time to some extent in the team facilities). Second, the system is both more informal and more permeable. That is, there is greater informality in training and orientation (which may reflect generally high seniority and skill levels in the work force); and there is greater movement in and out of the teams (which is, of course, a product of the system of rules). Given the high levels of economic performance of these groups under these circumstances (informal training and extensive job movement), there is evidence to suggest that this mode of work organization is really quite robust.

Diffusion of Autonomous Work Practices

While the initial autonomous work groups emerged under unique circumstances, there are indications that they are at the forefront of a larger transformation in work organization at Xerox. A recent visit to the Webster complex revealed that a number of new autonomous work groups had emerged of their own accord in various plants.

An important test of the autonomous work group concept in the components manufacturing operations occurred recently when Xerox offered an early retirement program for managers and other nonbargaining unit personnel. In about a half dozen cases, work groups whose supervisors took early retirement have petitioned to operate on their own. Gradually, managers are evolving a set of questions to put to these groups to assess their readiness to operate in this mode and preliminary indications are that groups will be established in most of these cases.

Further, across the facilities in the Webster complex, there are emerging increasing levels of complementary informal activities. Both managers and union officials indicated a wide range of work groups, while formally under the responsibility of a supervisor, that have begun to operate more autonomously in one or more of the following activities: handling their own scheduling/assignments; monitoring their own inventory; meeting on their own with suppliers; maintaining their own records on quality; maintaining their own records on absenteeism; taking an active role in work redesign, especially around the introduction of new technology; and engaging in safety planning. Thus, in a quiet way, the very organization of work is undergoing a dramatic change.

TRANSFORMATION OF THE
MANAGEMENT ORGANIZATION

Based in part on the successful experiences in the manufacturing organization (and in part on lessons from other organizations), the chairman and chief executive officer of Xerox, David Kearns, embarked on an effort to transform the way the entire management structure operates. Termed *leadership through quality* (LTQ), the initiative began with a meeting of Kearns with the senior executives who report directly to him. Treating each other as ''customers'' for their respective output, they sought to define standards for quality performance and to establish regular meetings or other mechanisms for meeting these customer requirements. In turn, these senior executives met with their direct reports to engage in the same exchange of requirements and plans for meeting these requirements. Preceding each of these sessions, the individuals were given training in communications skills, decision-making skills, and various LTQ principles. Following the same format as these top-level sessions, this interactive process has continued, as one individual put it, ''cascading down the organization.'' In a sense, this puts in place a process of continuous two-way negotiations that has the potential to allow for high degrees of adaptability throughout the management structure.

When the training of senior managers in the manufacturing portion of Xerox began, however, a source of tension emerged. It was clear that senior union officials were among the main "customers" for the senior manufacturing managers, but the LTQ plan did not contemplate union participation. Indeed, there were some in the union who feared that management was seeking to create a strategic alternative to QWL that did not depend on joint governance. A specific concern of the union was its desire to preserve its say in the sort of training that would be received by its members. Further, the LTQ team of trainers were using techniques and materials similar in many ways to those used by the union and management QWL facilitators, raising an issue as to who would provide this training. The first critical development to emerge out of this tension was the establishment of a core committee with top union leaders, top managers, LTQ trainers, and QWL coordinators. The main task confronting this committee was this bundle of integration issues.

It was decided that LTQ would occur in manufacturing but in a modified form. This first session included not only top managers but also top union leaders (a significant event) and the QWL coordinators. These QWL coordinators, along with the LTQ trainers, jointly delivered the subsequent sessions as they "cascaded" down the manufacturing side of the organization. As well, the content of the LTQ process was modified to fit a unionized setting. Today, every single manager and union official in manufacturing has been through the three days of LTQ training and almost every union member has been through the same sessions subsequently with their respective managers.

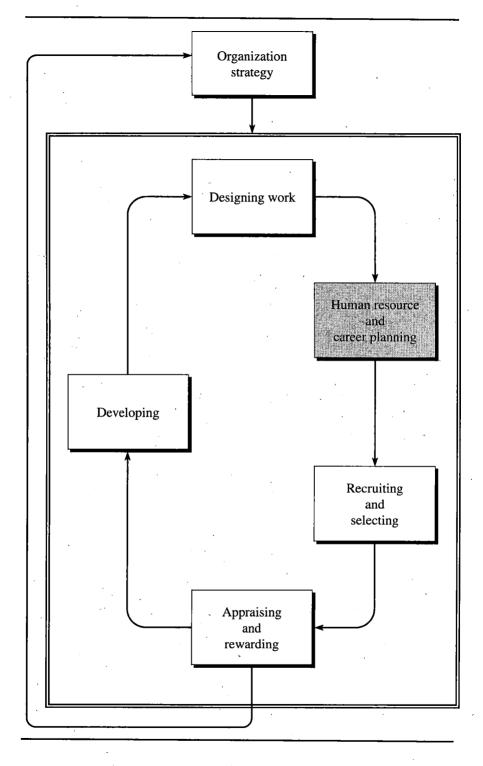

Organization
strategy

Designing work

Human resource
and
career planning

Developing

Recruiting
and
selecting

Appraising
and
rewarding

CHAPTER 5

HUMAN RESOURCE AND CAREER PLANNING

INTRODUCTION

As our review in Chapter 1 indicated, organizations today exist in complex environments. Technology is rapidly advancing, creating the need for employees with more sophisticated skills. Government regulations are requiring more intensive hiring of minorities and women, while at the same time, competition is increasing for qualified employees. Values are changing and so are the expectations people have of their jobs. Flexible work schedules, work done away from the office, and more fluid organizational structures affect the kinds of jobs organizations offer. All of these combine to create a situation in which good planning in the recruitment and use of human resources has become critical. We must understand the changing internal and external environments of organizations and consider how these will affect the type and quantity of employees we will need. We cannot assume that future organizational needs will be similar to those that presently exist and we cannot assume that the human resources we need will be available whenever we want them and in the quantities and types that we need. Instead, we must develop human resource planning programs that anticipate the types and quantities of people that will be needed and career development programs that will help people to develop to meet those needs. Let us consider human resource planning first.

STEPS IN HUMAN RESOURCE PLANNING

Human resource planning takes the objectives of an organization, as developed in its organization strategy, and the work designed to accomplish

85

them, and uses them to determine the staffing levels and types of employees needed. Human resource planning makes sure the right people are hired for the right jobs, that the organization is able to anticipate and adjust to changes in its environment, and that its human resource policies and practices are consistent with what the organization is striving to accomplish.

Figure 5–1 details the steps in human resource planning. The first step in the process begins by clearly establishing present and future organizational objectives. These objectives become the guide for determining the organization's human resource needs. It is important to remember that human resources are not static; they grow and change. Whatever human resources are like now, they will be different in the future. Before recruiting and development plans can be formulated, therefore, the organization must understand how changes will affect what human resources are available in the future. Based on the human resource needs and the human resources available, recruiting and development plans can be developed and implemented to close the gap. Once this has been accomplished, constant monitoring and evaluation will be necessary to make sure the organization and its employees stay on track.

FIGURE 5–1
The Steps in Human Resource Planning

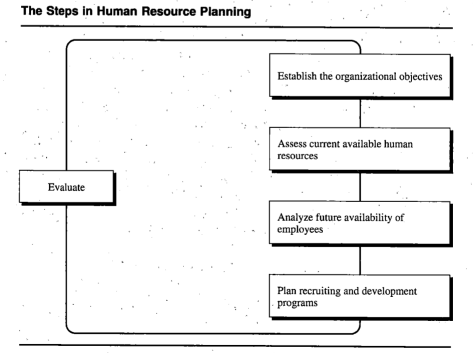

Human resource planning involves the following steps:

1. Establishing organizational objectives and human resource needs.
2. Assessing the skills, interests, and experience of current employees.
3. Analyzing the future availability of employees.
4. Planning recruitment and development programs to meet future human resource needs.
5. Evaluating human resource planning programs.

ORGANIZATIONAL OBJECTIVES AND HUMAN RESOURCE NEEDS

The business objectives determine the types and quantities of employees needed in the future. Organizational objectives identify the number and types of products and services the organization plans to offer in the future. Using this and information about the technologies and methods of production that are to be used in the future, the number and type of employees needed in each of the areas can be predicted. For instance, if one product line is expanding and another declining, technicians and managers from one can be shifted to another if skill requirements match. A computer firm moving to production of the next generation of computers will likely be able to shift the production work force from the old products to the new products because production will require the same set of skills. If, however, the new computers are a new type that is sold to a different market, the sales force probably cannot be transferred. Apple computer, for example, found that their Macintosh line of computers could not be sold through the same distribution channels both to businesses and to individuals for personal use. A whole new sales force was needed in order to sell Macintosh computers to businesses. Knowing which product lines will be expanding and which will be contracting helps identify what managerial and technical talent the firm will need in the future.

Competitive Advantage

The organization develops a proactive human resource plan by identifying its competitive advantage: what it does best and how it can capitalize on its strengths, identifying the types and quantities of people needed to maintain that competitive advantage. If the competitive advantage is mass producing consumer goods, then human resources are recruited, trained, and rewarded to accomplish that objective. If the competitive advantage is producing quality innovative products, then human resources are recruited, trained, and rewarded to accomplish that objective.

The concept of competitive advantage can also be extended to implementing human resource strategy. The corporation competes in the labor market for the employees necessary to reach its strategic objectives and uses its unique resources to attract and retain them. For example, a fast-growing, high-technology firm may need bright, creative engineers, but so does every other high-technology firm. Engineers are in such short supply that competing head-to-head with other firms looking for this limited human resource probably will not yield results. If, however, a firm has a competitive advantage in education, training, and development programs, it can find young people who are interested in engineering and train and develop them to yield top-quality engineers committed to the organization.

Analog Devices, for example, has a unique way of maintaining a competitive advantage for recruiting engineers. The firm produces state-of-the-art electronic equipment and needs a continuous supply of engineers familiar with its products. Most universities do not provide their graduates the applied experience Analog needs in the people they recruit. One alternative is for Analog to recruit on the open market from other firms. The main problem in recruiting from other firms is that the type of engineers Analog needs are in short supply and nearly impossible to find. Those that are available command a high enough price as to be unaffordable. Analog Devices takes another approach. They fund research and provide equipment for local colleges. The stipulation to receive the funding is that research must be in the applied area defined by Analog. Each year, Analog funds projects that come closest to its area of business. The result is that professors and students are doing research on problems Analog defines as important using equipment provided by Analog. Graduate students are very familiar with the unique equipment and products of Analog devices because they work on them doing research through their graduate programs. When the time comes to look for a job, the natural choice is Analog because they are already familiar with the products and equipment of the corporation. Thus, Analog has a competitive advantage in recruiting.

To identify and use the organization's competitive advantage for human resource management, the following questions are asked: What human resource does the corporation need to accomplish its objectives, and what unique resources or opportunities does the corporation have for attracting, developing, and rewarding employees who will contribute to the strategic objective? How will the competition for employees change in the future?

Life Cycle

Proactive human resource planning is concerned with predicting and understanding what an organization's human resource needs will be in the future and then developing and implementing plans to meet them. One way to do this is by using the life-cycle concept. A product goes through a cycle that moves from development and growth to maturity and on to decline (see Figure 5–2). At each stage of the product's development, the organization's human resource needs are different. Development requires innovators and entrepreneurs: maturity requires managers who will hold down costs and decline requires managers who understand what is involved in liquidation. By knowing what phase a product is in, an organization can recruit, reward, and develop the appropriate human resources. It can also predict where the product will be in the future and develop the proper human resources needed for that stage of the product's life.

FIGURE 5–2
Human Resource Implications of the Product Life Cycle

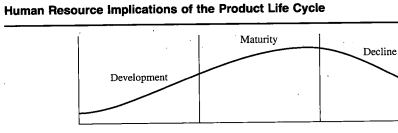

| | Maturity | |
| Development | | Decline |

Staffing	Expansion	Stable	Contraction
Major focus of compensation	Equity	Incentives	Salary
Structure	Flexible	Fixed	Reduced

For example, consider how the compensation system should vary to support the business objective at each stage of a product or organization. In the development phase, the organization needs to attract and reward innovators and entrepreneurs. Equity, a share of the business, is an important part of the compensation package. As the products and organization grow, the portion of equity the employees have through ownership grows. Share of profits is probably not as important during this phase. In fact, because money is devoted to development and building the market, profits will be low. In the maturity phase, employees should be rewarded for the ability to hold market share and cut costs. Incentive systems linked to growth and cost control are appropriate during these phases.

During decline, the focus should be on cost control and liquidation. Equity is not the main component of the compensation package because the business is declining. Incentive systems linked to profit, sales, or market share are also obviously not appropriate. Straight salary becomes the critical component of the compensation package. With salary, employees can be compensated according to their ability to successfully liquidate the product or organization.

Employees also advance through a career cycle of exploration, advancement, maintenance, and eventual decline. At each stage, employees can make unique contributions to the organization. Newcomers just learning and exploring bring a level of energy, innovation, and drive that, if channeled properly, can be a tremendous asset. As they advance and grow, their probing and questioning of old ways of working may lead to substantial improvements in the operating of the business. Those who are in the mature phase of their careers can make tremendous contributions as they apply all they have learned. Those who are declining in energy and interest possess a wealth of information and experience that can be tapped to train new employees.

Knowing where in the life cycle a product or organization is also helps in understanding where it will likely be going. A developing organization will likely mature. A mature organization or product will likely decline and diversify into new products. The human resource practices and procedures must be developed for now and in the future. The organization must anticipate and plan for the future.

The challenge of managing human resources strategically is to match the employee and product life cycle and to recognize that employees in different stages of their careers can all make unique contributions to the organization. A life-cycle approach to human resource strategy asks the following questions: Where in the product life cycle is the product? Do personnel programs such as recruiting, compensation, and benefits meet the needs of that stage of the product? Are the proper programs available to identify, counsel, and assist employees in their own life cycles? How do employees' and products' life cycles fit together?

Portfolio Mix

Strategy also deals with the relationship among the business units of an organization. Products at different stages in their life cycles are played off against each other to support an overall corporate strategy. The money generated in a mature business where expenses are low and market share already established may be used to develop a new business or improve the market position of one that already exists. Resources are transferred from one business unit to another as needed. Business units are organized to complement each other and employees recruited, rewarded, managed, and trained to contribute the maximum to each business unit and portfolio mix.

One of the best known models for analyzing a business portfolio was developed by the Boston Consulting Group (BCG). Their model uses two dimensions to categorize businesses: rate of growth and size of market share (see Figure 5–3).

A business with a high market share and a high potential for growth is referred to as a *star*. This business is doing well and looks like it will do very well in the future.

A business that has a large market share but does not appear to have the potential to grow in the future is referred to as a *cash cow*. Cash investments will not expand the market or improve profits in this business, so the best action is to reap a cash harvest by selling as much as you can.

A business with high growth rate and low market share is referred to as a *question mark*. The business may either grow quickly and establish a dominant market share or wither and die because of a lack of customers. Which way the business goes is determined by management's decisions and investments.

A business with low growth potential and low market share is referred to as a *dog*. The dog is best thought of as a declining organization. Dogs are usually sold, liquidated, or revitalized.

The key to successful management of multiple businesses within one firm is to balance off one against the other. Cash from the cash cow

FIGURE 5–3
BCG Portfolio Mix (Stars, Dogs, Cash Cows, and Question Marks)

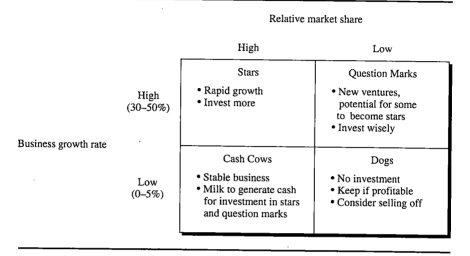

or the liquidation of the dog can be invested in turning the question mark into a star. Innovation from the question mark can be used to turn the dog around.

The portfolio of businesses in the firm also has implications for the management of human resources. For example, those working in a dog business are likely to be very discouraged unless they understand that their job is to get as much money out of the dying business as possible to invest in other businesses. When the business finally dies, their careers are not ended; they will move on to other good opportunities.

Human resource programs should recruit, motivate, and train the type of people the business needs. For example, those recruited with an aggressive entrepreneurial style would probably fit best in the question mark business. Those with an orientation to cutting expenses and controlling costs would fit best in the dog or the cash cow, and those good at developing client relationships and expanding market share will probably do best in a star business.

Organizations also have a portfolio mix of human resources. People have varying areas of competencies and interests. Some are innovative and entrepreneurial. Others are aggressive cost-cutting managers. Just as other resources can be transferred from one unit to another where they are most needed, so can people. Talented managers from a unit that is being sold may be moved to an established or growing business. Mature managers reaching the end of their careers can become mentors to those just beginning.

Proactive human resource management requires understanding the unique competencies of people and matching them to the needs of the business units. The portfolio mix of human resources is managed to complement the portfolio mix of products; as needs change, so people must change. A portfolio mix approach to analyzing human resources suggests the following questions: What is the people mix? What is the product mix? How do they fit together? What people mix will be needed in the future? How will the people mix be obtained now and in the future? Should investments for the future be made now or should needed human resources be bought later? Based on projections of business trends, human resource needs can be identified. Projections identify the quantity and types of people needed in the future plus explain how they can best be managed to accomplish organizational needs.

ASSESS AVAILABLE HUMAN RESOURCES

Once human resource needs are established, you should determine what types of people are currently employed in the organization. The other important component of the data needed to accurately assess the state of human resources in an organization is the human resource information system that describes its employees and how they are performing. This description should include the following information:

- Personal information.
- Career progression.
- Appraisals of the employee's work.
- Skills.
- Interests.
- Training/education.
- Target positions.
- Geographic preferences.
- Promotability ratings.

The amount of information that should be maintained on each employee will be determined by the nature of the individual's job. One word of caution: In constructing a human resource information system, make sure you have a purpose for the information you collect. It is easy to say you need particular data, but do you really? Make sure the information you collect will be useful before you go through the expense of collecting it.

Using information about both jobs and employees they can be matched so there is a fit. Then as jobs become vacant, the information system can be used to identify potential candidates within the organization.

ANALYZE FUTURE AVAILABILITY OF EMPLOYEES

Once you understand your future needs and present employees, you can develop plans for meeting those needs. The first step is to analyze what changes may take place in the present organization's work force: (1) possible retirements, terminations, and resignations, and (2) possible promotions, demotions, and lateral moves within the organization. The next step is to decide what human resources will be needed from outside the organization and how to recruit them.

The future staffing needs of the organization can be determined by the flow of employees into and out of the organization. Reaching the proper staffing level is a matter of controlling this flow, which is a complex process because it tends to be unpredictable. It is difficult to predict exactly how many employees will resign or advance or how many employees you will be able to recruit from other organizations or universities. The best you can do is make some educated guesses and then develop alternative plans if your guesses turn out to be wrong. You must also recognize that all your decisions in this area will be interrelated. The number of people you promote and terminate will have an effect on the number you will have to recruit. For example, if you are faced with a very tight labor market and you promote and terminate a fairly large number of employees, you may not be able to recruit enough qualified people to fill all the empty slots. You must consider all the components of the human resource flow when you are analyzing the future availability of employees. Let us discuss each step.

How Many and What Type of Employees Do We Have Now?

The human resource information system should provide data on current job holders, their personal characteristics, skills and experiences, tenure in the job, promotability, and performance.

Who Is Likely to Be Promoted or Transferred to Another Job?

You can predict what promotions will occur in a firm based on its past history or on its anticipated future needs. The rate of promotion will vary depending on the experience and performance level of those on the job and the need for them in higher level positions. As an example, consider three levels of engineering jobs in an organization: entry-level engineer, supervisor, and department manager. Figure 5–4 presents the transition matrix for these jobs. The transition matrix shows the probability of moving from one job to another over the last five years. If you assume the probabilities will remain the same, you can anticipate that 15 percent of the entry level engineers will be promoted to supervisors, that 26 percent of the supervisors will be promoted to managers, and that 15 percent of the engineers and 26 percent of the supervisors as a whole will either be promoted or transferred to jobs in different areas of the organization.

FIGURE 5–4
Transition Matrix for Engineering Department

	(E1)	(E2)	(E3)	Promoted or Transferred to Other Units in the Organization	Exit Organization
Entry-Level Engineer (E1)	.55	.15	.05	.15	.10
Supervisor (E2)	0	.40	.26	.26	.12
Department Manager (E3)	0	0	.25	.25	.10

How Many Jobs Will Be Vacant?

You can fill vacant jobs by three different means: (1) hiring from outside the corporation, (2) promotions and transfers from within the department in which the vacancy occurs, and (3) promotions and transfers from other departments within the organization. The first place to look for an employee to fill a vacancy is within the department in which the vacancy occurs. Once you have determined that no intradepartmental transfers are possible, you can begin to consider transfers from other departments and external hiring.

Because all the jobs in an organization are connected, changes in one job will affect others. You must look at the whole picture when implementing human resource programs. Consider our engineering example: What happens if some of the conditions we cited above are slightly changed?

• Rather than a 15 percent promotion rate from engineer to supervisor, assume that at some time during the five years, 25 percent of the engineers are ready for promotion. If there are only job openings projected for 15 percent of the engineers, then 10 percent of the engineers are likely to be frustrated because they will not be promoted. Matters would be even worse had you recruited two supervisors from outside the organization to fill the slots.

• Assume that none of the managers are promoted and that a tight labor market exists; even though the managers would like to go to another organization, they cannot because no one else is hiring at their level. Not only are they stuck in their jobs, but also, because they are not moving, they become obstacles to those below them. Now none of the supervisors can be promoted and, because the supervisors are not moving, the engineers cannot be promoted either.

• Within five years, you need eight people who are ready to assume the responsibilities of manager. Assume you promote the five qualified supervisors and then recruit three others. Because of labor market conditions, you cannot find qualified applicants, so you decide to promote some more supervisors. They are not really qualified either, but they are the best you can do. Now there are vacancies at the supervisory level that you had not planned on. You will have to recruit more candidates or promote more engineers.

• Assume you have an affirmative action program for women and minorities. You conscientiously hire and recruit qualified women and minorities at the entry level. Your goal is to have 50 percent of the supervisory and managerial slots filled by women and minorities. Assuming that the same percentages for promotions hold, if 50 females and minorities are hired, 7 of them will be promoted during the next five years. After 10 years of affirmative action, if you have focused on the entry level alone, only 10 percent of your managers will be minorities or women. It will take you 150 years to reach your goal of 50 percent minority representation at the managerial levels.

Various ways of analyzing and using the information generated by the analysis of the flow of human resources have been developed. The more complex approaches use a computer to model the flow of personnel and see how it is affected when hiring, promotion, and termination rates are changed. Simpler approaches do not consider changes in the rate of the flow but simply look at the vacancies. One of the most popular, nonstatistical approaches in use is replacement or succession planning. In its simplest form, replacement planning identifies possible successors for each position (see Figure 5–5). More complex approaches include rates of movement and development plans. The main questions, however, remain the same in all human resource planning models: What types of people will we need in the future and where are we going to get them?

PLAN, RECRUIT, AND DEVELOP PROGRAMS TO MEET FUTURE HUMAN RESOURCE NEEDS

Once you have analyzed your human resource needs, you can develop and implement a personnel program to meet those needs. There is nothing new or profound about this stage of the process. It simply says, based on the type and quantity of people you need, develop and implement all those recruiting and development programs that can most efficiently obtain them. Consider all the available programs and adopt those that will be best able to help your organization reach its goals.

The number and type of employees that you can hire from outside the organization to meet future human resource needs will be determined by a number of factors external to the organization: laws and

FIGURE 5–5
Replacement Chart for Human Resource Planning

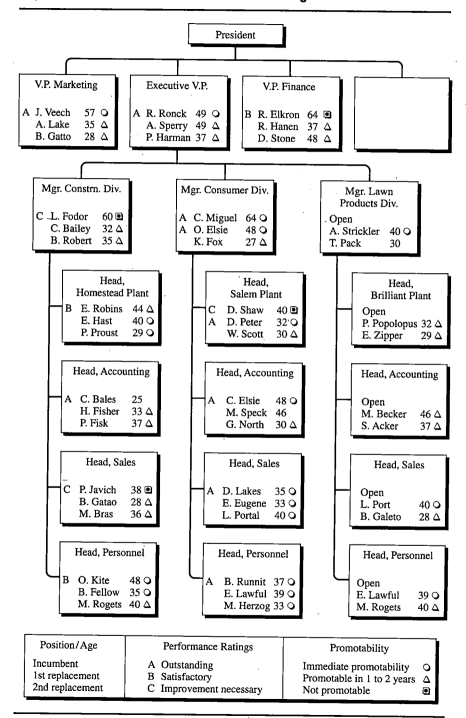

Source: Adapted and used by permission of Henri Tosi, University of Florida.

regulations, labor unions, and labor markets. Increasingly, organizations are recognizing that they cannot develop their human resource plans without taking into account what is happening in the environment. Environmental scanning is the method they have developed to understand and anticipate what is happening in the environment.

Environmental Scanning

In organizations such as General Electric, Honeywell, Xerox, and AT&T, environmental scanning is a formal procedure where line managers, staff specialists, and technicians are assigned to scan publications, conferences, and broadcasts; attend meetings, discussions, and presentations; and project the future availability of potential employees. Right now, for example, those doing environmental scans for engineering firms are projecting a critical shortage of educated engineering talent in the future.

Several years ago, those doing environmental scans for oil companies predicted a severe shortage of geologists and geophysicists. Based on this information, firms cut back their exploration plans, stepped up their recruiting efforts, began cooperating with universities in the training of new geologists, and developed programs for retaining the geologists they already had.

The data used in scanning the environment comes from many sources. Government documents are a prime source because they report on a regular basis the nature of the work force and project education levels for the future. Other sources are reports from professional groups, newspapers, and journals. These sources are available to everyone regardless of whether a formal environmental scanning program exists or not. Whether a formal program exists or not, part of the manager's job is staying in tune with the environment and knowing the quantity and quality of employees that will be available in the future.

Recruiting

Based on the projections of future needs and the environmental scan, the organization can gear its recruiting effort to fill both present and future human resource needs. By orienting a portion of your recruiting toward the future, the employees you hire now will have gained the kind of experience they need to accept greater responsibilities in the future. For example, banks are now facing competitive pressures from insurance companies and stock brokerage firms. They will need to recruit people with knowledge and skill to buy and sell in the stock market in order to remain competitive in the future. These people will need to understand the bank, its customers, and the legal and social constraints within which the bank operates. Banks need to hire those skilled at stock brokerage now and give them experience working in the bank and becoming familiar with its practices and procedures so that when they are needed in the future, they will be ready.

Development

Another way of developing the work force you will need in the future is by providing your current employees with the proper career experiences. For example, if you know that slots will be available in general middle-level management in five years, you can move some top candidates from production to marketing to give them the broad experience necessary to function well in those positions; note that career planning is an integral part of human resource planning.

Or, perhaps you anticipate that your firm will need senior scientists and engineers in five years. Based on past trends, you know that most senior scientists and engineers eventually accept positions in management and move out of the technical fields, leaving vacancies that are difficult to fill. To prevent this from happening in your firm, you suggest developing dual promotion ladders to keep your good scientists and engineers in their own fields rather than in administration. If they can enjoy the same or comparable money and power in their present jobs as they would as managers, they will be less likely to transfer, and thus your organization will have the qualified high-level scientists and engineers it needs in five years.

Recruiting and development play off each other. If enough workers are not developed internally, they must be recruited from outside the firm. If enough workers are not recruited, they must be developed from within the firm. What portion of the needed work force is recruited from the outside and what portion is developed internally is a managerial decision. Recruiting always seems easier because there is a bigger pool to draw from. If you decide to develop employees, you are obviously limited to those who already work in the organization. Compelling reasons exist, however, for trying to develop people from within to fill future jobs rather than recruiting them from outside the organization. Those who are already employees know how the organization and its systems work. They do not have to learn all the formal and informal rules and procedures that run the organization. By developing from within, you also provide career opportunities for present employees. They see that the organization is interested in having them perform over a full career and is willing to spend the time and money to prepare them for future jobs. With this knowledge, they are less likely to resist new technology and other changes because they know it will not be eliminating their jobs, but giving them new opportunities.

EVALUATING HUMAN RESOURCE PLANNING PROGRAMS

A critical phase in human resource planning is evaluating your program to see if you are achieving the desired results. Were you able to find the right people to fill the jobs you had open?

An informal evaluation of the effectiveness of a human resource planning program involves using the data available to do a qualitative analysis in each of these areas. For a more formal evaluation, you can set standards and evaluate performance against them. These standards might include:

1. Actual staffing levels versus established staffing requirements.
2. Actual personnel flow rates versus desired rates.
3. Programs actually implemented versus those planned.
4. Program results versus expected outcome (e.g., applicant flows, quit rates, replacement ratios).
5. Labor and program costs versus budget allotments.

These comparisons will alert you to problems areas. In each case, you will need to analyze carefully why the deviation occurred. The plan may not have been realistic, the information used may have been inaccurate, or the plan may not have been implemented properly. Failure to reach the planned level of staffing is not necessarily good or bad; it depends on why the failure occurred. The firm's situation may have changed in such a way that projected staffing levels were not needed, or it may be that the plan was inadequate to meet the needs of the firm. A careful analysis will reveal why these discrepancies occurred and what should be done to correct them in the future.

CAREER PLANNING

If the human resource plan considers the future needs of the organization, the counterpart for the individual is the career plan. Why should the organization be concerned about career planning when developing their human resource plans? Because the purpose of management is to create conditions such that all employees are able to make the greatest possible contribution to the organization by reaching their full potential for productivity in their present and future jobs. This can only be done by recognizing that employees change. Not only must the organization place its employees on the right job at the beginning of their careers, but as they grow and develop, it must give them new responsibilities and opportunities. This progression of jobs and responsibilities is referred to as an employee's career.

Why Should Employees Worry about Managing Their Careers?

For most people, work fills a major portion of their time. As such, it is a primary factor in determining the quality of their life. Most people have a need to feel involved, successful, and competent at work; when they put forth effort, they want to feel productive, recognized, and appreciated. This is most likely to happen if the abilities, skills, and interests of the person match the requirements of the job. It is in a person's own best interest to manage his or her career so that the time spent on the job will be personally rewarding.

There are many external factors at work that make it even more necessary for a person to manage his or her own career attentively. Economic conditions inside and outside the organization are a major influence on individual career paths. A boom in the economy or a new product demand will increase labor demand and the rate at which individuals advance and move through positions. Similarly, low unemployment rates may induce people to quit present jobs in order to look for more suitable opportunities. For those remaining in their old positions, this allows for more mobility and opportunities within the organization.

Demographic and educational changes over the last 30 years have had the most profound effect on people's careers. Because of population shifts, those now beginning a career are faced with a large group of people just ahead of them who are filling the jobs they would like to have. Birthrates have created a population bulge that has been described as a melon being digested by a boa constrictor. In the 1970s, this bulge consisted of 20 to 30 year olds. In the 80s, this large group of cohorts moved into their 30s and 40s and in 1990s, they will be 40 to 50 years old. A person just beginning a career is now faced with a large group of people in the 20- to 30-year-old category with whom they will have to compete for jobs and promotions.

People born during the baby boom are new in the labor force and are also highly educated. Forty percent of them have attended college. Because of their education, their expectations have been raised, but because of their numbers, and the large number of competent workers just ahead of them, they may face slower advancement and depressed incomes. For a lucky few, advancement will come quickly. The need for qualified managers will present opportunities to a few who will quickly be given major responsibilities. The rest will have to wait, and the wait may be a long one. In the 1990s, the large group that entered the work force in the 70s and early 80s will have experience but there will be few advancement slots to absorb them. They also have just ahead of them a large group of employees whose promotions have been stalled because there are fewer senior level jobs available.

The nature of jobs is also changing. The traditional hierarchical progression in which a person started his or her career as a specialist in a functional department (e.g., assistant engineer) and moved up through the organization in that area (e.g., engineer, supervisor of engineering, plant manager) no longer dominates. Project teams, matrix organizations, and other structural types do not offer the same clear career paths that traditional organizations once did. In new organizations, it is not even clear which way is up and which direction others have followed in their careers. In order to find the types of job moves they want, employees will have to search out information and actively manage their own careers.

Because the competition will be great and the career paths unclear, those who wait and let the natural course of events determine their careers will likely be disappointed, while those who consciously think about their future will have a much greater chance of success.

MANAGING CAREERS—THE INDIVIDUAL'S PERSPECTIVE

In most of this book, we refer to you in your role as a manager. In this section, we look at one of your unique responsibilities, managing your own career. Personal development does not end when you become an adult and start work. Your abilities and interests continue to change, as do your jobs. Some of these changes are predictable and can be managed; others seem to just happen and you have to adjust to them.

Understanding adult development is helpful in three ways. First, by anticipating possible changes in ourselves, we can better prepare for them. We will be much happier and productive if, as we change, our jobs change to match our new interests and abilities. Managing our careers can help make this possible. Second, the problems we face in each stage of our development are different. We need to develop new skills for coping with life and work if we are to achieve a sense of competence and fulfillment. Third, transitions from one stage of development to another are often hard. Entering a new phase of life can be painful, but by understanding the stages of our development and the relationships among them, we may be able to manage transitions and substantially enhance our career.

Let us look at the general stages of adult life and then consider the implications each has for career management. Obviously not all stages will fit exactly every person's life, but most of us will move through six basic stages of adult development: ages 16–22, leaving the family; ages 23–28, reaching out; ages 29–34, questioning; ages 35–43, mid-life explosion; ages 44–50, settling down; and over 50, mellowing.[1]

In this cycle, the early years are dominated by a search for personal identity. It is the beginning of the career and a time to find out who you are and how you fit into organizations. It is a time of questioning and adjusting. Mid-career is dominated by crisis; it is a period of accepting one's limitations and becoming realistic about one's career potential. The late career raises the question of retirement; it is a time to enjoy what you have achieved in the organization and prepare to move out of organizational life. Let us look at the problems and issues that good managers and employees have to face at each of the stages.

Early Career Issues

Because the early career is dominated by a search for identity and desire to fit into an organization, problems of how to enter an organization and become socialized in it dominate. The "psychological contract"

---

[1]For a complete discussion of the stages of adult life, their relationship to career management, and the strategies for managing your career, see Douglas T. Hall and James G. Goodale, *Human Resource Management: Strategy, Design, and Implementation* (Glenview, Ill.: Scott, Foresman, 1986), pp. 389–413.

summarizes this process. When people take a job, they have certain expectations of what they will receive from the organization as well as what they will give to it. The organization also has expectations about what it will receive and what it will offer the employee in return.

Problems arise when these expectations are not met. The new employee may expect his or her own office, secretary, or parking space, while the organization may not be able to offer any of these things due to problems of available space, budget, or location.

These four sets of expectations (what the individual expects to give and receive; and what the organization expects to give and receive) make up the psychological contract between employer and employee. It is not a legal contract, nor is it often written, but it will have a tremendous impact on what is accomplished in the organization and what happens in a person's career. Even minor violations of these expectations can have serious implications. For example, consider an employee who joined an organization because a manager told her she would be transferred to the West Coast after one year. She was not particularly committed to the West Coast, but based on her expectation, she started to make plans to move. Two years later, she found out the organization had no plans to transfer her. Even though she was not particularly interested in the move initially, after two years of anticipation and planning, she was very upset. In this case, the organization ran the risk of losing a competent employee because it created a false expectation.

While organizations sometimes misrepresent the jobs they offer, job candidates have also been known to overstate their qualifications. They describe interests and skills they do not have in order to land a job. Once on the job, they perform poorly and are soon in real trouble.

Realistic expectations are crucial for career success. Managers and employees should make a conscious effort early in the game to develop expectations that are mutually understood and acceptable. From an organizational perspective, setting realistic expectations will probably increase the cost of recruiting because more people will have to be rejected, but the employees that are hired will be more successful because their qualifications will match the requirements of the job. From the job candidate's perspective, setting realistic expectations will probably increase the time and effort involved in finding a job, but once accepted, the position is more likely to match personal interests.

After accepting a job, new employees must adjust to the job and organization. Once they are on the job, they have to learn "the ropes";

that is, what is required of them, how they fit in, how they should behave, and what others expect of them. In other words, they have to be
socialized into the organization.

There are three stages of socialization:[2]

1. *Getting in.* New employees begin to learn about the organization
   before they actually enter it. They try to form a mental picture of
   what it will be like to work there. The more accurate the information they are given before they enter, the quicker their adjustment will be once they have arrived.

2. *Breaking in.* At this stage, the person has become an employee
   and is a participating member of the organization. During this
   period, the employee establishes new relationships and learns
   the job, becoming familiar with what he or she is expected to
   achieve as well as receive within the organization.

3. *Settling in.* After resolving problems of adjustment to the new
   job and work group, two types of conflicts emerge: conflicts between work life and home life, and conflicts between one's own
   group and other work groups in the organization. Conflicts between work and home life can arise over an employee's schedule
   (hours off, vacation time, etc.), the demands of family life, wor-
   ries associated with the job that can carry over into home life,
   and so on. Conflicts between work groups may emerge because
   employees in other departments may have expectations that differ from those of one's own work group. Each of these conflicts
   must be resolved if the employee is to be productive.

The purpose of managing the socialization process is to communicate the expectations of the organization clearly and to match what the
organization wants from the employee and what the employee wants
from the job. Discussions should be held not only on the employee's
current job, but also on jobs that may be available in the future, and the
best way to talk about future expectations is to investigate career paths.
A career path is a series of jobs that move the employee through the
organization. Because different paths provide vastly different experiences and opportunities, it is important for both the employee and the

---

[2]For a review of these stages of socialization see Daniel C. Feldman, *Managing Careers in Organizations* (Glenview, Ill.: Scott, Foresman, 1988), pp. 71–99.

organization to understand what options are available. A progression plan should be developed that will give the employee learning experiences and opportunities.

Three types of career paths aremost common in organizations: functional, cross-functional, and radial.[3] A functional career path moves up through a single area in the organization; for example, a person could start as an engineer, then become a supervisor of an engineering group, and then the engineering manager. This type of career path would give an employee extensive experience in one specialized area, not a broad understanding of all the areas of the organization and how they fit together. In a cross-functional career path, the employee moves across departments and up the organization gaining exposure to all the operational areas of the organization. He or she may start in marketing, then move to a supervisory position in production, then over to finance and then to personnel. The advantage of lateral movement is that it provides experience in many different units. It gives employees an appreciation of each organizational area, enables them to develop skills in each, and affords them a better perspective of the overall operation of the organization. The disadvantage is that the employee may not become truly competent in any of these areas. This path will develop general managers, but it will not provide the experience necessary to become a specialist in any one of them.

The radial career path starts at the circumference of the organization and gradually works in. Someone who starts on the staff of the corporate president, then moves to head of the staff and into a top-level line position would have followed a radial career path. This kind of progression provides excellent knowledge of how top management operates and a chance to develop a specialized high-level skill. It does not give a good perspective of how the bottom of the organization functions.

Obviously, each of these paths provides different experiences. Employees' career paths should match their interests, so it is best to discuss these interests early in their careers so that they can plan a progression that makes the best use of their abilities.

In sum, the early career is a time for finding out about the world of work and how you are going to fit into it. It is a time to test out skills and

---

[3]Edgar H. Shein, "The Individual, the Organization, and the Career: A Conceptual Scheme," *Journal of Applied Behavioral Science*, 7(1971), pp. 401–26.

develop plans for the future. At this point, so many options will be open that you must be particularly active in managing your own career.

Mid-Career

Mid-career is a time for reassessment. Your skills have been tested, you have adjusted to work and the complex relationships it creates in the organization and at home. Three tasks must be completed at mid-career: reappraising, adjusting, and resolving.

Reappraising. Mid-career begins when a person starts seriously questioning the structure of work that has emerged out of the early career period. This need to reconsider comes from an awareness that time and opportunities are running out and that what remains of the career must be managed wisely to make the best of it.

It is a time of questioning your work, your position, your progress and your own interests. You will probably ask yourself questions such as:

1. What have I accomplished in my career?
2. What are my central values and how are they reflected in my work?
3. What are my greatest talents and how am I using (or wasting) them?
4. How satisfactory is my career experience so far? How can I change it to provide something better for the future?

As you reappraise your career, you will discover some success and some failure. You will have to come to grips with reality and some of that reality will be painful when you realize that long-held assumptions and beliefs about yourself and others may not be true.

Adjusting. Gradually people must come to realize that they cannot do everything they had planned in their career. They have to readjust and reorient their expectations. As you make choices and plans for the future based on more realistic expectations, mid-career firmly takes hold.

This is a time when drastic changes in lifestyle which affect your career are likely—increased or decreased financial obligations, divorce, remarriage, children leaving home, social shifts, and so on.

The primary purpose of making these changes is to create a solid foundation for a future that may be considerably different from one's past and each will have significant implications for what you do in your career.

Resolving. There are tensions in most lives that often become particularly intense at mid-career. Before going on, one must come to grips with these tensions, and resolve them one way or another.

First is the tension between youth and age. At mid-career, people are both young and old. They are thought of as old by those just beginning their careers, and as young to those who are retiring. People at mid-career must decide which they are and with whom they will identify, or they must become comfortable in a schizophrenic world and be both young and old. The important thing is to understand that this new tension exists and cope with it.

Second is the tension between the need for independence and the need for dependence on others that exists in any organization. The person wants to be free to create and achieve but can do neither without the support of the organization.

Mid-career is a time of recognizing one's limitations and opportunities. It is a time of reorienting oneself to make more effective use of one's time and energy. Managed properly, mid-career becomes the springboard to an even more satisfying and productive career. Mismanaged, it becomes a source of frustration. One's limitations are not recognized, one's dependence on others is not appreciated, and time and energy are wasted.

Late Career and Retirement

Late career is a time of adjustment to one's position in one's life and career. You have either been promoted to the position that you worked toward and planned for or you have been passed over, never to reach your goal. For some, it is a time to plan what to do after retirement; for others, it is a time to plan a career extended beyond the normal retirement age.

The three major issues the person has to cope with in late career are: (1) adjusting to the end of one's career and the successes or failures it has provided, (2) developing ways to continue to make meaningful contributions to the organization, and (3) preparing for retirement.

Adjusting to the End of One's Career.   Adjusting to the end of one's career does not necessarily mean sitting back and waiting for the inevitable. It may mean retraining, developing new interests and talents, or beginning a new career. Sometimes, however, people assume they have made their contribution and do sit back and wait for retirement; they are referred to as shelf sitters. Shelf sitters are not productive; their careers hold no future. Rather than make productive changes, they do the minimal amount of work necessary to maintain their employment. Their careers become a source of frustration to themselves and to others. Because they are not performing well, they are not promoted and they become blocks to others behind them.

Developing Ways to Make More Meaningful Contributions.   In addition to moving on to more productive jobs, there are two other ways a more mature employee can make contributions to an organization. One is to serve as a mentor; that is, to become involved in the development of junior members of the organization. The mature employee has a vast amount of experience to draw from. He or she can help others develop their skills or guide new employees in learning about the culture and norms of the organization. Mature employees can also act as sponsors by introducing their proteges to their contacts in the organization. Because of their greater visibility and involvement, mature employees can ensure that younger employees receive the kinds of assignments and the exposure they need.

Another way more experienced employees can contribute to the organization is by sharing the information and understanding they have collected over the years with younger, more inexperienced employees. They may not be in a position of power, but they certainly have the kinds of information that is important for decision makers to have.

Preparing for Retirement.   Retirement in the 1990s will be very different from what it was in the 70s and 80s. Two interesting phenomena have recently occurred that have had a tremendous impact on the more experienced worker: first, the mandatory retirement age has been increased from 65 to 70 for most jobs; and second, early retirement has become an acceptable option for many workers.

Those who retire later because of the change in the law will have more problems of old age to cope with: health, adjustment to a retired life after working for so many years, and so on, particularly if the person continues to work because of economic requirements rather than because he or she really enjoys work.

Those employees who retire early may do so in order to begin a second career or to slow down and relax. In either case, the change is not as abrupt as a late retirement. A second career will move them into new challenges and put them back into mid-career problems and opportunities. Slowing down and relaxing will move them out of a career and into other types of activities that they enjoy.

Managing Your Own Career

Managing a career uses the same principles as other kinds of management. First, choose objectives for the short and long term. Second, select a course of action. Third, work for results. Fourth, evaluate your results in relation to your objectives.

Objectives will vary with personal career orientations. Edgar Shein's study of Massachusetts Institute of Technology masters degree graduates in management identified five basic career orientations, or career anchors, each based on a different set of needs.[4] These are:

1. *Technical/functional competence.* An orientation toward the actual work done, which induces individuals to avoid general management positions or hierarchical climbing if it is not accompanied by increased use of their specialized skills.
2. *Managerial competence.* A reverse orientation of the first, in that hierarchical climbing is deemed more important than the development of functional competence. Individuals focus instead on developing managerial abilities such as analytical, interpersonal, and communication competencies.
3. *Security.* An orientation toward long-term employment in one particular firm or area, which takes precedence over level of position or skill.
4. *Creativity.* Similar to the first orientation, but more concerned with the creation of something new, original, and specifically the individual's. This may be a company product, a personal

---

[4]Edgar H. Shein, *Career Anchors: Discovering Your Real Values* (San Diego, Calif.: University Associates, 1985).

gain, or even a whole new organization. It is taking functional competence to its utmost extreme.

5. *Autonomy/independence.* An orientation toward self-determination, self-employment. These individuals, seeking to avoid constraints of place, position, or organizational procedures, may free lance or become consultants to gain more personal control.

Shein found the first two orientations to be most prevalent, though in his study of only 44 individuals, he found repeated instances of the other three. Whatever an individual's personal orientation, there are methods of career management useful to all.

The key elements of managing your own career are planning your job experiences and evaluating your progress. The more aware you are of your own goals, the more you will know about your organization and the better you will be able to manage your career. In addition, research suggests certain strategies that can be particularly helpful in career management.[5]

Develop Career Competencies

Four skills are important for successful career management: self-appraisal, goal selection, planning, and problem solving.

- *Self-appraisal* is the ability to assess yourself and how well your job is meeting your career objectives. Counseling and testing are common ways of obtaining this kind of information. Career planning workbooks can also provide excellent structured exercises and questionnaires for self-assessment. The purpose of all of these tools is to help you gain a better awareness of what you want out of a career.
- *Goal selection* is the ability to clearly identify future career positions. Only by having career objectives can you monitor your progress and development.
- *Planning* is deciding how to achieve the career goals you have set. Without it, goal setting is of little value. Planning how you will attain your goals directs your activity into projects that will be most productive for you.

---

[5]For an in-depth explanation of career management strategies, see Douglas T. Hall, *Careers in Organizations* (Pacific Palisades, Calif.: Goodyear Publishing Company, 1976), pp. 181–89.

- *Problem solving* is necessary when unexpected obstacles arise in one's career. When positions that look interesting fall through or goals change, career objectives and plans have to be modified. Managing your career will often require reevaluation and adjustment, and problem-solving skills will be crucial in this process. To manage your career well, you have to be able to analyze your progress and solve the problems that are preventing you from achieving the results.

Get a Challenging First Job and Perform It Well

Your first job will have a great impact on your future in two ways. First, how you perform on this job will determine what options you have in the future. The better you perform, the wider your future options will be. Only successful employees will be given opportunities to move on to other jobs. While a challenging first job will likely motivate you to perform well, a job that is not motivating will likely be a handicap because if you are not performing well, your chances for transfer to a more interesting position are slim.

Your first job also puts you on a career path. It closes some options and opens others. For example, if someone with a marketing education takes a job working in industrial marketing research, he or she will gain valuable experience for certain types of jobs. This experience will probably not be particularly valuable for jobs in such areas as industrial sales, advertising, customer relations, or purchasing, nor will it be applicable to jobs in such fields as finance, education, or accounting. After your first job, you will have started a career path that leads in a certain direction; transfers to other types of jobs are still possible, but they become increasingly more difficult to obtain.

Practice Self-Nomination

Actively managing your career means that you do not wait until the organization wants to move you to a different job. It will probably transfer you when it needs you somewhere else, not necessarily when it is best for you, and it may move you before you have learned all you can from the job you have. By managing your own career, you have a better chance of holding and maintaining a job that fits your needs. Decide what you want and then aggressively pursue it.

Maintain Contacts

You should always be searching for the next job. Life is not stable enough for you to assume you will have one job forever. The best jobs are found when you do not need one, so maintain your contacts. Stay active in professional organizations, get to know recruiting firms in your field, meet people in other organizations who do the kind of work you would enjoy, and take colleagues and potential employers to lunch just to get to know them. Staying active and visible outside of your normal circles can pay off.

Be Visible

High performance is not enough for career mobility; your performance has to be visible. In order to get where you want to go, people have to know who you are, where you are, and what you can do. Working quietly and assuming the organization will take care of you is often counterproductive; it is easy to become invisible and anonymous in a large organization.

Become a Crucial Subordinate

One excellent way of getting where you want to go is by following some- one else. Working for a person who is advancing is a good way to ad- vance yourself. If you are working with good supervisors, you can learn a lot from just watching them, and when they get promoted, you may go with them. If advancement with them is not possible, you may be se- lected to fill the job they vacate.

Recognize Obstacles to Your Career and Move around Them

In the same way that a successful supervisor can facilitate your career, unsuccessful ones will block it. You cannot learn from them, and they will not leave their jobs unless they are fired. Thus, you cannot move up into their jobs. You will have to move around them by transferring to an- other unit or by moving out of the organization entirely. Do not become a crucial subordinate to an incompetent, immobile supervisor. You will be there forever.

CAREER MANAGEMENT PROGRAMS

Why Should Organizations Worry about Managing Their Employees' Careers?

While career management is essential for all employees, it is also in the best interest of organizations. Organizations need a skilled and committed work force: employees who not only can do their jobs now but can also redesign their jobs so that they are more productive and then move on to other jobs in which they can make even greater contributions. Organizations need people who learn from their experience, who can develop their own abilities, and who are competent and involved in the firm.

By developing competent employees, the organization not only improves organizational performance, it can also create a pool from which to draw future managers and higher-level professionals. Career management programs can have a positive impact in many areas:

1. *Equal employment opportunity.* Not only should minorities and women be employed, they should be given advancement and development opportunities. Not only should minorities and women be hired from the outside, but career management programs can develop and position them from the internal labor market. This will require identifying career paths and eliminating barriers to upgrading their positions and skills.

2. *Competition for personnel.* Competent professionals, high-performing managers, and all well-qualified employees will prefer to work in organizations that are supportive of their career goals and have programs that will facilitate their attainment.

3. *Obsolescence.* Changes in technology, demographics, and economic conditions make certain skills obsolete. Career management programs will help employees update their skills, inhibit stagnation, and maintain organizational and individual flexibility.

4. *Turnover.* One of the major reasons for high turnover is unrealized expectations on the part of the employee or the organization. By improving communication and information systems, career development programs help reduce turnover in two ways. First, they help employees take on suitable jobs so that they are

not forced to go elsewhere because their skills are obsolete or mismatched to the position. Second, they help employees develop career paths that match their career aspirations.

The methods employed will vary with the size and nature of the organization. Large ones will have more formal programs, probably incorporated into the personnel process. Smaller organizations will have less formal career management programs, probably run from the administrator's office or lunch table instead of the personnel office. The chief executive may personally meet with employees, and assist them and the firm by forming efficient career paths for them.

Regardless of size and formality or informality, the specific programs employed have similar purposes. In some career programs, which focus on training and counseling, the purpose is employee development; in others, which focus on career information systems, human resource planning, and career pathing, the purpose is to provide information so that employees can find the jobs they want and are suited for.

Organizational responsibilities in career management fall in many areas, such as internal and external recruitment (promotions, transfers), separations, and retirements. The mechanics involved in each function differ. In initial hiring processes, it is the responsibility of the organization to orient new employees. The company should provide new employees with information about the company's policies, goals, and history, as well as the rules, hazards, benefit systems, and operations concerning individual employees. Orientation programs can be both too casual and uninformative as well as too formal and overwhelming. Managers should tailor their programs to the nature and size of the organization, and to the positions of the new employees.

Internal recruitment procedures also vary. They can be open or closed; that is, filling a position can involve an open system like job posting or a closed system where the responsibility rests with the supervisor who has the vacancy. In private organizations, open and closed systems are equally used for technical and professional positions, but managerial positions tend mostly to be filled through closed systems, and clerical or blue-collar positions through open systems. In government and unionized organizations, open systems tend to prevail regardless of the position in question.

There are many factors that must be taken into account and balanced by the manager when making a promotion, demotion, or transfer decision. Seniority and past experience or performance are, of course, crucial, but more ambiguous factors also come into play. For example, a problem may arise when one employee is slotted for an opening because it fits his or her career development schedule, and another because he or she is most qualified or suited for it. Salary rates are another factor. When an employee has been with a company for 30 years and accepts a demotion or transfer to a lower-paying position for reasons other than poor performance, should that person receive the lower salary? Effective career management programs will have to take issues like these into consideration.

In addition to its responsibilities to its new and growing employees, the organization has a responsibility to its potential retirees. Almost all firms have retirement pension plans and programs to assist in the transition to retirement. Some have preretirement seminars and preparation programs to familiarize employees with the problems and opportunities of retirement so that employees will have a positive outlook and be happier after separation. Some firms also have postretirement programs that provide counseling and social events or clubs to retain contact between the organization and the retiree. Phased retirement is a new program that aims at progressively reducing the mature employee's workday and workweek while increasing annual vacation time. It seems to work best when it is voluntary and when salary rates do not drop substantially.

Training and Development Programs

Training and development programs are covered in depth in Chapter 9, so they will only be covered briefly here. The difference between training and management development programs is their content, not the way they are conducted or their duration. Training programs are oriented towards performance on the present job and personal skill development, whereas management development programs are more oriented toward future positions and helping employees move from one job to another.

Management and supervisory training and development programs run the gamut from one- or two-day skill-training sessions to extended programs including on-the-job experience. Those programs that are oriented specifically towards career development emphasize future jobs. For example, each year, the career development program of one company identifies 10 to 12 promising middle managers and relieves them of their immediate job responsibilities to attend an eight-week program that provides an overview of the company. The candidates then attend a two-week management institute. When they return to their old jobs, they are considered candidates for top-level management positions. Other organizations have apprentice training positions; these are usually entry-level positions that offer employees the opportunity to learn on the job. Apprentice programs are most common for technical jobs where skills are learned by practice. The apprentice works directly with a more experienced employee. The assumption is that apprentices learn by watching others do the job and then by doing it themselves under close supervision.

In higher-level managerial and professional positions, the same concept of training through experience is included in mentor programs where those who have experience help new employees learn their jobs. The mentor may be the new employee's supervisor, someone else in the organization at a higher level, or, very often, a peer.

Career Counseling

Career counseling can and should be involved in most personnel practices. Employment interviews should deal with the present job as well as possibilities for the future. Performance appraisals should include discussions of career development and future responsibilities. Testing and assessment programs should provide information about employee skills and interests that will be relevant for both the short and long term; even day-to-day supervision should be geared to career development as well as current performance. In addition to being part of ongoing personnel practices, career counseling is a formal responsibility of the personnel department. It can provide self-assessment techniques and information about career opportunities.

Career Information Systems

Career information systems are designed to provide employees with information about available jobs within the organization. Job posting is a common method used to inform employees of new opportunities. The company newsletter and/or bulletin boards usually describe open jobs so that any employee who wishes to be considered can apply for them. Career information can also be disseminated in career counseling sessions with individual employees.

Human Resource Planning

Human resource planning includes all of the techniques used in organizations to predict future employment needs and to plan recruiting, promotions, terminations, retirements, and so on. This planning takes into account organizational growth and changes in the market and in the internal and external labor force. By projecting human resource needs, the organization can provide employees with information on future job openings in the firm. This can then become the basis for career planning. The employee and the firm can plan job progressions that will be productive for both.

Career Pathing

Career pathing is a sequence of jobs that makes the greatest possible use of the employee's skills and interests. In fields such as retailing, the paths are clear; there are only one or two tracks to follow. When the paths are clear, the normal performance appraisal and reward systems will move people along them. When the paths are not as obvious, they need to be clarified so that employees can progress through them.

DEVELOPING A CAREER PLAN

After understanding the individual and the organization, you will be prepared to help an individual develop a career plan and begin managing it.

We suggest you help the employee answer the following 11 questions:

1. Where Do I Want to Be?

Describe in as much detail as possible what you want to be doing in the future. The description should include both the types of activities you enjoy and the results you would like to accomplish. If possible, identify some jobs that would allow you to engage in these activities and results. Try to list more than one type of job but be as specific as you can. Also, explain how you will measure achievement of your career objectives; that is, how you will know whether you are on course, whether you have reached your objective, or whether you should make a change in your career plan. You should develop career objectives for 12 months, 3 years, and 5 years. The further in the future, the harder it will be to be definite, but make your descriptions as specific as you can. Remember that your career objective must take into account other facets of your life: your family, your community interests, and your personal goals.

2. Where Am I Now?

Describe where you are now in relation to your goal. What experiences have you had? What job do you now have and how does it relate to the jobs you would like to have in the future? Try to describe as accurately as possible the difference between where you are now and where you want to be. Identify the major and minor skills you will have to develop. Decide how your future job will differ from the one you have now. If you are a student, consider that as your job; how will your future employment differ from that of being a student? Think carefully about that.

3. What Personal Strengths and Internal Resources Do I Possess that Will Help Me Reach My Goal?

Identify the skills and personal strengths you have demonstrated in life so far. Think of actual incidents that have demonstrated that you possess the skills you have listed. Be specific and list career-related skills. Be cautious about listing skills you think you possess but have never had a chance to demonstrate. Careers are built on good concrete accomplishments, not on wishful thinking.

After listing the skills and personal strengths you have demonstrated in the past, list some you think you may have but are untested as yet. Make this a second list to emphasize your uncertainty about them.

4. What Personal Shortcomings Will Hinder My Progress toward My Goal?

Describe the activities you presently cannot do well. What are you unable to do now that you will need to be able to do in the future to obtain your career goals?

5. How Will I Overcome Each Internal Barrier?

Develop a plan for acquiring the skills you need for your career. Specify when you think you can develop them. Be realistic about this; remember that you have many components in your life, all of which continue to demand time and energy.

6. Who Can Help Me Overcome My Internal Barriers, What Will I Ask Them to Do, and When?

Other people can provide you with the counseling, information, and career guidance necessary for your growth and development. You will need an aggressive plan of how to use their assistance.

7. What External Barriers or Obstacles Will Hinder My Progress toward My Goal?

Identify obstacles that your organization or society in general places in your way. These may be blocked career paths, prejudicial attitudes, or organizational practices. The list should be as extensive as possible. After you have identified these constraints, decide which affect you most directly.

8. What Opportunities and Resources Are Available within and outside of the Organization?

Describe the opportunities and resources the organization provides. Consider not only the types of jobs available, but also the people with whom you can work and projects you can undertake. In describing the opportunities outside of the organization, list only those that are easily accessible. Which ones can you take advantage of?

9. How Will I Get around Each of the External Barriers I Face?

Develop a plan for overcoming the obstacles you face. Give a specific and detailed description of the actions you can take.

10. How Will I Take Advantage of the Opportunities and Resources Available to Me?

Develop a plan for taking advantage of the opportunities and resources available to you. Give a specific and detailed description of the action you can take.

11. Who Can Help Me Overcome External Obstacles, What Will I Ask Them to Do, and When?

Identify specific people and state how they can help you. Remember to consider people inside and outside of your organization.

One obvious caution: As you—the manager—work with employees to develop their career plans, you will raise their expectations. They will expect assistance in meeting their career plans, and rightfully so. It is to your benefit to have employees constantly improving. Career advancement will increase their ability and interest in contributing to the organization.

APPLICATIONS

1. Do not assume that future organizational needs will be like those that now exist. Develop human resource planning programs to anticipate the types and quantity of people that will be needed and develop those employees that now exist to meet human resource needs.

2. Identify your organization's competitive advantage and then recruit, train, and reward human resources to maintain that advantage.

3. Identify where a product is in its life cycle and match organization structure, systems, culture, and human resource management practices accordingly.

4. Determine the types and quantity of employees your organization will need based on the number and types of products and services the organization plans to offer in the future.

5. Determine the types of people currently employed in the organization through a human resource information system that describes employees and how they are performing.

6. Make sure your human resource information system contains only necessary information. Unnecessary information just adds expense.

7. Analyze changes that may take place in your organization's work force by looking at:

   a. Possible retirements, terminations, and resignations.

   b. Possible promotions, demotions, and lateral moves. Then decide what human resources will be needed from outside the organization and how to recruit them.

8. Identify future jobs and skills that will remain unfilled. Rewrite and develop people to fill them.

9. Recognize that employees change. Give them new responsibilities and opportunities so they can continue to grow and develop their careers.

10. Carefully manage the socialization process of a new employee so that the performance expectations of the organization are clearly communicated and can be matched with what the employee can and wants to do on the job.

11. Don't allow mid-career questioning to become a frustration. Help those in a mid-career crisis to develop their jobs to be even more satisfying and productive.

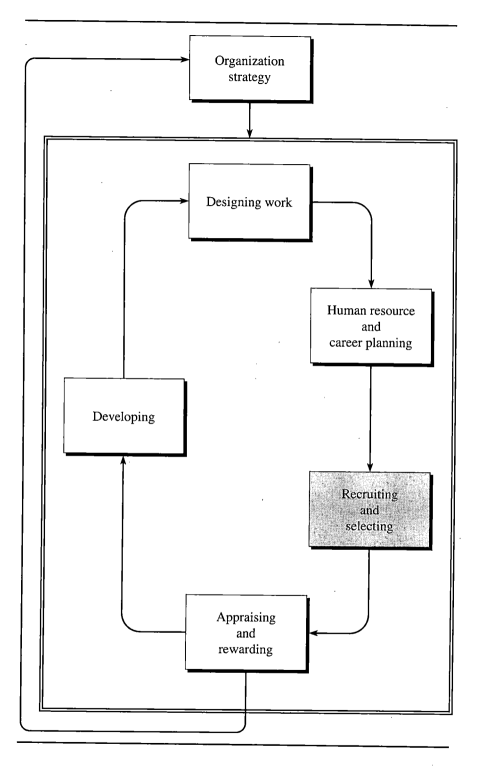

CHAPTER 6

RECRUITING AND SELECTING

INTRODUCTION

The staffing of organizations is a critical concern for the modern manager. Organizational growth, employee advancement or separation, and job change will all create a need for new employees. Recruiting qualified employees to consider applying for a job, selecting the most qualified from those who apply, and convincing them to accept the job offer are among the manager's most important jobs. Recruiting and selecting need special attention if the right employees are to be found. In order to staff their organizations properly, managers must answer the following questions:

1. What type of people do we need on the job?
2. How can we find available and qualified applicants?
3. Of those available, which ones should we select?
4. How can we convince those we select to accept our offer to join our organization?

Let us consider each of these questions.

WHAT TYPE OF PEOPLE DO WE NEED ON THE JOB?

Recruiting, like so many other human resource management activities, is something done now to affect organizational performance in the future. We recruit people because we think they will be able to perform in the organization. Naturally, we would like to hire those who will perform best. We do not really know how well the new recruits will do until they

125

are actually performing on the job, so we are forced to recruit and select based on how well we predict they will do. Performance on the job is referred to as the criterion and the measures we use to predict how well people will perform in the future are referred to as predictors.

Consider the following example. Each year, college basketball coaches must rebuild their teams by replacing players that have graduated. They recruit from the ranks of high school players those they think can perform on their teams. Before they can recruit, coaches must have a good idea of what performance is on their team. Usually a coach is looking for someone who can score and/or play defense. The criteria are the number of baskets made for the team and the number of baskets prevented for the opponent. The coach's job is to find players who will score and defend. To decide which high school athletes to recruit, the coach will use predictors of future performance. As a predictor of the number of baskets a player will make on the college team, the coach will likely look at the number of baskets scored, percentage of shots, and number of free throws made in high school games. The assumption is that those who have scored well in high school will score well in college.

Predicting future defensive ability will be a little harder. Defense is effective if the other team is prevented from scoring baskets. The coach will have to look at high school game films and scouting reports to form judgments of how good the players are at defense. Again, the assumption is that if they were good at defense in high school, they will be good at defense in college. The criteria are scoring and defense in college games. The predictors are scoring and defense in high school games.

Managers are often not as lucky as coaches. People just starting their careers will probably never have performed the type of work for which they are being recruited. Even people recruited from other organizations with substantial work experience usually will not have worked on the type of job for which you need them. The predictors will have to be the potential employees' performance on similar jobs, the skills they possess, and their interests and motivation. For example, a bank needing a loan officer looks for someone who has demonstrated motivation as evidenced by superior academic performance, written and spoken communication ability, and analytical and quantitative skills, because it has found over time that people with these skills do well as loan officers. Academic performance has been found to be an accurate, valid, and reliable predictor of future performance as a loan officer.

HOW CAN WE FIND AVAILABLE AND QUALIFIED APPLICANTS?

One excellent source of people to fill available jobs can be found among current employees, but only if the new job represents a promotion, a needed change of pace, a learning opportunity, or a chance to work with new colleagues. By searching internally first and offering job opportunities to those already employed, the manager can foster greater loyalty and commitment to the organization among employees, and vice versa. Because of their familiarity with the organization, current employees can learn their jobs more quickly and have a shorter adjustment period. If there are no qualified candidates internally, then you will have to search externally. Let us look at several methods of internal and external recruiting.

Internal Recruiting

Self-Selection. Job posting allows employees to apply for positions by responding to public announcements of jobs available. Announcements, which are often posted on bulletin boards or published in company newsletters, usually give the salary level of the position, experience requirements, responsibilities, and any other information that would be useful for prospective candidates.

Job posting is most common for office, clerical, administrative, and technical positions, and it is often considered a key component of affirmative action programs. The openness of the system allows all employees to apply; it is therefore a good method for communicating job availabilities to protected groups. Bank of America, for example, publishes a job opportunities bulletin each week. The bulletin lists job openings with brief descriptions of job responsibilities, qualifications, salary level, and location. Copies are posted on bulletin boards, placed in lounges and entrances, and generally made available to employees. Employees interested in the position fill out the application on the back of the bulletin and mail it to those who are doing the recruiting for that job.

Another way the personnel manager can allow employees to select themselves is to have them identify in career plans the jobs in which they are interested. Based on this information, the manager can then inform employees when jobs that interest them become available.

Skills Inventories. Rather than post jobs, some organizations maintain an inventory of employee skills. The inventory lists skills relevant to jobs in the organization. As a job becomes available, the organization can search the records to find qualified candidates and then contact them to find out whether they are interested in applying.

Referrals. A very common way of finding new employees is through friends and acquaintances of present employees. The acquaintance network has always been a very powerful way of finding employees. The problem with referrals is that employees will tend to recommend people who are similar to themselves, and this will perpetuate the existing racial and sexual composition of the organization's labor force. Minority workers, for example, are unlikely to hear of available jobs if they have no friends in the organization. Because of the likelihood of exclusion of certain types of people, care must be taken to make sure a broad range of people know about the jobs available. With referrals as with other methods, the manager must keep meticulous records so that the organization can evaluate its recruitment procedures and meet affirmative action goals.

External Sources

College Recruiting. College recruiting is a major source of professional, technical, and managerial talent. Over 50 percent of such hires in organizations come from college recruiting. To students, college recruiting is the most often thought of method for finding employment.

Like other recruiting, campus recruiting is best thought of as a series of activities. For college students, the most visible activities are the interviews on campus and the letters that follow inviting them for further interviews and offering them jobs or informing them that no jobs are available. The organization, of course, has done substantial work that is not visible preparing for the campus visit. They have identified what types and how many employees are needed by the organization. They then have decided on which campuses to recruit. This decision is based on many considerations. The organization may decide that recruiting at a prestigious university is important for their image. They may have contacts at the university and even though the organization has no jobs to offer, they may want to keep up the contacts for future recruiting. They may have found people at the university to be a good source of information about the labor market and economic conditions, so they come to campus not only to make some contacts with students, but also to talk with other recruiters and professors to gather information.

Once on campus, the recruiter must attract students to sign up for interviews. Students sign up for interviews based on their overall impressions of the company and the jobs being offered. To be effective, the company and the recruiter must have sufficiently advertised both. Placement office notices, company literature, and prior visits and discussions with groups of students all create an image of what the company is and what jobs are available. A lot of preliminary work has to be done to convey the right image and hopefully attract the right students to sign up for interviews.

After the campus interview, the organization must decide which if any of the students to invite to the organization. Rarely will job offers be made based on campus interviews. Rather, the students who look like potential employees are invited to the organization for further interviews with the department or unit that has job openings. After a series of interviews at the site and with the personnel/human resources department, employment decisions are made and job offers extended.

The campus recruiting office serves as a contact between students and employers. The advantage of working through the campus recruiting office for organizations is that they can quickly meet numerous students and gather valuable information about them before spending money to bring people into the organization. The advantage for students is that they can make contact with numerous organizations in a short period of time and all at one location. The campus recruiting office can become a valuable tool for students, which they should learn how to use. Students should remember, however, that it is only one tool. Most jobs in the organization are not filled through the college's recruiting office. They are filled from internal recruits, other educational institutions, employment agencies, professional associations, unions, and media advertising that generates walk-in applicants.

Other Educational Institutions.   Organizations also recruit at educational institutions other than colleges; high schools and vocational schools provide a rich source of talent. Recruiting in these institutions is different than college recruiting because there are usually no formal interviews or programs. Employment opportunities are usually announced by teachers or counselors or made known through bulletin boards or career days; the students then contact the organization.

Employment Agencies.   Many public and private employment agencies seek to match employers with employees. The United States Employment Service (USES), for example, operates 2,400 employment agencies throughout the United States and deals primarily with clerical, production, and technical workers, though their services are available free of charge to all job seekers.

Private employment agencies typically specialize in one field of employment. For example, executive search firms, or "headhunters," as they are called, are a prime source of executive and managerial talent. Recently, employment agencies specializing in women executives and minority employment candidates have emerged. Because these private organizations are so specialized, they can often find better qualified candidates than the organization's own recruiting department.

Professional Associations.   Most professional associations provide placement services for their members. Often, organizations can announce job openings in the association newsletter or journal and then arrange interviews with candidates at professional meetings. Usually a member of the profession will do the recruiting and interviewing, rather than someone from the personnel department.

Unions.   Some unions provide employment services for their members; in fact, some contracts require employers to recruit first among union members. Employers can submit requests for work at union hiring halls, and applicants are then referred to the organization.

Media Advertising.   Newspapers, magazines, television, and other print and broadcast media provide an excellent resource for recruitment of employees. The main advantage of media advertising is that it reaches large numbers of people. Its main disadvantage is that it cannot be narrowly focused; thus, a large number of unqualified candidates will be attracted.

The most common medium used to advertise is the help wanted section of the newspaper. A quick scan of this section shows what jobs are available and provides a good summary of conditions in the labor market. Other popular media include billboards, magazines, posters in public places, and radio and television announcements. In selecting among these alternatives, the considerations are cost and effectiveness in reaching the desired audience. Billboards and posters can be cheaper, but will not reach the large numbers of people that other media will.

As with all recruiting efforts, material used for recruiting should accurately describe the job and the qualifications necessary to perform. Advertisements should not state age, race, religion, national origin, or sex requirements that are not job related. Often, if discrimination exists in the organization, it has been initiated in the recruiting process. If the organization can remove discrimination from recruiting and employment practices, it has a better chance of removing it from the organization.

Managing the Recruiting Budget

Sometimes recruiting is viewed as a process initiated and controlled by the organization. In practice, however, both the employer and the prospective employee are active participants. The employee finds and chooses the organization just as the organization finds and chooses the individual. Recruiting is thus the matching of the needs and interests of the individual to those of the organization.

Because everyone will not accept offers, an organization must initially contact many more people than it will finally hire. Four ratios can be used to predict how many leads should be obtained to yield the desired number of hirings. Yield ratios are the ratios of leads to invitations, invitations to actual interviews, interviews to offers, and offers to hirings. Time lapse data will indicate the average time intervals between such events as the extension of an offer to a candidate and his or her acceptance and addition to the payroll. Together, the ratios and time lapse data will tell you how many leads you should generate and how long it will take you, on the average, to complete the hiring process.

These data should be based on past experience and will vary depending on the organization, the type of job available, the labor market conditions, and the efficiency of the organization's recruiting program. If no previous data are available, information from other companies or best guesses will have to be used. Consider the following as an example of how these ratios work.

Recruiting Ratios

A certain firm trying to fill several technical positions finds it must extend offers to two candidates in order to gain one acceptance, an offer-to-acceptance ratio of 2:1. If it needs 100 engineers, it will have to extend 200 offers. Further, if its interview-to-offer ratio has been 3:2, then 300 interviews must be conducted to extend 200 offers; and if its invitations-to-interview ratio is 4:3, then as many as 400 candidates must be invited to interview to yield 300 interviews. Finally, if it finds it must contact six leads for every invitation to interview it offers, its lead-to-interview ratio is 6:1, and it must make 2,400 contacts.

			Ratio
Hires	_____		
Offers	_____	Offers to hires	2:1
Interviews	_____	Interviews to offers	3:2
Invites	_____	Invitations to interviews	4:3
Leads	_____	Leads to invitations	6:1

What Approach Should We Use?   After deciding how many leads you will need to yield the number of hirings you want, you will have to decide how to find those leads. Both cost and effectiveness will have to be considered.

Media advertising can be expensive, but it effectively reaches large audiences. Recruiting at professional meetings is relatively inexpensive and is an effective means of finding specialists in narrow fields. The very specialization of this form of recruiting, however, can be a drawback. You may be less likely to find minority candidates among members of professional organizations than you might elsewhere.

The recruiting approach you use should be determined by the jobs you are trying to fill and the available budget. The key is having a clear understanding of what the different approaches can accomplish and how much they will cost.

Who Should Do the Recruiting?   It may come as a surprise to some, but it is not always the personnel department that can do the best job of recruiting. For specialized jobs that require high-level technical skills, or for jobs that involve a considerable amount of work done in groups, it may be better for those who are currently on the job to do the recruiting. For example, the professionals of universities and scientific organizations are often assigned the responsibility of recruiting their colleagues because they have the contacts and are better able to evaluate potential employees. Also, graduates from a particular university may be assigned to return to that university to recruit. When close group work is necessary on the job, very often the group itself is given the responsibility of recruiting new group members. Because of its involvement in the recruiting process, the group will have a greater commitment to integrating new members and helping them succeed.

The recruiting process is critical to the success of the organization, and therefore recruiters should receive proper training. Their competence in representing the organization to the outside world will determine what kind of work force the firm can attract; this should not be left to chance.

OF THE AVAILABLE CANDIDATES, WHICH ONES SHOULD WE SELECT?

Once a number of applicants are found, the organization must decide to which candidates it will make an offer. Some managerial and legal requirements must be satisfied when making this decision. Let us consider these requirements and then discuss how the selection process can be conducted.

Management is interested in job performance. Decisions about selection should be based on recruits' anticipated ability to perform the job. This requires first, that when selecting, you have a clear understanding of what constitutes good performance; second, that you select your candidates based on job-related criteria; and third, that you use an understandable, usable, and cost-effective selection method.

Training will often help you meet the first two of these requirements. For instance, you can learn interviewing techniques through training. The requirement of cost effectiveness is a little more complicated, however, since it relates to the degree of precision that can be applied to the selection process. How sure do you want to be about the ability and motivation of a candidate before making him or her an offer? An auto company in Canada wants a high degree of certainty; its selection process involves inviting the candidate to work on the job for one week. It established a small production line where job candidates work for one week at minimum wage. After four days of work, they are given feedback on their performance and either offered a job or given an explanation of why they probably would not fit into the organization. The firm's experience with this method has been very good. Those who are offered jobs usually accept; they have a good understanding of the job and usually perform well. Also, because of their exposure to the job, the new employees know what they are getting into and therefore stay longer. In addition, their performance is enhanced because there is less training time. The potential employees also do some self-selecting. Because they actually experience the job, they are able to decide whether they like it or not.

This selection process reflects future performance fairly accurately; that is, it is a relatively valid indicator of true performance. The problem, of course, is that it is very costly; special machinery, supervision, and observation are all necessary. However, some organizations have decided that the reliability of the results is worth the expense.

Other firms choose different, less costly, and often less valid methods for selection. Cheaper selection methods such as interviews and standardized tests may select candidates who will not perform well. These problems must then be solved by training or increased supervision. In one sense, it is a matter of where you want to incur costs; the less valid your selection method, the more problems you will have and the more you will have to pay later. Of course, the best selection method will be the one that offers the greatest possible validity while still remaining within the budget constraints of the organization.

The legal and managerial requirements for selection methods are very similar. The law states that the selection method used must be a valid indicator of a person's ability to perform on the job. A good way to understand what the courts will accept as a ''valid indicator'' is the classic case of *Griggs* v. *Duke Power Company* mentioned in Chapter 3. Duke Power Company required a high school diploma or a certain cut-off score on a standardized intelligence test for their employees. As a result, the company employed very few blacks. Griggs was a 30-year-old black man who failed to meet the company's requirements for hiring. His claim was that neither the high school diploma nor the standardized test were very good indicators of how he would perform as a lineman. The court agreed, and using Title VII of the Civil Rights Act, found that the methods used by the Duke Power Company to select its employees were invalid. The following are excerpts from the court's decision:

(a) neither standard is shown to be significantly related to successful job performance, (b) both requirements operate to disqualify Negroes at a substantially higher rate than white applicants, and (c) the jobs in question formerly had been filled only by white employees as part of a longstanding practice of giving preference to whites.[1]

Congress did not intend Title VII to guarantee a job to every person regardless of qualifications. The act does not command that any person be hired simply because he or she was formerly the subject of discrimination, or because he or she is a member of a minority group. Discriminatory preference for any group is proscribed. What is required by Congress is the removal of artificial and unnecessary barriers to employment that discriminate on the basis of racial or other impermissible classification. Quoting again from the court's decision:

> Nothing in the Act precludes the use of testing or measuring procedures; obviously they are useful. What Congress had forbidden is giving these devices and mechanisms controlling force unless they are demonstrably a reasonable measure of job performance. Congress has not commanded that the less qualified be preferred over the better qualified simply because of minority origins. Far from disparaging job qualifications as such, Congress has made such qualifications the controlling factor, so that race, religion, nationality, and sex become irrelevant. What Congress has commanded is that any tests used must measure the person for the job and not the person in the abstract.

Companies are thus legally responsible for developing and using valid selection methods; that is, measures related to job performance. The government, by its application of discrimination laws to selection processes, is asking managers to do nothing more than they should already be doing—developing methods that identify prospective employees who are most likely to perform on the job.

The Selection Process

Selection is a process of considering those candidates who have been recruited and deciding which ones should receive job offers. Let us examine the steps involved in this process.

---

[1] U.S. Supreme Court, *Willie S. Griggs et al.* v. *Duke Power Company*, March 8, 1971.

Step 1: Preliminary Screening.   The organization should develop some rough guidelines for a review of the candidates. These guidelines should be used to weed out those applicants who are clearly unsuitable for the job so that neither the organization nor the individual will waste time.

Step 2: Completion of an Application.   The candidate's past experience, and personal, experiential, and attitudinal characteristics should all be taken into consideration when the organization reviews his or her application. This is a very common and useful way for the organization to begin to know the candidate.

Step 3: Employee Interviews and Other Selection Tools.   Interviews and tests are often used to gather complete information about a person's ability to perform a job. Interviews may either be of the structured or unstructured type. In the structured interview, the interviewer prepares a set list of questions that are chosen to obtain job-relevant information. The advantage of the structured interview is that it will cover all the relevant information. The disadvantage is that if the interviewer sticks exactly to the prepared agenda, neither party will be able to probe areas not on the list. Therefore, some flexibility is recommended. A totally unstructured interview is not recommended because there will be no guidance to the conversation. It is not likely that relevant information will be obtained if no agenda has been set.

In addition to interviews, many tests can be used to assess performance potential. In fact, structured tests have proven to be more valid than interviews because they are not as subjective. These tests can be either of the paper and pencil type or may be simulation exercises. Because of the cost of developing such tests, organizations often purchase exams. This is acceptable where jobs have standardized components such as typing skill, manual dexterity, and certain personal characteristics, but they are not as valid for jobs requiring unique skills.

Step 4: References.   References are a very common way of gathering information about a person's experience and performance on previous jobs. The accuracy of the information is determined by how thorough a reference check is conducted. The easiest and cheapest way to check references is to request that the applicant submit three letters of recommendation from past associates. These letters can provide useful information about the applicant's previous jobs, but they are rarely useful for evaluating the person's performance on the job; applicants will, of course, ask those they expect to give positive recommendations. A more extensive reference check can be conducted, however. Those supplying references can be contacted by phone and their responses probed. Past associates and employees can be contacted and interviewed and a full investigation conducted.

Step 5: Employment Decision.   After all of this information is collected, the organization must decide whom it wishes to employ, based on the requirements of the job.

HOW DO WE CONVINCE THOSE SELECTED TO ACCEPT OUR OFFER TO JOIN OUR ORGANIZATION?

Four conflicts exist when individuals and organizations are scouting each other:[2]

Conflict 1.   Conflict 1 involves the need of the organization to attract good candidates versus the candidate's need to make an honest assessment of the organization. In order to make a good choice, the individual needs complete and accurate information. The organization, on the other hand, needs to attract the best possible candidates and might have a tendency to present itself in the best possible light by providing only positive information.

Conflict 2.   Conflict 2 addresses the need of the organization to find the right employee for the job versus the candidate's need to be employed. Candidates also feel that they must make themselves as attractive as possible in order to obtain as many good job offers as they can. They will tend to highlight their good qualities, not present information about their bad qualities, and describe themselves in terms they think fit the organization's expectations. The organization, of course, would like to acquire an honest picture of the individual.

---

[2]Lyman Porter, Edward E. Lawler III, and J. Richard Hackman, *Behavior in Organizations* (New York: McGraw-Hill, 1975), pp. 133–36.

Conflict 3. Conflict 3 reflects the need of the organization to make its job openings known versus its desire to attract only qualified candidates. To attract employees, the organization often provides more positive than negative information about itself. By doing so, however, it will attract many candidates that are either unsuitable or unqualified.

Conflict 4. Conflict 4 is due to the candidate's need to make him- or herself known in the job market versus the candidate's desire to receive offers for suitable jobs only. Candidates will tend to present positive information about themselves and will consequently attract job offers that do not match their skills or needs.

These conflicts demonstrate that the problem organizations face is not only attracting people to the organization but attracting the right people. Organizations have taken two approaches to solving this problem: the positive approach and the balanced approach. The positive approach attempts to sell the organization by presenting only its good aspects with a view toward attracting as many candidates as possible. Those advocating this approach are more interested in filling their jobs with qualified candidates than in meeting the candidates' career needs. They are not concerned with what needs people have and how these needs will fit the job, partly because needs cannot be measured very well and partly because their concern is performance on the job and not how satisfied people are. Their assumption is that if enough people apply for the job, the organization can then select those who are best able to perform. They assume that any dissatisfaction that arises from inflated expectations due to the overly positive picture of the firm presented during the recruitment process can be handled later; as new employees adjust to the organization, they will develop a more positive attitude.

The balanced approach provides both positive and negative information to prospective employees. Its purpose is to attract only those candidates who will perform well and be satisfied with the organization. When a firm presents both positive and negative information, candidates are more likely to sort themselves out; the number of applicants will be fewer, but their needs will be better met by the organization, and vice versa.

These two approaches produce very different results. The positive approach tends to intensify the conflicts discussed above. By providing only positive information about itself, the organization limits the candidate's ability to make a good decision. The balanced approach, on the other hand, promotes better decision making. It makes it more likely that the organization will attract qualified candidates who understand what they are getting into and who will become productive employees. Of course, some cost and risk are involved. The organization will have to contact a larger number of people because some of them will choose not to apply, but those who do apply will tend to be better candidates because those who feel that the job is not suitable will have already weeded themselves out. The costs of recruiting and selecting will probably increase, but better people will be hired, so the long-term costs will probably decrease. In fact, one area in which costs have been shown to decrease dramatically as a result of using the balanced approach to recruiting is turnover. Because candidates have more realistic expectations, they are not as often disappointed, and they tend to remain on the job longer; this creates fewer job openings and thus decreases future recruitment costs. Therefore, we recommend that organizations provide as much realistic information as possible to the candidates they recruit.

The balanced approach to recruiting is an attempt to match the needs of the individual and those of the organization. The organization attempts to achieve this match by presenting an honest assessment of itself throughout the recruiting process. If it wishes to convince a candidate to accept an offer it has tendered, it should maintain this forthright approach by explaining exactly how this individual will fit into the firm and how the organization can meet his or her career needs. In order to be able to meet these needs, the organization should select candidates whose abilities match the requirements of the job and whose personalities are well suited to the climate and culture of the firm. The way to attract these people is to recognize the conflicts inherent in the recruiting and selecting processes and to provide as much realistic information to prospective employees as possible. Proportionately fewer people may want to talk to you and fewer may accept your offer, but the ones who do will more than compensate you for these losses by becoming productive and loyal employees.

APPLICATIONS

1. Decide what type of people will be needed on the job by gathering and defining job descriptions.

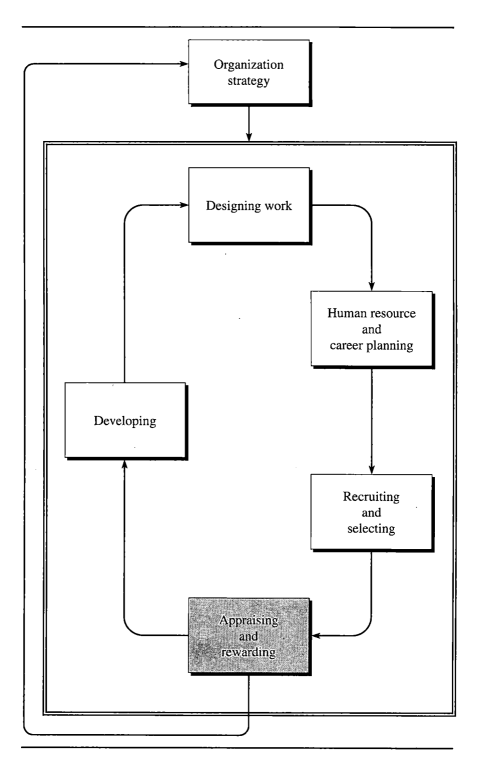

CHAPTER 7

APPRAISING AND REWARDING PERFORMANCE

INTRODUCTION

Appraising and rewarding are basic elements of good management. They are the link between what is being accomplished in the present and what needs to be done in the future. Without appraisals of performance, neither managers nor employees can know whether what they are doing is productive. They have no basis for assessing past performance or planning future performance. Without proper rewards and recognition, employees are not likely to devote time and effort to being productive in the future.

Despite their importance to organizations, good performance appraisals are difficult to do because they require an understanding of not only performance on the job but also how to give positive and negative feedback. Providing proper rewards is often neglected because managers do not feel they control rewards. Let us look at what performance appraisal is and how it fits into human resource management. Then we will be prepared to consider how rewards can be given based on performance.

WHAT IS PERFORMANCE APPRAISAL?

Performance appraisal is the process of identifying, measuring, and developing human performance. Performance appraisal systems must not only accurately measure how well an employee is performing a job, but they must also contain mechanisms for reinforcing strengths, identifying deficiencies, and feeding such information back to employees so they can

143

improve future performance. Thus, performance appraisal has both evaluative and developmental purposes, but it is exactly because it serves a dual purpose that it is so difficult to do.

In order for performance appraisal to succeed, managers need to recognize that any time they help employees understand their responsibilities, collaborate with them to decide what must be done to meet their responsibilities, and provide feedback on performance, they are involved in the appraisal process.

When managers see appraisal as an ongoing management responsibility, it becomes possible for them to be supportive when problems arise, help employees develop skills they are lacking, and provide specific feedback focused on problems as they occur. Then at the end of the year there will be no surprises. When feedback is consistently given, problems are solved as they arise. Yearly performance appraisals become a chance to summarize past performance and make plans for the coming year. If all the information is saved until the end of the year, the chances for development and change are lost. Performance appraisal becomes an "I gotcha" system. This method of performance appraisal is exemplified by a manager who waits until the end of the year to give you any feedback or assistance. While you may have had the wrong approach all year, the manager waits until the end of the year to say you were wrong. At this point, you have lost a whole year of opportunities to change and improve. This may sound all too familiar to many employees.

In sum, performance appraisal is the continual process of identifying, measuring, and developing human performance. It is both an ongoing part of daily management activities and a periodic summary (usually yearly) of how the employee is doing. A good performance appraisal system has the following characteristics:

1. *Performance definition.* The appraisal system should measure performance as defined for the job.
2. *Job design.* Activities on the job should relate to the results to be accomplished. Measures of performance must come from a very careful analysis of what the job is and what is to be accomplished on it.
3. *Selecting and recruiting.* Since employees are selected and recruited for jobs based on their potential, the performance appraisal should be useful for predicting performance on present and future jobs.

4. *Feedback.* The performance appraisal should be used to give feedback identifying areas where performance is good and areas that need improvement.

5. *Rewarding.* Rewards should be given based on the appraisals of performance.

6. *Training and development.* Appraisals identify skills and knowledge that can be improved by training and development.

7. *Promotion and transfer.* After being on the job for a period of time, employees may develop abilities that are useful in other parts of the organization, or they may not be able to perform adequately and may have to be moved to another job or out of the organization. In all these cases, action taken should be based on the performance appraisal.

PERFORMANCE APPRAISAL AND THE LAW

The U.S. courts also have an interest in performance appraisal. Much of the impetus for developing accurate measures of performance has come from corporate failure to comply with race and sex discrimination laws. The initial intent of the Equal Employment Opportunity Commission (EEOC) "Guidelines on Employee Selection Procedures" and the Office of Federal Contract Compliance's (OFCC) "Order on Employee Testing and Other Selection Procedures" was to eliminate discrimination in the selection of employees. The basic purpose of both was to ensure that all tests (i.e., formal, scored, quantified, or standardized techniques of assessing job suitability) were accurate measures of potential job performance.

The courts very quickly went beyond this narrow concern for the correct use of performance measures and focused on issues that went to the very heart of management practices. They questioned the validity of the measures themselves. If selection decisions were to be based on how well the person can be expected to perform in the future, the courts argued that the organization should have an accurate definition and method of measuring good performance. Unfortunately, the ratings offered to the courts by organizations were often a supervisor's appraisal of a subordinate or job candidate's traits; for example, helpfulness, punctuality, initiative, and so on. The courts then asked, "Do supervisor ratings evaluate performance accurately?" The answer was often no. Performance appraisal methods must yield accurate results before the courts will accept them as the basis for management decisions.

The courts broadened their definition of a selection decision to include any decision that might affect the future employment status of an individual. This broad definition included the use of any formal or informal device for evaluating employees for such purposes as layoffs, transfers, promotions, and so on. This quite clearly included decisions made at all stages of the performance process.

The results of court cases state that a performance appraisal process should have the following characteristics in order to meet legal requirements. Note how closely the following characteristics match what you as a manager would want your performance appraisals to include.

- The overall appraisal process should be formalized, standardized, and (as much as possible) objective in nature.
- The performance appraisal system should be as job related as possible.
- A thorough, formal job analysis should be made of all positions being rated.
- Subjective supervisory ratings should be considered only one component of the overall evaluation process.
- Evaluators should be adequately trained in the use of appraisal techniques.
- Evaluators should have substantial daily contact with the employee being evaluated.
- If the appraisal involves various measures of performance, the weight of each measure should be fixed.
- Whenever possible, an appraisal should be conducted independently by more than one evaluator.
- The administration and scoring of the performance appraisal should be standardized and controlled.
- Opportunities for promotion or transfer should be posted and the information made available to all interested individuals.

CHOOSING AN APPRAISAL INSTRUMENT

Choosing an appraisal instrument is a matter of deciding what kind of data is to be collected and the best way to collect it. The various types of data and formats serve different functions. An instrument should not be chosen just because it is cheap and available. The choice should be based on a thorough understanding of the job and the purposes of the particular appraisal. Let us look at the various types of formats and then discuss the reasons for choosing one versus another.

Appraisal instruments vary in focus; some evaluate traits and skills, others determine the processes and behaviors necessary to do the work, or the results and outcomes of performance. Trait measures assess personal characteristics such as dependability, effort, initiative, job knowledge, cooperativeness, planning ability, punctuality, and attitude. Process measures focus on the way people go about their work and how they interact with others. Let us first look at how these measures can be used and then at some specific examples of the variety of performance appraisal instruments available.

Measures of performance vary according to their degree of subjectivity; that is, how much the interpretation of the evaluator affects the rating. More objective measures include production data (e.g., volume, dollar sales, number of errors, amount of scrap, distance, time) as well as human resource data (e.g., turnover, absence, and tardiness). These measures are often referred to as "count" data because they can be counted and the result will be the same no matter who is doing the evaluating. In fact, because the data is objective, it can often be collected by computer or other mechanical means. Subjective measures necessarily involve an evaluator. These ratings either compare the work of the person being evaluated to that of other employees or to some absolute standard. Let us consider the advantages and disadvantages of the various ways of appraising performance.

Trait Scales

The most common method of appraisal is the trait approach, in which the rater evaluates performance on a list of individual characteristics (see Figures 7–1 and 7–2).

Advantages.   This method is easy to administer because few forms are needed and they can often be obtained commercially. The criteria used are often broad enough to be applied to many different types of jobs.

Disadvantages.   The traits evaluated are usually so general that they do not specifically apply to any one job, which raises questions of

FIGURE 7–1

Trait-, Behavior-, and Results-Based Performance Appraisal Systems

A. Trait-Based Appraisal

Rate the employee on each of the following traits:

1. Loyalty to Company   very low   low   average   high   very high

2. Communication Ability   very low   low   average   high   very high

3. Cooperativeness   very low   low   average   high   very high

B. Behavior-Based Appraisal

Using the scale below, rate the frequency with which the employee exhibits the following behaviors:

1 = never   3 = sometimes   5 = almost always
2 = rarely   4 = frequently

_____ 1. Greets customers in a pleasant and friendly manner.

_____ 2. Is unable to explain technical aspects of a product to a customer.

_____ 3. Fills out charge card slips correctly, getting approval from supervisor for all charges above $300.00.

C. Results-Based Appraisal

From your production and employee files, please provide the following information for this employee:

1. Number of units produced this month: _____

2. Number of units produced that were rejected and scrapped by quality control: _____

3. Number of units produced that were rejected and returned for repair by quality control: _____

4. Days this month the employee was absent without certified medical excuse: _____

Source: C. Fisher, L. Schoenfeldt, and J. Shaw, *Human Resource Management* (Boston: Houghton Mifflin, 1990), p. 423.

their validity. Because the scales usually range from high to low with no descriptions of what these ratings mean, a "halo" effect may be created that results in a lack of consistent discrimination between good and poor performers.

Best Uses. Trait scales may be useful for low-level positions where the number of different jobs makes it impractical and too costly to es-

FIGURE 7–2
Typical Graphic Rating Scale

Name _____	Dept. _____		Date _____	
	Outstanding	*Good*	*Satisfactory*	*Fair*	*Unsatisfactory*
Quality of work Thoroughness (neatness and accuracy of work) Comments:	☐	☐	☐	☐	☐
Knowledge of job Clear understanding of the facts or factors pertinent to the job Comments:	☐	☐	☐	☐	☐
Personal qualities Personality, appearance, sociability, leadership, integrity Comments:	☐	☐	☐	☐	☐
Cooperation Ability and willingness to work with associates, supervisors, and subordinates toward common goals Comments:	☐	☐	☐	☐	☐
Dependability Conscientious, thorough, accurate, reliable with respect to attendance, lunch periods, reliefs, etc. Comments:	☐	☐	☐	☐	☐
Initiative Earnestness in seeking increased responsibilities. Self-starting, unafraid to proceed alone? Comments:	☐	☐	☐	☐	☐

Source: George T. Milkovich and John W. Boudreau, *Human Resource Management,* 6th ed. (Homewood, Ill.: Richard D. Irwin, 1991), p. 100.

tablish personal objectives for every job or where the purpose of the appraisal is to measure effort. Some of the disadvantages of the trait approach can be overcome by developing separate trait checklists for functional areas. Even in these cases, however, it should be used with caution because of its susceptibility to bias.

Behavior Scales

Behaviorally Anchored Rating Scales (BARS) (see Figures 7–1 and 7–3) are popular with those who want to focus on job behavior. They are developed for a class of jobs and use specific examples of behavior to illustrate kinds of employee behaviors at various levels of performance.

Advantages. (1) The scales are developed for specific jobs and are much more relevant to that job than a general form would be. (2) Observable behaviors rather than personal characteristics are rated. This increases the reliability of the rating because the raters are reporting what they observe rather than what they think of the person.

Disadvantages. (1) Because the behaviors are job specific, it is impossible to develop a form that can be used for a multitude of jobs—separate forms must be developed for each job category. (2) The long process necessary for developing the scales is costly. (3) The nature of

FIGURE 7–3
Behaviorally Anchored Rating Scale (BARS)

Performance Dimension

Concern for individual dorm residents: attempts to get to know individual dorm residents and responds to their individual needs with genuine interest. This resident adviser could be expected to

Rating Scale

Good (1)	(2)	(3)	(4)	(5) Poor
Recognize when a floor member appears depressed and ask if person has problem he or she wants to discuss.	Offer floor member tips on how to study for a course he or she has already taken.	See person and recognize him/her as a floor member and say "hi."	Be friendly with a floor member; get into discussion on problems, but fail to follow up on the problem later on with student.	Criticize a floor member for not being able to solve his or her own problems.

Source: George T. Milkovich and John W. Boudreau, *Human Resource Management*, 6th ed. (Homewood, Ill.: Richard D. Irwin, 1991), p. 101.

the scales causes people to focus on behaviors when results may sometimes be more important.

Best Uses.   Behavior scales are particularly useful where results are hard to identify and measure.

Management by Objectives

Management by objectives (MBO) is a popular results-oriented approach to performance evaluation. Using this approach, employee and supervisor agree on performance objectives; these goals are then stated in terms of results, and progress is monitored. At the end of an agreed-on period of time, the appraisal is made by comparing actual results with predetermined objectives. This is referred to as a results-based appraisal (see Figures 7–1 and 7–4).

Advantages.   (1) This evaluation method focuses on results, not traits or processes, which are harder to measure; thus, it offers greater validity, reliability, and freedom from bias. (2) Specific goals provide a focus for employee efforts.

FIGURE 7–4
A Typical Management by Objectives (MBO) Performance Report

Objectives Set	Period Objective	Accomplishments
1. Number of sales calls.	100	104
2. Number of new customers contacted.	20	18
3. Number of wholesalers stocking new product 117.	30	30
4. Sales of product 12.	10,000	9,750
5. Sales of product 17.	17,000	18,700
6. Customer complaints/service calls.	35	11
7. Number of sales correspondence courses successfully completed.	4	2
8. Number of sales reports in home office within one day of end of month.	12	10

Source: George T. Milkovich and John W. Boudreau, *Human Resource Management*, 6th ed. (Homewood, Ill.: Richard D. Irwin, 1991), p. 98.

Disadvantages. (1) Each employee is rated on different factors and different scales, making comparison among jobs difficult. (2) Because each job has its own goals, it is possible that varying standards will be used to establish performance objectives. (3) The system is difficult to implement and administer. (4) Once goals are defined, employees tend to focus exclusively on those goals, often missing key opportunities that suddenly appear.

Best Uses. MBO is useful in positions where results-oriented goals can be set. It is particularly appropriate for positions that control everything necessary to accomplish the objective. MBO is also valuable as the basis for incentive awards based on results.

In sum then, there are many performance evaluation methods from which to choose. Each one involves a trade-off between ease of development and use versus validity and reliability. The more objective performance appraisal systems—those that are based on observations rather than attitudes—are usually more costly to develop and administer, but they are also more valid and reliable. For this reason, the performance appraisal instrument you choose should be as objective as possible, given the practical limitations of your situation.

WHO DOES THE EVALUATING?

The traditional evaluator of an employee's work has been the supervisor, but valuable information can also be obtained from peers, subordinates, persons outside the organization, and self-appraisals. The evaluator should be chosen on the basis of the position to be appraised and the perspective desired.

The right and responsibility of the supervisor to evaluate performance is accepted in most organizations. Supervisors bring the organizational perspective to the evaluation, and control many of the rewards and punishments that may result from the evaluation. The superior's evaluation should be considered an important source of performance data, but it should not be considered the only source.

Several problems emerge if the supervisor is the only source of performance appraisal information. First, the superior is thrust into the conflicting roles of judge and counselor. Second, being appraised by someone who controls organizational rewards may threaten subordinates so much that they focus only on the reward or punishment and not on the job and how they can improve their performance. In this case, communication will be one-sided, with the supervisor doing all the talking. If the employee says anything, it will tend to be defensive and little problem solving will take place. That is why it is often important to have other sources of performance data in addition to the supervisor's appraisal. When performance is analyzed from different perspectives, the validity of the results is increased, and the superior and subordinate can then focus on problem solving.

Peer appraisals are valuable whenever there is a high level of personal interaction on the job and when information about the employee's performance is uniquely available to his or her peers. These situations most often exist among professionals such as professors in a university, physicians in a clinic, or scientists in an industrial organization. In each of these cases, the professional's peers will have the background and experience to evaluate his or her performance while the supervisor may not. In these situations, peer evaluations are valuable substitutes for, or complements to, supervisory evaluations.

Subordinate appraisals are not usually a component of an employee's performance evaluation. However, there are situations such as those in which leadership potential is to be assessed where subordinate appraisals are valuable (if leadership is the ability to influence subordinates, it is logical to ask the subordinates how well the manager is doing). Subordinates can also provide managers with valuable feedback on their performance that can help them develop their own style of management.

Specialists in performance appraisal from within or outside of the organization can also be used as evaluators. Outsiders may be able to make a valuable contribution because their specialized expertise or objectivity may be better able to meet legal requirements. In addition, by allowing one person to do many evaluations, they may help the organization avoid problems that often arise when a number of evaluators, each with his or her own perspectives and standards of performance, all conduct appraisals. The major disadvantage to the use of specialists or outsiders is that the employee's supervisor may not be involved in this critical component of the management process and may, therefore, find it hard to give meaningful feedback to the employee in the future.

Self-appraisal is important in conjunction with other kinds of appraisal as well as in and of itself. It is particularly valuable when the purpose of the evaluation is developmental. Personal growth, self-motivation, and organizational development take place when employees know where they are and where they want to go. When employees consistently appraise themselves, they have been found to be (1) more satisfied and constructive, (2) less defensive, and (3) more productive on the job. This is because the employees have become more involved in managing themselves. Self-appraisal presents some obvious problems, however. When it is used for evaluative purposes, employees will naturally give themselves unreasonably high ratings, which will lead to disagreements about relevant performance standards. While it is productive to discuss these differences and resolve them, this may become a conflict-laden and destructive process if not managed properly. In sum, then, self-appraisal is useful for fostering personal growth and for identifying and resolving conflicts, but not for the purposes of evaluation and rewarding.

REWARDING PERFORMANCE WITH MONEY

Once performance has been evaluated, good performance must be recognized and rewarded. Without proper rewards, employees are not likely to continue to perform in the future. Money is an important reward for most people. People want it and they need it to buy food, clothes, shelter, and all else they desire. Employers should construct a compensation system that maximizes dollar investment by making employees feel economically and psychologically rewarded enough to choose to work with the organization, to stay with it, and to produce at high levels. To do this, the employer will have to decide on fair and adequate pay levels to differentiate between jobs and compete with other firms in the same field. Consider the following examples:

> Morris—the "finicky cat" of TV food fame—earns more than two and a half times the average earnings of many American actors.
>
> Robert Parish, the oldest player in the National Basketball Association at 39, earns $3.5 million per year.
>
> Top rock groups earn tens of thousands of dollars for one night's performance, whereas the annual salaries of members of top symphony orchestras range from $30,000 to $60,000.
>
> A minister in Chicago is paid $10,500 annually, while Roger Clemens, a pitcher for the Boston Red Sox, earns more than $10,500 for a single game.

A typical professor of liberal arts makes $45,750; a New York garbage collector is paid $36,350.

A pilot of a 747 is paid $90,000 and a bus driver makes $23,500.

There is nothing intrinsic about a cat that makes it worth more than a person, and a rock star does not necessarily have hundreds of times more talent than a symphony member. The market, supply and demand, and competition all help determine salary levels. The employer will have to take all of these factors into account to construct a fair, cost-efficient, motivating compensation system. Is that possible in today's organizations? How can money be managed to obtain the greatest benefit for both the organization and the employee? These are the questions to be answered in our discussion of compensation and benefits. We will first look at what motivation theory says about how compensation should be used to motivate performance and then review how those principles should be implemented when an organization establishes compensation and benefits systems.

Money motivates so well because it is a generalized reinforcer; that is, people can use it to satisfy most of their needs. Not only does it buy food, shelter, and other commodities, it is an indicator of the esteem in which an employee is held. It may not buy love, but it determines what groups you can associate with, what activities you can afford, and what opportunities for growth and development you can take advantage of. Because money does all of this, people will work hard to obtain it and will be very concerned that their pay is fair.

People generally determine the fairness of their rewards by comparing them with those received by others. For example, I expect my reward to be the same as that given to someone else who has expended the same effort and achieved the same results. I also expect to be rewarded less than someone who has produced more. My satisfaction will thus be determined by comparing my inputs and results with those of others either within or outside the organization or by judging them against some internal standard.

Comparison with an Internal Standard
We each have developed a sense of what our work is worth. This standard usually comes from our past experience and is modified as we gain more experience. Students who have just graduated use internal standards shaped by part-time and summer work at minimum wages. Once

they enter into full-time employment where salaries are typically higher, they will soon discover others are making more. They will tend to adjust upward their perception of what they are worth.

Comparison with Others in the Organization

When comparing your pay to that of others in the organization, you will generally consider two groups: those doing the same work and those doing different work. If you are making less than others doing the same work, you will surely be dissatisfied. If you are making less than others doing different jobs you think are less valuable than yours, you will also be dissatisfied.

Comparison with Others Outside the Organization

Again, the two groups you will compare yourself with outside the organization are those doing the same work and those doing different work. If you have a strong professional orientation and identify more with the type of work you are doing than the organization you work for, then you are most likely to compare yourself with others who do the same work outside the organization. If you have a strong identification with your organization, you are more likely to compare against others outside the organization doing different types of work.

   Because employees are constantly endeavoring to judge the fairness of their salaries, managers must be sure that their salary ranges are in line with other jobs both inside and outside their own organizations. This will require continuous surveying of salary conditions to keep the pay structure of the organization up-to-date.

ESTABLISHING THE COMPENSATION SYSTEM

The purpose of a compensation system is to establish salaries that reflect the relative worth of each job to the organization. Notice particularly that we are talking about paying jobs, not people. In establishing the system, we are concerned with what range of salary is appropriate for the job as it contributes to the accomplishments of the organization; and what the individual employee receives will then fall within that range. Let us consider the overall compensation system first and then consider how individual wages and benefits should be determined within that system.

Develop Job Descriptions

All jobs need to be placed in a wage structure so that employees doing them will be paid according to their relative worth to the organization. Rather than define the exact wage for each job, which would be tedious and very imprecise, you should group the jobs together according to common characteristics and then establish salary ranges for each group.

In order to place jobs in the correct clusters, it is necessary to have accurate job descriptions. Previously written job descriptions may be used for this purpose.

Establish Criteria for Comparing Jobs

From the job descriptions, extrapolate a number of components common to all jobs in the organization. Then weight these components according to their relative importance.

This is clearly a very subjective process. The components and weights should be determined by people who are familiar with the jobs. In order to have the weights and components as widely understood and accepted as possible, it is important to have as broad a representation as possible.

Evaluating the Jobs

The next step is to evaluate the jobs according to their relative worth in the organization by using the criteria you just identified so that equitable levels of pay can be established. Develop a profile of each of the job categories and compare them to each other by using one of the four most common methods for evaluating jobs: ranking, factor comparison, classification, and the point system. A job evaluation can be formal or informal, developed internally or brought from an outside source. Informal job evaluation systems are only used in very small businesses where evaluations are usually made on the basis of intuitive judgment and local experience. Formal systems are more complicated and expensive, but also more accurate and applicable for larger organizations. Regardless of which approach is taken, it will be used for similar reasons to compare the relative worth of the job evaluated to other jobs in the organization.

Each method of job evaluation is based on several assumptions. First, it is assumed that those jobs contributing the most to the organization should be paid the most. Second, employees will feel that the pay system and the organization are more equitable if pay is based on job value. Finally, it is assumed that basing salary on job worth will further the goals of the organization itself. The following methods are most commonly used.

Ranking.   Ranking is the simplest approach to job evaluation. Jobs are simply arranged in an ascending scale according to their relative worth to the organization or from simplest to most complex. This method does not allow for consideration of the different components on the job; it merely provides an overall rating. The larger the organization, the less effective this system tends to be. The major problems with this system stem from its lack of strict standards or guidelines. There is no way to scientifically examine the results of the evaluation.

Factor Comparison.   The first step in factor comparison is to identify which jobs have correct salary levels. These jobs are then ranked according to their components. The most commonly used factors are mental and physical skills required, degree of responsibility, and working conditions. Dollar amounts are then assigned to each factor and the total job value determined. Other jobs can then be evaluated by comparing them to this initial set of jobs.

Classification.   In this method of evaluation, a limited number of jobs are classified into broad categories such as skill and responsibility levels, which are then arranged in grades. Each grade is assigned a value in terms of how much it contributes to the organization. Each job is then fitted into one of these categories.

The Point System.   The point system rates jobs according to how much they exhibit certain factors that are valuable to the organization. Each of the factors is assigned a number of points according to the degree to which it exhibits the skill or trait. After the job is rated according to each of these factors, the points are added and the total score is then compared to those of other jobs. Because it is so systematic, this method is the most frequently used. Provided that an adequate number of job factors—3 to 10—are considered, and that they exhibit definable, distinguishable differences between jobs, this method will have few complications. As with other methods, the evaluators should be objective and the process understood and accepted by both employees and managers.

Evaluations are best done by a committee of 5 to 10 members to ensure that the ratings will be reliable and verifiable. Each committee member should conduct an initial evaluation independently so that extreme differences and reliability can be checked; then these evaluations can be compared. Where disagreements exist, discussion leading toward consensus will be necessary. Disagreement that is extremely difficult to resolve is an indication that the factors employed in the evaluation have not been defined clearly enough, and they should be reconsidered.

The best job evaluation systems will depend on the nature and structure of the organization. Some organizations may even opt to use two plans, finding that management cannot be adequately evaluated on the point system used for the production workers, and vice versa. Whichever plan is chosen, it should always illustrate the job aspects deemed valuable, the levels of each aspect found in each job, and on the basis of this information, the relative worth of each job to the organization.

Establishing Pay Grades and Salary Ranges

The next step is to convert your evaluations into pay grades. Monetary values can be assigned to the points, classes, or ranks; this is referred to as pricing the job structure. Usually a range of pay for each job is developed based on the evaluation. Frequently, these ranges are assigned to job groups; thus, all jobs in the group will receive the same base pay rate.

Comparisons with similar jobs inside and outside the organization, and with different jobs inside the organization, will have to be made to set up the salaries to be attached to each range. Budgets can be manipulated to allow the organization to pay more, the same, or less than the comparable averages in each range. However, some factors influencing pay rates are not subject to organizational manipulation.

The government, through laws and regulations, and indirectly through fiscal and monetary policies, influences pay structure. A healthy economy and low unemployment rates may increase salaries and wages as organizations compete to recruit and retain employees. In a recession, wage and salary rates may go down. Further, differences in pay rates may be the result of union actions and collective bargaining, or may be affected by differences in locality or country (for international organizations). Employers will have to assume that the differences will exist, and allot their organization's resources within the environment in a way that attracts, retains, and motivates their work force. There are several tools that may aid employers in this effort.

Conducting a Compensation Survey

Job evaluations establish internal equity of compensation. Compensation surveys determine what salaries will be competitive with other organizations. People are always comparing their pay with others who do comparable jobs. Salary surveys formalize the comparison and ensure that all the relevant organizations are included.

The first step in conducting a salary survey is to determine which organizations should be included in the comparison; that is, those that offer comparable jobs. Those organizations that you compete with for employees are likely choices. You may compete primarily in a local market for clerical and technical employees or on a national scale for managerial and highly trained scientific staff. Remember to limit your survey to the comparable industries as well; that is, the main competition for nurses will be in hospitals and health care institutions and that should be the focus of your analysis.

Note that the data you need may already be available from consulting firms, professional associations, or even the government. Government publications from the Bureau of Labor Statistics are the place to start, but make sure to use only information about comparable jobs. If you wish to develop your own data, apply the principles just discussed to your survey. Choose organizations that will be competing with you for employees, but note that it may be difficult to gain the cooperation of these organizations. If they are your competitors for human resources, they will be willing to cooperate only if they receive something of value from the survey, which usually means you will have to share all your information with them. For this reason, it is often helpful to have a professional association or some unbiased third party serve as your main source of data.

If you choose to do your own survey, make sure that the organizations you include are truly representative so they will provide good benchmarks. It is easy to use only those organizations with which you are personally familiar, but your results may be very biased. Collecting this information from a good sample of organizations will provide an excellent body of data for establishing a compensation system.

·Based on the findings of your survey, you may have to adjust the pay ranges that were established with the job evaluation to match market conditions. Remember that you will be adjusting the total pay range and everyone in it. Changes are made based on market conditions and not on personal attributes or job performance. Employees should understand what portion of their pay is a function of market conditions and what portion relates to their performance on the job.

Determining How an Employee's Pay Will Vary within a Salary Range

The simplest way to handle salary ranges might be to simply pay everyone who does the same job the same amount. This is rarely done, of course, since it does not take into consideration any differences in personal skill levels, expertise, or seniority. Rather than pay everyone the same, most organizations will choose to establish graded rate ranges and leave some flexibility to vary salary within the range.

Rate ranges could be established per job or per group of jobs. Dollar amounts and minimums and maximums will have to be determined, as well as differentials and overlaps between ranges. Finally, any salaries that are currently out of line with the established system will have to be restructured.

There are several ways of varying pay within the salary range; each has its advantages.

Automatic Progression. Automatic progression gives pay raises according to job tenure. As long as an employee remains on the job, the size and timing of the raises are set; for example, a $1,000 raise after six months on the job. Automatic progressions are therefore best for jobs in which performance level is more dependent on technology than skill or motivation.

Automatic progressions are less costly and easier to administer than other approaches. The manager needs only to keep track of how long a person has been on the job to determine his or her salary. However, this method of determining salaries is not likely to motivate employees to do better since it does not reward performance.

Merit Progressions. Merit progression assigns pay according to performance on the job. The employee starts at the beginning level and progresses according to his or her performance. If merit progression is working properly, the top performers will be at the top of the pay scale and the low performers at the bottom.

This system is more difficult to administer than the previous one. Performance appraisal methods must be fair and accurate, and the relationship between level of performance increase and level of merit pay increase must be proportionate. One problem is deciding how much of an increment is enough to feel like a merit reward.

Another problem with merit progression is sticking with it. The tendency is to give everyone a general cost-of-living increase and then add merit progression. However, those who have been performing poorly may make more than top performers who have recently joined the organization.

Limitless Range Progression.   With most salary ranges there is a maximum that can be earned. This may cause motivational and performance problems as the good performers reach the limit and see nowhere to go from there. One option is to move them into jobs where the range is higher; another is to allow salaries to go beyond the maximum for good performers.

It is not recommended that you remove the maximum pay limit. Without it, salaries of average and low performers will gradually creep up through automatic progression to where they are being paid more than others on more valuable jobs. If you retain the ranges, you must at least consciously justify exceeding maximums. One way of avoiding a maximum pay limit for a position and also ensuring that pay varies with performance is to institute an incentive system where salary is tied directly to performance with no set maximum. This can be done if performance can be clearly defined and measured on an ongoing basis.

Combination Programs.   Any combination of merit and automatic progression programs is possible. For example, when employees join an organization, raises may be rewarded automatically during the initial period; as they gain experience, raises can be distributed on a merit basis.

These combination programs have all the advantages and disadvantages of merit and automatic progressions. Sometimes they are simply the result of an uncontrolled merit system. They are hard to administer because you must constantly monitor and reward performance. They are sometimes perceived as inequitable because average and low performers who have been on the job for a while will be earning as much as good performers who have just arrived. In many instances, however, a combination program works best. First, it rewards employees for staying on the job as they learn, and then it rewards them for performing well.

Job evaluations result in recommended pay ranges for each of the jobs in the organization. If the evaluations are done conscientiously, the range for each job will be equitable. It should be remembered, however, that job evaluation is an ongoing process. You cannot just do it once and resolve all the salary inequities and problems in your organization because conditions are bound to change. The external market may drive up the salary necessary to attract and hold people in certain job categories, and the value of various jobs to the organization may also change. You will have to repeat your job evaluation as internal and external forces make the existing system less and less viable.

While job evaluations and salary surveys will determine general compensation levels, some policy decisions concerning such questions as maximum and minimum salaries, relationships among pay levels, the number of jobs to be included in each pay category, and how the compensation dollar could be split among base pay, incentive pay, and benefits, will have to be made by top management and based on organizational objectives.

Let us consider some of the questions you will have to answer when establishing a compensation system.

How Many and What Type of Pay Categories Should We Have?

The number and type of pay categories in an organization are partly determined by the kinds of jobs it offers and partly by how much discretion managers have to vary salaries within each category. If there are many types of jobs, there should be many pay categories. It is usually better to err on the side of too many than too few. Employees will be very concerned about how their salaries compare to those of others in the organization. If they perceive that others in their pay category are doing different jobs, they will be concerned about the equity of the compensation.

The problem created by having too many categories is overlap; that is, when the higher paid employees in one category (one hopes these will be the good performers) make more than the lower paid employees in another category. Most compensation systems have up to 50 percent overlap. If overlap is greater than 50 percent, there are too many pay categories. Two pay categories that overlap greatly should probably just be one.

Fewer categories will give the manager making the pay decisions more latitude, which may also be a disadvantage. If managers distribute rewards properly, employees the organization wants to keep will be compensated differently from those it wants to encourage to leave; if they do not distribute rewards properly, however, all the employees will be bunched at the top. Broad ranges can give great power to managers that, if used properly, can have a positive effect on performance because managers can then distribute rewards on a more individualized basis.

Should the Compensation System Be Open or Closed?

Should people know what others are making? The answer depends on the inequities that exist in the system, how well you can measure performance, and the type of behavior you want to encourage. Open systems are found mostly among hourly workers, public-sector salaried employees, and unionized wage employees. Closed systems, where the information concerning pay is known only to top management, the employee, and the personnel department, are most common in the private sector.

Let us start by saying that compensation systems should be open and then modify that statement. In far too many cases, organizations assume that their compensation systems should be closed. Rather than analyze the situation critically and correct the problems that prevent the adoption of an open system, they find it easier to keep pay secret.

Closed systems offer numerous problems. People usually overestimate what their peers are making and become dissatisfied. Rumors always exaggerate reality. Letting your employees know what others are making will encourage them to have more realistic expectations.

Closed systems also have less motivating power. People cannot compare salaries, and therefore they do not know whether they are doing well or not. The biggest problem with a closed pay system is that it increases the possibility of abuse on the part of managers. If employees do not know what others are making, they are less likely to question how managers determine salaries and this is often exactly why managers want to keep the compensation system closed. If employees find out that they are being paid differently from others doing the same job, they will want to know why, and explaining why might not be easy. For example, if performance is hard to measure, it will be difficult to justify differences based on it. You should either develop accurate measures or pay everyone the same salary, unless you want to use some criterion other than performance, such as seniority, to distribute compensation.

Market conditions may be another source of inequities in the compensation system. A person hired as an engineer five years ago who was given a normal 5–10 percent raise will probably be making less than an engineer who is hired today. This is another case in which the tendency will be to keep information secret so as not to create problems. What should be done, of course, is to conduct a salary survey and adjust salaries so they are competitive for long-term as well as newly hired employees.

One crucial consideration before opening a compensation system is the kind of behavior you wish to generate among your employees. Although sharing salary information is likely to increase competitive behavior, the nature of the salary structure will determine the nature of the competition. If one person's gain is another's loss, intensely competitive behavior among employees will result. If salaries can be increased through cooperation, or if a person can gain by helping others, this behavior will be manifest. It is important for the organization to make sure that the natural competitiveness that results from an open pay system is channeled in the right direction.

In sum, it is advisable to open up the compensation process if at all possible. If that is not possible, find out why and see whether the obstacles to establishing an open system can be overcome.

Should Automatic Adjustments or So-Called Cost-of-Living Raises Be Given?

In theory, cost-of-living raises are supposed to adjust salary levels to keep up with inflation. Examples of true cost-of-living adjustments are the automatic raises tied to the consumer price index included in some union contracts. In practice, there are very few actual cost-of-living adjustments. In order to be a true cost-of-living adjustment, the raise should be tied to the cost of purchasing goods (the consumer price index) and should be automatic. However, this assumes that the organization can increase rates regardless of market conditions, and that public-sector organizations have unlimited flexibility in their budgets. Furthermore, pay structures are distorted by automatic, fixed-amount adjustments.

All other so-called cost-of-living raises are actually across-the-board raises given to all members of an organization. It would probably be better to take the same amount of money and use it to adjust job categories in order to remain competitive with other organizations. Across-the-board raises result in very little satisfaction or increased productivity because they do not reinforce good performance nor do they meet the expectations developed by market conditions.

Should Past, Present, or Future Performance Be Rewarded?

Incentive systems are built on the premise that salary should vary according to individual performance. But how do you reward past and future performance? Any time seniority or tenure is included in a salary decision, past performance is being recognized. Seniority may be included in pay either directly—for example, by having some portion of the salary dependent on the number of years an employee has served the organization—or indirectly—for example, by allowing for an incremental adjustment in salary based on years of service. Also, any time a percentage raise is given, it partially rewards past contributions to the firm. For example, a person making $15,000 per year who is given a 10 percent raise will be receiving a different reward from a person making $20,000 in the same job who received the same raise. The latter receives a $500 bonus either because of greater seniority, better performance, or higher starting salary.

The practice of not lowering salaries is a subtle way of rewarding past performance; and no matter what present performance levels are, lowering of salaries is uncommon. Organizations generally carry employees at their present salaries, which recognize past performance, rather than reduce salaries to precisely reflect present performance.

Rewarding present performance is a commonly accepted organizational norm. Those who perform better should receive more compensation. Rewards can come in the form of fixed sums of money for performance levels or they can be percentage raises, with higher percentages given to those who perform better.

Future performance is rewarded by paying higher salaries to those who are likely to make substantial contributions to the organization in the future; for example, employees with advanced degrees. Workers who are particularly good may have their salaries increased beyond what can be justified for their present job in order to keep them in the organization until there is a vacancy in a more advanced position.

Past, present, and future performance are all important. Management must decide how much each should affect salary levels in the organization by carefully analyzing the salary structure and then consciously choosing which will be most rewarded.

WHY COMPENSATION SYSTEMS DON'T WORK AND HOW TO FIX THEM

The purpose of compensation and benefit programs is to attract and retain good employees, to encourage and reward good performance, and to develop the talent the organization will need in the future. A good compensation system will do all of these things, but only if it responds to changing internal and external conditions. It cannot be put in place and forgotten on the assumption that it will continue to work. Management has to analyze its compensation system constantly and assess its success. Listed below are some general reasons why compensation systems fail and some suggestions about what can be done about them.

The System Has Not Been Explained Well
Often, a compensation system has been properly established—pay is competitive and equitable, performance is rewarded, and the benefit package is generous—but the employees do not understand it. They react to what they know and assume they are underpaid. Management should explain the compensation system clearly and often. New employees particularly need clear explanations of how their salary and that of others have been determined. If the compensation system has been explained well and employees are still not satisfied with it, they may have unrealistic expectations. In this case, employees may need more complete information about how the system was established and how it works.

Compensation and Benefits Have Not Been Related to the Nature of the Job or to Performance
Compensation and benefits should be determined by the value of the job relative to other jobs and by the employee's performance. If employees do not perceive that their compensation is related to these two factors, the fault may lie in the compensation system itself or in how it is understood. It is usually a bit of each and management will have to work on both problems.

The Compensation Offered Is Not Viewed As Rewarding
Managers must always remember that it is the employees who decide whether the compensation they receive is rewarding. If an organization offers something employees do not want, they will not perceive it as a reward. For example, if an organization offers an overtime incentive program when what the employees really want is time off, or if it gives pay raises to employees who are in such high tax brackets that much of it goes to the government, or if it increases the health benefits of employees who are already covered through their spouses, these rewards are not likely to be found very satisfying by the employees involved. The attitudes and perceptions of the organization's employees must serve as the basis of any compensation system.

The Merit Awards Are Not Properly Managed
A pay raise or an incentive tells workers how their work is valued by the organization. It is common for employees to get the wrong message from incentive pay. This may happen for one of several reasons:

Conflicting Reward Schedules.   One set of rewards may be in direct opposition to another. For example, giving the best manager a free trip to Hawaii may set up competitive behavior among managers who are supposed to be cooperating. Introducing a cost-reduction program may directly conflict with the quality and quantity improvement programs already in place. These conflicts will invariably cause confusion. A compensation system must be considered as a total package. One part of it cannot be changed without considering how the rest of the system will be affected.

Inequities Exist in the System.   If the compensation system is not based on a good survey, or the system has not been kept current, there will very likely be inequities in it. These will have to be corrected before a merit pay system will work. When analyzing the causes of inequities, it is important to remember that you will be dealing with employees' feelings. It may be that compensation is equitable but is not seen that way by employees. This happens most often when employees do not have accurate information on which to base their opinions (which often happens in a closed system); research has shown that in this case, employees tend to overestimate the salaries of others. For example, when an employee who is rated above average receives an 8 percent pay increase, he may be dissatisfied, believing that the average increase was 10 percent when in fact it was only 5 percent. In order to avoid such dissatisfaction, employees need as much information as possible about the merit pay system.

The Portion of the Compensation System that Is Based on Merit Is a Threat to Employees' Self-Esteem. Most people rate themselves above average. The merit awards will signal to some that they are only performing at an average or below average level. This will be a threat to their self-image. Support systems such as counseling and training will have to be developed to help the poor performer who wants to improve.

Those Who Establish and Manage the Merit Awards Are More Concerned about Maintaining Employee Satisfaction than about Improving Job Performance. A well-run merit system will create organizational loyalty so that when performance is low, employees will strive to improve. Notice that satisfaction is not the main objective here. A good compensation system will tend to foster dissatisfaction in those who are performing poorly and encourage them to do better. If management places more emphasis on satisfaction than performance, it will probably respond to any dissatisfaction among employees by giving them more money and benefits; this may well increase satisfaction, but it will do very little for performance. In fact, high performers may well become dissatisfied because they have been unfairly treated.

The Organization Expects Its Merit System to Solve All Its Motivation and Productivity Problems while Ignoring the Role of the Job, the Manager, and the Technology in Improving Performance. The merit system is only one of a number of factors that can be used to motivate performance. It cannot be relied on to do everything; and it must be supported by management action and the rest of the organizational structure. An employee's job, for example, will have a tremendous impact on what he or she can accomplish. No merit system can overcome the negative effects of a badly designed job.

REWARDING PERFORMANCE WITH BENEFITS

Benefits are increasingly important forms of rewards employees receive for being part of the organization. Also, the level and type of benefits are often determined by your position in the organization. As you are promoted, benefits increase. Benefits such as pay for time not worked, subsidized health care, and retirement, and employee services actually deserve much consideration by employees and employers alike. The types of benefits that a company should offer depend on both the individual and the company. The ideal balance of required and optional benefits should be decided on by careful evaluation of purposes and costs. For example, no one argues the benefits of a health care policy, but which one you choose must be determined by the types of employees you have and the costs of providing the benefits.

Benefits were not always taken for granted. Before the 1930s, almost no public or private organization offered any substantial benefits. In 1929, the average cost of employee benefits was about 3 percent of total compensation. Personal well-being was assumed to be the responsibility of the individual. All employees could expect from their employers was a paycheck.

A great boost in benefits began during the 40s, when wartime wages were strictly regulated. Employers started offering fringe benefits to attract employees, while unions pushed for nonwage compensation to assist their members. By 1949, the percentage of total compensation accounted for by benefit costs had increased from 3 percent to 16 percent. By 1990, the figure reached over 30 percent.

The growth in benefits has occurred for many reasons. Originally they were offered for humanitarian purposes, for the welfare of the employees during the trying times of the Depression. A responsibility was felt to protect the employees from risks and uncertainties such as serious illness, accidents, layoffs, and retirement.

During the 40s, benefits were often used as recruitment lures. Today, the purposes of benefits are varied. In addition to the above-mentioned reasons, some organizations also use them to keep unions out or keep them appeased, to give employees a feeling of security, to decrease turnover, or to increase employee satisfaction, efficiency, or productivity. Depending on the benefits offered, they *can* have a positive effect on recruitment and retainment, increase the well-being and security of employees, and appease unions or decrease their influence. However, there is no evidence that they increase productivity or satisfaction.

For this reason, organizations should give much thought to the benefits they offer. With benefit costs over 30 percent of compensation and climbing, employers will want to be sure they are getting a good return on their investment and not offering services that are of little help to employees or the organization.

There are several types of benefits an employer may offer, some of which are legally required and some of which are determined by the company. Union and government regulations may influence types and levels of benefits, and so will labor market conditions, the economic standing of the organization and the nation, the goals of the organization, and even the nature of the individual employee.

Legally Required Benefits

Federal and state legislation have mandated three types of benefits: workers' compensation, unemployment compensation, and social security. Workers' compensation, also known as workmen's compensation, was unheard of at the turn of the century. It was only after publicity about hundreds of accidents resulting in death or serious injury that left families with no income that state compensation laws began being passed in 1910. Until then, employers were not held liable because of the following common law defenses:

1. *Assumption of risk doctrine.* Employees assume the risks incident to the employment they take on; therefore, the employer is not liable.
2. *Fellow servant rule.* If an accident results from co-worker negligence, the employer is not held liable.
3. *Contributory negligence.* If an accident results in any part from the injured party's negligence, the employer is not liable.

The Workmen's Compensation Act was passed by the New York State legislature in 1910; by 1948, all states had passed laws with similar coverage. What the laws are generally based on is the concept of liability without fault; an injured employee is entitled to some form and amount of compensation regardless of who or what causes the accident. If an employee works for a covered employer in a covered job (85 percent of workers in the United States are covered), the laws generally mandate payments to them or their families in the event of on-the-job accidents, death, or illness. Originally, this referred only to immediate physical injuries, but now some latent physical or psychological problems are also included.

Unemployment compensation is another benefit required to be carried by most companies. Coverage varies from state to state and industry to industry, but the total cost of the coverage tax is carried by the employer. The benefit was designed to provide subsistence to employees who found themselves without work suddenly or through no fault of their own, and who were currently looking for work. Payments now average about one half or two thirds of previous income and are receivable for 26 weeks, or in times of high unemployment, 52 weeks.

Like workers' compensation, the entire tax is paid by the employer. Payments will be higher for employers with a history of overuse of the fund and high unemployment rates, and lower for those with low rates. Payments to employees will also vary, depending on salary and on particular laws in effect in their locality.

The major controversy surrounding unemployment compensation is fraud. Some feel that the program fails because it is designed to financially assist the unemployed as they look for work, but that it actually encourages their not finding it. Many studies indicate that the closer to wages and salaries the payments come and the longer they are available, the longer the unemployed remain so.

Unemployment compensation was only part of what resulted from the Social Security Act of 1935. Originally passed as the Old Age Survivors Insurance Act, it provided a system by which employee and employer contributed equally to a fund used to subsidize retired workers. Full payments were disbursed to employees when they reached age 65; partial benefits were available starting at age 62. The size of the payments depended on the employee's final salary and length of service. Nearly all privately and self-employed individuals were eligible for coverage.

The system has undergone more changes over the decades than any other mandatory benefit. From 1935 to 1949, the maximum annual contribution was $30 each from employee and employer on the first $3,000 earned, or 1 percent per year. By 1983, the taxes had risen to 6.7 percent,

or \$2,392 on the first \$35,700. By 1990 the figure had risen to 7.65 percent—or \$3,924 on a base salary of \$51,300. Many predict it will continue to rise.

In addition to these three legally mandated benefits—workers' compensation, unemployment compensation, and social security—other legislation has been passed that regulates both optional and mandatory
systems. The Welfare and Pension Plans Disclosure Act of 1958 imposes
strict guidelines on employers and unions regarding the reporting and
record keeping of pension and welfare plans. The Employee Retirement
Income Security Act of 1974 (ERISA) imposes strict regulations on private pension plans when they are offered. The 1978 amendments to the
Age Discrimination in Employment Act allow for the private-sector retirement age to be increased from 65 to 70. The Revenue Act of 1978
gives employers more options in designing innovative and different benefit systems. The Equal Pay Act of 1963 makes it unlawful for an employer to discriminate between men and women in the provision of
benefits. The Pregnancy Discrimination Act of 1978 requires that preg-
nant workers receive the same benefits as workers suffering disabilities.
All of this legislation, with more being passed every year, coupled with
that mandating certain benefits, has relieved countless burdens employees at the beginning of the century had to face unassisted.

Company-Determined Benefits

Most companies offer far more benefits than simply those required by
law. The types of benefits offered and the reasons for offering them vary.
The constituency of a firm will have an effect on the choices. For example, a firm whose employees are mostly young and straight out of school,
and who stay for short periods of time, will feel less need to offer retirement benefits. Instead, they may wish to lure and retain employees by
offering discount policies or flexible time schedules. If the organization
is made up mostly of older employees with families, group health plans
might be most important.

The reasons for offering one type of benefit over another go beyond
employee preference. However, budget constraints limit the number and
level of benefit provisions; there will only be so much money available
for compensation and benefits must compete with pay and services.

Most organizations offer three major types of optional benefits:
security- and health-oriented benefits, paid nonworking days, and

employee services. Security- and health-oriented benefits come mainly in the form of private pension plans, and health, life, and disability insurance.

Private pension plans were established partly as a complement to social security benefits. Since neither alone provided a standard of living equal to that of preretirement, providing both seemed to be a good idea.

Benefit plans have a vast variety of coverage. Major medical insurance covers surgeries, hospitalization costs, and as of 1978, expenses incurred in pregnancy. Some plans also cover outpatient care or ongoing treatments for mental illness, physical therapy, or drug and alcohol addiction.

New additions to health insurance coverage are dental and orthodontic care, visual care covering not just regular prescriptions but also accidents and surgery, chiropractic service, and to a small extent, psychiatric counseling. An increasing number of organizations are now including preventative medical coverage, such as for physical and diagnostic exams.

Life insurance coverage is provided by most organizations for the benefit of the employee's family in the event of his or her death. A typical benefit payment is double the employee's annual salary, and like health insurance coverage, it is increasingly noncontributory. The employee very rarely pays any part of the premium. Many organizations now provide some level and form of life insurance for their employees after retirement.

Disability insurance is offered by many organizations to provide basic support to employees if they are unable to work because of an accident or illness that temporarily or permanently disables them. Workers' compensation does not cover the entire cost in such cases, so roughly 75 percent of organizations provide noncontributory illness and accident coverage. As of 1978, the law requires that if an organization offers a health insurance plan, it must cover pregnancy; no time limit is allowed to be put on the absence due to pregnancy and the benefits payable must equal those of any other medical disability or problem.

The second major type of company-determined benefit is payment for time not worked. This includes vacations, holidays, and paid days off—all of which were very rare prior to this century. Employees once worked up to 16 hours a day, 6 days a week, every week of the year. If they did not show up for work one day regardless of the reason, not only did they lose their pay, they stood a good chance of losing their jobs.

Vacations began being offered around the same time as all the other benefits, during the 1930s and 40s. Vacation time varies with length of service. Typically, an employee is eligible for one week's paid vacation after six months to a year, two weeks after 1 to 3 years, three weeks after 5 to 10 years, and four weeks after 15 to 20 years. Many organizations offer a maximum of five weeks paid vacation annually, though there are a few that offer six. Paid vacations are one of the costliest benefits, and some employees are even arguing for bonus pay to cover vacation expenses.

In addition to vacation, most organizations offer all of their employees 7 to 10 paid holidays a year. These typically include Memorial Day, Labor Day, Thanksgiving, Christmas, and New Year's Day.

Paid nonworking days are offered for many reasons. Employees are allowed a set number of personal days off and days off due to reasons beyond their control. Personal time off is given for jury duty, death or illness in the family, civic or military duty, marriage, maternity and paternity leave, union duty, medical or professional appointments, religious observations, and even birthdays. Extended leaves at reduced salary are often available for college professors and some executives in the form of sabbaticals.

Employee services are the third major discretionary benefit offered by many organizations. These are the most varied, differing widely from organization to organization. Some may offer recreational facilities on the premises, such as gyms and health clubs. Some may provide educational services in the form of free in-house classes or tuition refunds for related course work done outside the organization. Financial and personal services are also often available. Organizations may also provide credit unions, savings plans, emergency loans, estate planning, transfer assistance, expatriate allowances for employees stationed abroad, plus programs to help with retirement and drug and alcohol rehabilitation.

COMPENSATION ISSUES IN MODERN ORGANIZATIONS

New modes of organizing, the flattening of organizations, delegation of authority downward, participative management, and a push to use teams all create new challenges for those managing compensation. As we have discussed, the intent of compensation is to reward those who have accomplished organizational objectives and provide them with feedback and an incentive to continue performing. One of the critical questions, then, is "Who accomplished the objective?" If the organization is flattened, the implication is that those lower in the organization are most responsible for accomplishing organizational objectives and thus more entitled to rewards. That may come as a bit of a shock to higher level managers. Most organizations wanting to reward lower level employees must obtain the needed funds by reducing the amount that goes to higher level employees.

Participative management and job enrichment is another example of current practice that has enormous implications for compensation. If all that happens with participation is an increasing of workers' responsibility but no increasing of recognition, rewards, or even punishments, employees will not participate very long. Compensation systems must be redesigned to recognize increased responsibilities. New job descriptions must be written, new pay grades defined, and new standards of performance established.

One of the most pervasive practices in modern management is the use of teams: Product development teams, quality circles, productivity improvement teams, process improvement teams, and many more dominate many organizations. If objectives are accomplished by teams, teams—not individuals—should be the focus of appraisals and rewards, a simple concept often forgotten by organizations. Problems often exist because those who organize work by creating teams are separate from those who design the compensation system. As much as possible, those who perform as teams should be evaluated and rewarded as teams.

Appraising and rewarding performance becomes even more of a problem when organizations move to network, collegiate, or loosely coupled structures. Assigning the responsibility for accomplishing an objective to one individual becomes just about impossible. Even identifying a group is a problem because the organization and thus the work is done by networks with overlapping responsibilities. In such cases, people should be rewarded based on the overall organization performance. To do otherwise will only cause you to spend so much time figuring out who did what that you will lose your focus on your main responsibility—performing.

APPLICATIONS

1. Help employees understand their responsibilities, collaborate with them to decide what must be done to meet their responsibilities, and provide feedback on their performance.

2. The performance appraisal process should be formalized, standardized, and objective in nature.

3. Choose an appraisal instrument based on a thorough understanding of the job and the purposes of the particular appraisal, not because it is cheap and available.

4. In addition to the supervisor's appraisal, be sure to have other sources of performance data to increase the validity of results.

5. Evaluators should be adequately trained in the use of appraisal techniques and should have substantial daily contact with the employee being evaluated.

6. Use self-appraisals for fostering personal growth and for identifying and resolving conflicts, but not for the purposes of evaluation and rewarding.

7. Construct a compensation system that maximizes dollar investment by making employees feel economically and psychologically rewarded enough to choose to work with the organization, to stay with it, and to produce at high levels.

8. Choose an evaluation plan that illustrates the job aspects deemed valuable, the levels of each aspect found in each job, and, on the basis of this information, the relative worth of each job to the organization. Also be sure to obtain employee input and participation when making a job evaluation.

9. Develop a range of pay based on the evaluation.

10. Let your employees know what others are making in order to encourage them to have realistic expectations. But make sure the competition that results from this is channeled in the right direction by making success a function of what employees can gain by helping their peers.

11. Carefully analyze your organization's salary structure and then decide whether past, present, or future performance will be most rewarded.

12. Constantly analyze your organization's compensation system and assess its success to identify and correct the parts that are no longer working.

CHAPTER 8

CASE 3 USING COMPENSATION TO FOSTER PRODUCTIVITY AT LINCOLN ELECTRIC*

WHICH INCENTIVE PROGRAM DO I IMPLEMENT?

With all the talk about motivating people these days, it's easy to think that you're asking for trouble if you're not always looking for a brand-new incentive system. Many experts argue that, given the pressures in today's economy, compensation plans quickly lose their punch. So a lot of managers are continually tinkering—a bonus for teamwork, say, one year, and then one for quality the next. Consultants love it—it keeps them employed. But the irony is that some of the best incentive plans haven't been touched in decades. Just ask the folks at Lincoln Electric Company.

Lincoln Electric's Solution

Lincoln Electric, in Cleveland, Ohio, is a 93-year-old manufacturer of welding machines and motors—a company that might seem to be an unlikely candidate for survival, let alone success. Its biggest customers have been in such cyclical markets as oil, steel, and construction, and during downturns, Lincoln, like other machinery makers, has taken some licks. But, its managers argue, it has remained solvent—and keeps bouncing back—because of its approach to managing and rewarding people.

---

*Reprinted with permission from Bruce Posner, "Right from the Start," *Inc.*, August 1988, pp. 95–96.

Lincoln Electric's system has been in place since 1934, and the basic idea is as straightforward as can be: The company pays individuals on the basis of what they produce. Nearly all of Lincoln's 1,800 production employees—all nonunion—receive no base salary at all. Their earnings are based on their individual output and on bonuses from the company's profits. (Lincoln's professional people, such as engineers, are on salary, although most also participate in the bonus plan.) The original idea, described in "Incentive Management," by James F. Lincoln, brother of the founder, was to give nonmanagement employees direct and powerful incentives to manage their work as efficiently as possible and to be on the lookout for opportunities to do more. That's still the philosophy. And lest employees worry about working themselves right out of a job, the company has a long-standing policy of no layoffs.

How Piecework Works

For more than 50 years, the combination of pay by output, bonus, and job security has worked like a charm. Lincoln's employees produce an average of two to three times what their counterparts produce at competitive plants, including those in Japan. Hard workers who don't mind overtime have been known in a good year to gross more than $80,000, with bonus. Not everyone does that well, says Donald F. Hastings, a 35-year company veteran who is now president, but the philosophy has always been that top performers should not be constrained. "We think it's very important to give people the fruits of their efforts," Hastings says.

Overall, Lincoln is a no-frills company: there is no dental insurance, no paid holidays—not even sick days. (Employees do get paid vacations.) The main facility looks as though it's out of the 1950s, with two-tone green walls, no windows, and no air conditioning. Still, the company has gathered an almost cultlike following. For years, it has been a subject of business school case studies. Recently, in response to inquiries from managers, Lincoln began hosting seminars for people interested in the company's compensation system (refer to the section See for Yourself? at the end of this chapter). Though designed for a production-oriented environment, the Lincoln system has been adapted to businesses as diverse as fast-food outlets and financial institutions.

The basic element is paying people for their output, known as piecework. It requires understanding—and, so far as possible, measuring—every production sequence. Lincoln itself has documented thousands of discrete functions that go into making its line of products. Different jobs have different piecework ratings (and pay scales), based on such qualities as degree of skill and responsibility required. But no matter where employees are working, the incentive is clear. The more they produce, the more they get, with one caveat: quality problems get corrected on employees' own time.

The piecework method doesn't guarantee that everyone produces as much as is humanly possible. Not everybody arrives at 5 A.M., for example, to get things organized for the day. But some do; the beauty of the system is that people have a choice. To maintain credibility, management resists the temptation to revise ratings every time an employee does well. In fact, the only time piecework ratings are adjusted, says Richard Sabo, assistant to the CEO, is when there's a bona fide change in technology. And even then, employees have the right to challenge the new rates.

Piecework sets the overall tone. It also reduces the need for constant supervision, Sabo says. But it's really just the beginning of the Lincoln system. For more than 50 years, everyone, except the top three managers, has taken part in Lincoln's bonus plan, with payments based on the performance of both the company and the individual. Technically, whether to pay an annual bonus is left to the discretion of the board of directors, but the fact is that Lincoln has never missed a year.

Evaluating Performance

The company goes to great lengths to see that the bonuses aren't arbitrary. Every six months, each person in the company, including those on salary, is evaluated in four distinct areas: output, quality, dependability, and idea generation and cooperation. Supervisors are required to rank employees and to grade them. The average score is set at 100, with some scores as low as 60 and others as high as 140. Each score is reviewed by three or four layers of management before it's final.

How well do employees do? In a good year, a top performer can more than double earnings with the bonus. And even in bad years, the bonus often exceeds 50 percent of an individual's other pay. The average bonus in 1987 was $18,773, or about 70 percent of other earnings. Over the past decade, Lincoln has handed out checks totaling about $421 million—more than 12 percent of revenues. Why so much? Because, thanks to the system, there's more money to play with, Hastings says—and because the system's future depends on it. "Our goal is to make the bonus checks significant enough to make a difference to people."

The Payoffs

Clearly, money can be a great motivator. But the managers doubt that employees would be so dedicated if it weren't for the company's long-standing commitment to maintaining employment. Anyone who's been working at Lincoln for more than two years is virtually guaranteed a job somewhere in the company. The guarantee does two things: it assures the employees that they won't be done in by their own efficiency, and it protects them in downturns. Technically, the company pledges that it will give workers at least six months' notice before laying anyone off, but the last layoff was at least 30 years ago.

Job guarantees can be dangerous, but Lincoln's commitment has weathered even serious downturns. Back in 1982, for example, revenues fell by 40 percent from $450 million to $220 million, when Lincoln's major customers—especially those in the steel industry—hit hard times.

Hastings admits that it was a frightening period. "We had never seen anything like it," he says. "Every market we were in went down." The company trained some production people to sell, and put others on maintenance crews, rebuilding machines, and painting fences. Hourly workers went on a shorter, 30-hour week, and their earnings were cut in half—an average of $22,000 versus $44,000. But nobody lost a job. Since the company made a profit and paid dividends to shareholders, management went ahead and paid bonuses that year, an average 55 percent of earnings. "To skip a bonus would have been devastating," Sabo says.

Since then, business has picked up. Today, Lincoln is a $370 million company with no debt. What's more, it's a leader in its market, something that Hastings and his management colleagues—nearly all of whom are Lincoln veterans—doubt could have happened under another kind of system.

Dedication to Succeed

To be sure, Lincoln's work environment is not modeled after a company picnic. During busy periods, people are expected to work extra shifts and weekends, and, unlike a lot of companies of its kind, there's no seniority. People are producing all day long, and competing with their peers for bonus money. Tough as it is, it seems to work. Turnover rates are high—around 25 percent—during the first three months or so, as people learn that nothing is given away. But after that, most employees stay longer than 30 years.

"An employee has to *want* to be in a system like this," Hastings explained one afternoon, sitting in his windowless office. And the same might be said of managers as well. Clearly, it's not for owners who find competition among employees distasteful or who need to be totally in charge of the show. At Lincoln, says Hastings, it depends on trust. "If all an owner wants to do is make more money, my feeling is that he'd be very disappointed with this system. It's not going to work unless people feel they're being treated fairly."

SEE FOR YOURSELF?

Want to Know More? Lincoln Electric Will Be Happy to Show You

Since 1983, Lincoln Electric Company has been sharing the inner workings of its incentive management system with managers from all over the world. Most months, the company sponsors a four-hour seminar for outsiders at its plant in Cleveland. The sessions, which are free, include a plant tour, lunch in the cafeteria, and a question-and-answer period. To date, they've attracted more than 2,500 managers, and that doesn't take into account special tours organized for the likes of Ford and General Motors.

The purpose of Lincoln's sessions was—and still is—at least partly altruistic, insists Richard Sabo, assistant to the chief executive officer and organizer of the seminars. "We wanted other companies to see that it's possible to remain profitable during difficult times." Lincoln has never worried much about giving away free information to its competitors, he says, and there may, in fact, be a benefit to the exposure. "If other companies are profitable," Sabo says, "some of them may end up buying our products."

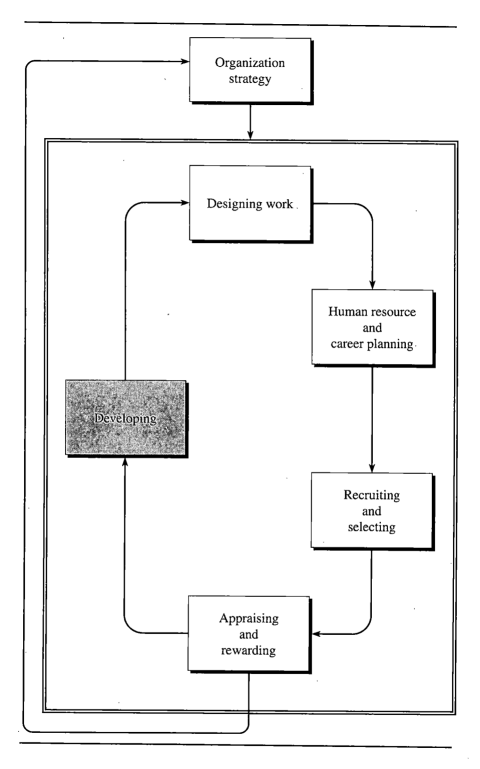

CHAPTER 9

DEVELOPING

INTRODUCTION

Both the employee and the organization in general must be developed so that they meet the demands of the operating environment. Employee development is anything that prepares employees to better perform their jobs. Organizational development is the process of integrating all of the components of the organization—structure, systems, skills of the people, culture, and so on—so that they support and work well with each other and provide productive and motivational work environments; it is the continuing effort to enhance the problem-solving and renewal process of the organization. Let us first consider employee development and then organization development.

EMPLOYEE TRAINING AND DEVELOPMENT

The first step in establishing a training program is to determine whether one is needed to help improve performance. Employees perform poorly for many reasons: Among them are such problems as:

1. Confusion about what is supposed to be accomplished on the job.
2. Lack of physical and mental skills and know-how to apply them to the job.
3. Lack of motivation or desire to perform because they have not been recognized or rewarded for accomplishments in the past.
4. Lack of feedback, so they have no knowledge that performance is bad.
5. Lack of resources or facilities.

185

Training programs aimed at familiarizing employees with their jobs and improving skills will help solve the first and second problems. The last three problems cannot be solved by training. In fact, training programs that improve employees' ability to perform but don't address these last three problems may only lead to frustration and withdrawal because of organizational constraints that limit employee performance.

DESIGNING AND IMPLEMENTING THE TRAINING PROGRAM

The type of training program you choose will be determined by what employees need to learn. The three general areas in which training and development focus are self-awareness, job skills, and motivation. Let us consider a few training programs that represent each of these approaches. This list is not meant to be exhaustive; rather, it presents some ideas about the wide range of approaches used to affect employee attitudes, behaviors, and accomplishments.

Self-Awareness Programs

Career Development.   Many self-awareness programs are oriented toward career development; that is, helping employees become more aware of their own interests and abilities and the jobs available in the organization. Career development is one of the first training programs that should be established in any organization. By helping employees think about careers rather than just the job they presently have, the organization can help them see their present job as a learning experience. Employees are more likely to develop long-term commitments to the organization if they understand career possibilities.

Personal Assessment.   Many training programs are designed to help employees understand their personal characteristics. Personal assessment is well illustrated by the T-P leadership style questionnaire (see Figure 9–1). Employees fill out the questionnaire, then compare their scores with the type of leadership style needed on the job. If people can accurately assess themselves and the needs of their job, they have a better chance of matching themselves and jobs on which they can perform. Another example of personal assessment is Mintzberg's questionnaire for self-analysis. Based on observations of five chief executives,

FIGURE 9–1
What Kind of Leader Are You?

Instructions

Complete the following steps to analyze what leadership style best fits a current management situation. You can focus on any group or organization. You might, for example, focus on a study group in your class. The items describe aspects of leadership. Respond to each item according to the way you would be most likely to act if you were the leader of a study group. Circle whether you would be likely to behave in the described way Always (A), Frequently (F), Occasionally (O), Seldom (S), or Never (N).

A F O S N   1. I would most likely act as the spokesman of the group.

A F O S N   2. I would encourage overtime work.

A F O S N   3. I would allow members complete freedom in their work.

A F O S N   4. I would encourage the use of uniform procedures.

A F O S N   5. I would permit the members to use their own judgment in solving problems.

A F O S N   6. I would stress being ahead of competing groups.

A F O S N   7. I would speak as a representative of the group.

A F O S N   8. I would needle members for greater effort.

A F O S N   9. I would try out my ideas in the group.

A F O S N   10. I would let the members do their work the way they think best.

A F O S N   11. I would be working hard for a promotion.

A F O S N   12. I would tolerate postponement and uncertainty.

A F O S N   13. I would speak for the group if there were visitors present.

A F O S N   14. I would keep the work moving at a rapid pace.

A F O S N   15. I would turn the members loose on a job and let them go to it.

A F O S N   16. I would settle conflicts when they occur in the group.

A F O S N   17. I would get swamped by details.

A F O S N   18. I would represent the group at outside meetings.

A F O S N   19. I would be reluctant to allow the members any freedom of action.

A F O S N   20. I would decide what should be done and how it should be done.

A F O S N   21. I would push for increased production.

A F O S N   22. I would let some members have authority which I could keep.

A F O S N   23. Things would usually turn out as I had predicted.

A F O S N   24. I would allow the group a high degree of initiative.

FIGURE 9–1 (*concluded*)

A F O S N	25. I would assign group members to particular tasks.
A F O S N	26. I would be willing to make changes.
A F O S N	27. I would ask the members to work harder.
A F O S N	28. I would trust the group members to exercise good judgment.
A F O S N	29. I would schedule the work to be done.
A F O S N	30. I would refuse to explain my actions.
A F O S N	31. I would persuade others that my ideas are to their advantage.
A F O S N	32. I would permit the group to set its own pace.
A F O S N	33. I would urge the group to beat its previous record.
A F O S N	34. I would act without consulting the group.
A F O S N	35. I would ask that group members follow standard rules and regulations.

Scoring Instructions

1. Circle the item number for items 8, 12, 17, 18, 19, 30, 34, and 35.
2. Write the number 1 in front of a *circled item number* if you responded S (seldom) or N (never) to that item.
3. Also write a number 1 in front of *item numbers not circled* if you responded A (always) or F (frequently).
4. Circle the number 1s which you have written in front of the following items: 3, 5, 8, 10, 15, 18, 19, 22, 24, 26, 28, 30, 32, 34, and 35.
5. Count the circled number 1s. This is your score for concern for people. Record the score in the blank following the letter P at the end of the questionnaire.
6. Count the uncircled number 1s. This is your score for concern for task. Record this number in the blank following the letter T.
7. Plot your scores on the two dimensions to give you a sense of how you compare with others.

Task
```
0        5        10       15 ·      20
├────────┼────────┼────────┼────────┤
low concern                high concern
for task                   for task
```

People
```
0        5        10       15       20
├────────┼────────┼────────┼────────┤
low concern                high concern
for people                 for people
```

Source: J. William Pfeiffer and John E. Jones, eds., "T-P Leadership Questionnaire: An Assessment of Style," *A Handbook of Structured Experiences for Human Relations Training* vol. 1 (La Jolla, Calif.: University Associates, 1974), pp. 10–12.

Mintzberg identified three categories of managerial roles: interpersonal, informational, and decisional (see Figure 9–2). Each of these roles is present in all managerial work, but the importance of each varies with

FIGURE 9–2
Mintzberg's Summary of 10 Roles of Managers

Role	Description
Interpersonal	
Figurehead	Symbolic head; obliged to perform routine duties of a legal or social nature
Leader	Responsible for the motivation and activation of subordinates; responsible for staffing, training, and associated duties
Liaison	Maintains self-developed network of outside contacts and informers who provide favors and information
Informational	
Monitor	Seeks and receives wide variety of special information (much of it current) to develop thorough understanding of organization and environment; emerges as nerve center of internal and external information of the organization
Disseminator	Transmits information received from outsiders or from other subordinates to members of the organization; some information factual, some involving interpretation and integration of diverse value positions of organizational influences
Spokesperson	Transmits information to outsiders on organization's plans, policies, actions, results, etc.; serves as expert on organization's industry
Decisional	
Entrepreneur	Searches organization and its environment for opportunities and initiates "improvement projects" to bring about change; supervises design of certain projects as well
Disturbance handler	Responsible for corrective action when organization faces important, unexpected disturbances
Resource allocator	Responsible for the allocation of organizational resources of all kinds—in effect the making or approval of all significant organizational decisions
Negotiator	Responsible for representing the organization at major negotiations

FIGURE 9-2 (*continued*)

Self-Study Guide for Managerial Activity

• Where do I get my information and how? Can I make greater use of my contacts to get information? Can other people do some of my scanning for me? In what areas is my knowledge weakest and how can I get others to provide me with the information I need? Do I have powerful enough mental models of those things within the organization and in its environment that I must understand? How can I develop more effective models?

• What information do I disseminate into my organization? How important is it that my subordinates get my information? Do I keep too much information to myself because dissemination of it is time-consuming or inconvenient? How can I get more information to them so they can make better decisions?

• Do I balance information collecting with action taking? Do I tend to act prematurely before enough information is in? Or do I wait so long for "all" the information that opportunities pass me by and I become a bottleneck in my organization?

• What rate of change am I asking my organization to tolerate? Is this change balanced so that our operations are neither excessively static nor overly disrupted? Have we sufficiently analyzed the impact of this change on the future of our organization?

• Am I sufficiently well-informed to pass judgment on the proposals made by my subordinates? Is it possible to leave final authorization for some of them with subordinates? Do we have problems of coordination because they, in fact, now make too many of these decisions independently?

• What is my vision of direction for this organization? Are these "plans" primarily in my own mind in loose form? Should they be made explicit in order to better guide the decisions of others in the organization? Or do I need flexibility to change them at will?

• Are we experiencing too many disturbances in this organization? Would they be fewer if we slowed down the rate of change? Do disturbances reflect a delayed reaction to problems? Do we experience infrequent disturbance because we are stagnant? How do I deal with disturbances? Can we anticipate some and develop contingency plans for them?

• What kind of leader am I? How do subordinates react to my managerial style? How well do I understand their work? Am I sufficiently sensitive to their reactions to my actions? Do I find an appropriate balance between encouragement and pressure? Do I stifle their initiative?

• What kind of external relationships do I maintain and how? Are there certain types of people that I should get to know better? Do I spend too much of my time maintaining these relationships?

• Is there any system to my time scheduling or am I just reacting to the pressures of the moment? Do I find the appropriate mix of activities, or do I tend to concentrate on one particular function or one type of problem just because I find it

FIGURE 9–2 (*concluded*)

interesting? Am I more efficient with particular kinds of work at special times of the day or week and does my schedule reflect this? Can someone else (in addition to my secretary) take responsibility for much of my scheduling, and do it more systematically?

• Do I overwork? What effect does my workload have on my efficiency? Should I force myself to take breaks or to reduce the pace of my activity?

• Am I too superficial in what I do? Can I really shift moods as quickly and frequently as my work patterns require? Should I attempt to decrease the amount of fragmentation and interruption in my work?

• Do I orient myself too much toward current, tangible activities? Am I a slave to the action and excitement of my work, so that I am no longer able to concentrate on issues? Do key problems receive the attention they deserve? Should I spend more time reading and probing deeply into certain issues? Could I be more reflective?

• Do I use the different media appropriately? Do I know how to make the most of written communication? Do I rely excessively on face-to-face communication, thereby putting all but a few of my subordinates at an informational disadvantage? Do I schedule enough of my meetings on a regular basis? Do I spend enough time touring my organization to observe, firsthand. Am I too detached from the heart of our activities, seeing things only in an abstract way?

• How do I blend my rights and duties? Do my obligations consume all my time? How can I free myself sufficiently from obligations to ensure that I am taking this organization where I want it to go?

Source: Figure and text from *The Nature of Managerial Work* by Henry Mintzberg. Copyright 1973 by Henry Mintzberg. Reprinted by permission of HarperCollins Publishers.

the nature of the environment, the level and function of the job, the characteristics of the manager, and the situation. Mintzberg suggests that managerial effectiveness is improved when managers understand each of these variables and adjust their behavior accordingly. To facilitate self-analysis, he developed a series of questions based on the three categories of managerial roles that help managers understand how to change their behavior to improve personal effectiveness.

Job Skills Programs

Many training programs are oriented towards improving skills. These range from those that help new employees adjust to the organization and the requirements of their jobs to those that focus on personal skills. Some more common types of job skills programs are reviewed below.

Orientation Programs. New employees need to learn the skills necessary to perform their jobs. Too often this is left to chance, and employees have to guess what they are supposed to accomplish and how. A good orientation program is the responsibility of the organization and the department within which the employee works and should prevent this from happening.

This initial orientation is particularly important because new employees will often have unrealistically high expectations of their jobs. If new employees do not understand the nature and purpose of their entry-level jobs, they are very likely to become dissatisfied, unmotivated, and maybe even quit. One solution to this is to develop more challenging entry-level jobs. Another solution is to provide realistic interviews and job descriptions so that applicants can have a clear understanding of the nature of the job being offered. Applicants will then know what they are getting into if they take the job.

On-Job-Training. The most widely used skill-training program is on-the-job training. As new employees do the job, other experienced employees or training specialists help them improve their skills. There are several advantages to on-the-job (OJT) training: the employee is directly involved in the job, so there is no problem transferring skills learned in the training to the actual job, the skills learned are directly relevant and applicable, and the program is much cheaper than most because there is no need for expensive equipment or facilities.

Motivational Programs

Some training programs are focused on improving employee's motivation to do the job. Examples in this category are programs based on the concepts of motivation to manage and achievement motivation.

Motivation to Manage. Miner's theory of employee motivation to manage states that certain attitudes and motives will affect a person's choice of whether to become a manager, how well he or she will perform

in the managerial job, and how fast he or she will advance in the organization hierarchy.[1] He identifies six attitudes that are key to determining a person's motivation to manage: favorable attitude toward authority,
desire to compete, assertive motivation, desire to exercise power, desire
for a distinctive position, and a sense of responsibility.

Miner suggests that those who have these attitudes will be effective managers. According to his theory, organizations can develop
their managers by improving their motivation to manage. He has developed a training program that uses lectures, video tapes, role plays,
and many of the conventional training techniques to help employees
increase their awareness of these favorable attitudes and develop them
in themselves.

Achievement Motivation.   McClelland and his associates have
developed a training program to improve manager effectiveness based
on the "need for achievement," which they define as the urge to improve or a desire to exceed some standard of behavior.[2] The overall objective of the program is to help employees develop a desire to excel in
their jobs by training them to think in terms of goals, accomplishments,
and feedback.

McClelland's theory of achievement motivation states that people's
motives are developed through childhood experiences and affect the way
we respond to experience. For example, when confronted with a situation, some of us emphasize the personal relationships involved, others,
the task to be done, and still others, the achievement of some objective.
In a training program, these tendencies can be assessed by asking the
participants to fantasize about certain situations and then by scoring their
fantasies according to the number of achievement-oriented works and
themes they include. The participants can then be taught to produce fantasies heavily loaded with achievement-oriented words and ideas. Once
they are able to do that, they can learn to apply the same achievement
orientation to their own work.

---

[1]John B. Miner, *Motivation to Manage* (Atlanta, Ga.: Organization Measurement Systems Press,
1977).

[2]D. C. McClelland, *The Achieving Society* (New York: Van Nostrand, Reinhold, 1961); and D.
McClelland, J. Atkinson, R. Clark, and E. Lowell, *The Achievement Motive* (Englewood Cliffs,
N.J.: Prentice Hall, 1953).

ORGANIZATION DEVELOPMENT

Organization development focuses on improving the ability of the whole organization or some subunit of it to perform and accomplish its objectives. Organization development involves change and improvement. Even though the competitive environment we face, the pressures for quality, the need to meet customer demands, and the requirements for reduced product development time all create pressures for change and improvement, there is still a natural resistance to change.

People don't resist all change. They don't resist increases in their salary. They don't resist improvements in their work environment. People resist changes they don't understand, which they feel might be to their disadvantage, or they simply have a low tolerance for change. But this resistance can be managed. The classic study of resistance to change was conducted at the Harwood Manufacturing Company, a pajama producer that gained prominence among managers and students of management because of a study done on its loss in productivity resulting from job change.[3] The study showed that Harwood's production workers resisted the job changes to such an extent that it took new workers seven fewer weeks to reach a standard of efficiency than experienced workers who were shifting from one kind of work to another. Many workers flatly refused to change, preferring to quit.

The Harwood study was conducted by Lester Coch and John R. P. French to determine whether work resistance to change would decline if employees had the opportunity to participate in changing their own jobs. In one set of groups, worker representatives decided how the work would be changed; in a second set, all members participated; in a third set, the workers were trained to implement changes designed by industrial engineers. For the next month, the workers' performance was carefully checked. Coch and French discovered that those groups of workers that did not participate in developing the changes made in their jobs showed the most resistance to change and a marked decline in performance. Those groups that participated through representatives did only slightly better, but the groups that involved all their members in developing these changes showed a rapid and sustained improvement in productivity.

---

[3]Lester Coch and John R. P. French, ''Overcoming Resistance to Change,'' *Human Relations,* 1, 1948, pp. 512–32.

We resist any change we think will make it harder for us to fulfill our needs. Consider, for example, how a move to a new facility might be viewed by employees with different needs.

1. Some will be most disturbed by the change in physical setting—"I will have to give up my old chair. I just arranged the office the way I wanted it."
2. Some will be most worried about the social aspect of the move—"My work group will be broken up. We have been friends for a long time. Why should I have to learn to work with new people?"
3. Others will be most concerned about the effect of their move on their careers—"I was just beginning to learn this job; now I'll probably have to start all over. How can I show the boss what I can really do if they keep shifting me around from job to job?"

Of course, none of these workers' fears may be realized. The physical surroundings may be better, the established work groups may remain intact, and the new jobs may be more rewarding. As long as people perceive a threat to their well-being, however, they may react negatively. People respond to what they expect to happen. If we don't know what will happen, we always assume the worst, and in that case, it is easier to remain in the present situation than to take a risk.

In sum, then, people don't resist all types of changes, they resist change that has perceived or actual negative consequences. Managers need to be able to reduce resistance by making sure that job changes meet their employees' needs as much as possible and, most importantly, by helping employees understand the reasons why these changes are being made. Three strategies can help accomplish this: (1) involve employees in decisions that affect their jobs, (2) develop open communications, and (3) build trust between workers and management.

Involving Workers in Decisions that Affect Their Jobs

Involving workers in the decision-making process increases their understanding and acceptance of job changes. When they understand those job changes, they can become more involved in implementing them and therefore more committed to making sure the changes are successful.

In order to achieve these results, workers must truly be able to influence the decisions that affect them. This means that managers cannot merely inform employees about what they have decided but must give them all the available information, an explanation of the constraints and opportunities of the situation, and a share of the authority to make the decision.

Developing Open Communications between Workers and Management

Managers need to know how their employees feel about the proposed change. Open communications is a basic requirement of managing change effectively.

Building Trust

Managers need to trust that their employees will use the information and authority given to them effectively. Workers have to trust that management will act in their best interest and be sensitive to their needs. This trust will be built up gradually as management and workers become used to working together.

Where resistance to change is based on fear and anxiety, organizations could offer facilitation and support to further build trust. Retraining employees to fit new job requirements, offering time off after difficult periods of change, providing emotional support and counseling therapy are some of the ways managers can ease the change process. Trust could be built in bargaining with resistors, especially those who stand to gain something of value to them by the change, or by conferring with them openly and directly.

These are the objectives of organizational development: to involve workers in the decision-making process, to develop communications between workers and management, and to build trust. Each of these techniques accomplishes its objectives in a different way, but they all have the same ultimate goal. In order for them to work, of course, the people in the organization must possess certain characteristics; they must want to get involved, they must be willing to trust the organization enough to take some personal risks, and they must be able to communicate their needs to management.

THE PROCESS OF ORGANIZATION DEVELOPMENT

Whereas training programs focus on developing individual skills, organization development programs focus on improving the performance of whole units or the whole organization. Organization development is best thought of as following the process of unfreezing, change, and refreezing.

Unfreezing

Unfreezing is the development of an acceptance of the need to change. All people have habits and familiar ways of doing things. Just as a stationary car requires a greater force to get it going than to keep it moving, people need a great initial force to put change in motion. A critical component of this force must come from the person involved in the change. He or she must see the need for change and must want to change. Without that desire for change, trying to motivate a person will be like trying to move a car with the brakes on and the motor off.

The field of organizational development has developed many ways of unfreezing attitudes and behavior. Most of the techniques involve a diagnosis or assessment that provides employees with information comparing actual behavior to performance objectives. To produce the desired results, the information must be provided in a believable and usable form. It must be seen as an aid to better performance and not a threat, and it should be expressed in a way that will increase employee trust and willingness to change.

Techniques for providing this information vary. Some deal with changing interpersonal behavior or improving groups' effectiveness, and others focus on improving the performance of whole units or the total organization.

One of the best techniques for helping people recognize change is force field analysis. Force field analysis recognizes those forces that promote change in people (or driving forces) and those that restrain it. Some driving forces might be the need for increased productivity, the desire for higher salary, or the need for recognition. Some restraining forces might be lack of skill, peer pressure, or poor equipment.

The driving and restraining forces push against each other to hold performance and productivity at a certain level. This level can be changed by either increasing the driving factors, or reducing the restraining factors. Pressure for better performance can be applied by increasing monetary incentives, by setting higher goals, or by providing more recognition for achievement. Restraints can be reduced by increasing skills, reducing peer pressure, or by obtaining new equipment. To manage change effectively, we should first decrease the restraining forces and then, if necessary, increase the driving forces.

The contribution of force field analysis is that it recognizes the forces that cause resistance to change and provides a structured way of dealing with them. In general, managers can be much more effective by reducing the resistance to change than they can by increasing the pressure to change.

Making Changes

After individuals and groups have identified problem areas and realize the need for change, the question is, what changes should be made? Changes can be technological, people-oriented, or structural.

Technological Approaches. Technological approaches are many and varied. One of the earliest was Frederick Taylor's *Scientific Management,* which we reviewed in Chapter 1. *Scientific Management* analyzed interactions between workers and machines to determine the most efficient way for workers to use the machines. Each was then paid according to how much he or she produced.

Later technological approaches include modification of equipment and production methods. Ergonomics, the study of how to best design equipment to fit the physical characteristics of the worker, is the latest technological approach.

People-Oriented Approaches. People-oriented approaches to organizational change focus on employees' behavior, skills, attitudes, perceptions, and expectations on an individual, group, unit, or organizational level. People-oriented programs for change are advantageous in that they can be as small or large as the problem itself. However, they still overlook certain relevant tasks, and structural and technological aspects of the problem.

Structural Changes. Structural change approaches are aimed at maximizing productivity by changing what is included in jobs and how the jobs are done. Job enrichment—structuring jobs so that they contain a variety of activities—is a recent example. Sometimes it is difficult to put structural changes into effect because they require adjusting not only what is done in one job but how it relates to many other jobs. For example, if my areas of decision making are increased, it often means someone else's areas of decision making are decreased.

Sometimes, the necessary change will involve developing new attitudes; at other times, it will involve acquiring new skills and behaviors or modifying the structure of the organization. It is important to remember that no change occurs in isolation. All units of an organization—no matter how diverse in function—are still parts of a single whole with a unified purpose. Alterations in the marketing department may benefit other departments. The ripple effects of any change, not just the local and immediate effects, should be carefully studied before any change is enacted.

Refreezing

When new behaviors are learned, new attitudes acquired, or new organizational structures developed, they need to be maintained. The tendency will be to slip back into the old familiar ways. For example, it is common for employees to learn a new skill in a training session and never use it afterwards because the right opportunities, feedback, and support are not available on the job. Soon, the new skill is forgotten.

Maintenance of change is not the final step in the organization development process because the new approaches, no matter how effective, soon become stale as the organizational environment continues to change. Continuous evaluation of current programs and identification of potential problems are necessary, then the cycle of unfreezing, change, and refreezing begins again.

TECHNIQUES OF ORGANIZATIONAL DEVELOPMENT

Techniques of organizational development focus either on interpersonal relations, the group, or the organization. Figure 9–3 offers a representative but not exhaustive list of techniques that can be used at these three levels.

FIGURE 9–3
Traditional OD Interventions

Interpersonal Level

Sensitivity Training   An analysis of interpersonal interactions typically done in small groups. The focus is on how to improve relationships.

Performance Appraisal and Feedback Training   Training on how to evaluate performance and give feedback to others so that performance is improved. Interpersonal communication skills are enhanced.

Group Level

Role Analysis   Ideally, all organization members should understand exactly what role they play in the accomplishment of the organization's goals, and all roles should be meshed so that goals can be achieved cooperatively.

Team Building   Enhancing the performance and developing the effectiveness of groups is one of the most popular OD interventions. Effective groups must be able to set goals and priorities, allocate work among themselves, and understand how group members relate to each other.

Organizational Level

Survey Feedback   To give everyone in the organization an understanding of its current status and an opportunity to participate in improving this status, some organizations use surveys and questionnaires. The information gathered is analyzed and fed back to those who supplied it in a format they can use for problem solving.

Grid® OD   Grid® OD was developed in the 1960s, based on Blake and Mouton's Managerial Grid®. It is a comprehensive, long-range training program that may unfold over four or more years. Participants work in teams to identify mission-oriented objectives, implement them, and simultaneously develop their problem-solving and conflict resolution skills.

Source: Adapted from information on Grid® OD, based on Robert R. Blake and Jane Srygley Mouton, *The New Managerial Grid* (Houston: Gulf Publishing, 1978).

Interpersonal Relations

Sensitivity training is one common way of providing feedback to individuals about how they affect others. Sensitivity training involves leaderless groups with no formal agenda. The facilitator helps the group and the individuals in it understand how they interact with and affect one another. No theory or conceptual material is offered; instead, the discussion focuses on interactions in the group and what might be done to improve relations.

Group-Oriented Programs

Many organizational development techniques are group oriented. In fact, some of the techniques that are individually oriented, such as sensitivity training, can also be used to improve group effectiveness. The techniques that focus on groups strive to improve the ability of people to work together. Team building is a good example of this kind of technique.

Team building follows the normal organizational development sequence of unfreezing by data gathering, changing by identifying alternatives and selecting the proper one, and refreezing by developing a support structure. The following are the steps involved in team building:

1. *Initial diagnosis.* The diagnosis consists of three stages. First, a series of interviews are held with a sample of supervisory and managerial personnel; second, group meetings are held with those interviewed to examine the results and to determine problem areas and priorities; and finally, managers and consultants meet to finalize the decision.

2. *Team skills training.* Foremen, general foremen, assistant superintendents, and superintendents participate with their peers in groups of approximately 25 in a series of experience-based exercises during a two-and-a-half-day workshop.

3. *Data collection.* Immediately following the team skills training, all participants complete two questionnaires. The first concentrates on organizational health and effectiveness, and the second asks participants to describe the behavior of their immediate supervisor, general foreman, or assistant superintendent.

4. *Confrontation.* In this phase, various work groups are asked to review the data described above and determine problem areas, establish priorities in these areas, and develop some preliminary recommendations for change.

5. *Planning.* Based on the conversations that occur during the confrontation, each group develops some recommendations for change and plans for the changes to be implemented. The plans include what should be changed, who should be responsible, and when the action should be completed.

Organizationally Oriented Programs

The organizational effectiveness questionnaire, developed by Organizational Dynamics Incorporated, is an example of an organizationally oriented program. The organizational effectiveness questionnaire is built on the concepts of employee involvement and participation in decision making; its diagnosis looks at many managerial characteristics that are needed to support a participative culture. A diagnosis done by employees, management, or staff groups will help to determine whether the organization has the desired characteristics (see Figure 9–4). Next, the organization must decide at which level it would like to be operating. The difference between the level at which it currently functions and that at which it would like to function becomes the basis for change. The organization can then develop and implement plans to narrow the gap.

Total quality management (TQM), introduced in Chapter 3 and discussed extensively in Chapter 10, is an example of a currently popular organization level development program. The thrust of TQM is performance improvement of the total organization by enhancing performance of individuals, groups, and the total organization.

The Learning Organization[4]

One of the most extensive new thrusts in organizationally oriented programs is creating and managing the learning organization. Both managers and researchers are finding that getting the current job done is not enough. Nor is delivering continuously improving quality enough for organizations to be successful. In the last 10 years, organizations have seen the speed of change and the complexity of markets, technologies, competitors, political environments, and human resources increase dramatically. For an organization to survive and succeed, not only members of the organization but the organization itself must have mechanisms for learning faster and more effectively. Modern writers have coined the phrase "learning organization" to describe this need. Improved organizational learning has many benefits. Individual members are encouraged to learn and improve their skills. They are better able to reach their full

---

[4]Adapted from Peter Kreiner and Paul Morrison, "The Learning Organization" (working paper of the Manufacturing Roundtable), 1991.

FIGURE 9–4
Organizational Effectiveness Questionnaire*

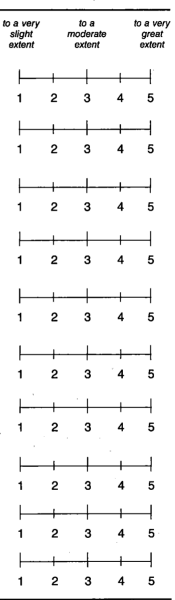

	to a very slight extent	to a moderate extent	to a very great extent

1. **Goal Setting:** Employees work toward clear objectives which fit in with organizational as well as personal career goals.
   1 2 3 4 5

2. **Feedback:** There is good two-way communication between managers and employees so that both sides are informed of employee performance.
   1 2 3 4 5

3. **Responsibility:** Employees are given enough authority to do their jobs and the freedom to determine how best to do them.
   1 2 3 4 5

4. **Participation:** Employees are encouraged to participate in making decisions, to speak up when they disagree with their bosses, and to make suggestions.
   1 2 3 4 5

5. **Leadership:** Managers provide vision and inspire commitment to quality and productivity by stressing excellence in everything that is done.
   1 2 3 4 5

6. **Teamwork:** The work is organized so that employees can work as a team and/or freely exchange ideas and opinions.
   1 2 3 4 5

7. **Coordination:** There is communication and cooperation, rather than competition, between different groups in the organization.
   1 2 3 4 5

8. **Standards:** The organization demands high quality work and insists that employees at every level give their best effort.
   1 2 3 4 5

9. **Reward:** Pay, benefits and promotions are administered well. Employees who do their jobs well are rewarded.
   1 2 3 4 5

10. **Recognition:** Employees who do their jobs well are recognized for their efforts.
    1 2 3 4 5

*Reprinted with permission, Organizational Dynamics, Inc. Five Burlington Woods Drive, Burlington, Massachusetts 01803.

potential and increase the contribution they can make to the organization. The organization is able to more quickly understand customer needs and design operating systems to meet them. Also, the organization has in place mechanisms for continuously improving its processes and products. The organization continuously transforms and improves itself.

In most companies, "learning" is viewed narrowly as the acquisition of knowledge and skills by individuals. The concept of a learning organization views learning much more broadly, as a way of doing business that touches all operating processes and constantly strives to transform the way work is done and the products and services that are produced. A learning organization consciously manages learning. It has in place programs, mechanisms, and procedures for all employees to constantly upgrade their skills, and for the organization itself to learn from its mistakes and experiences. It uses every interaction with customers and other constituencies in its environment to question what it is doing and how. It is constantly changing and adjusting to new environmental pressures.

Three factors characterize a learning organization. First is customer-driven continuous improvement. This focuses on controlling variation in the manufacturing process and products and services so that they meet customer needs. Every activity is continuously evaluated by those participating to assess whether it adds value and how it might be improved to add even more value. The organization has in place feedback mechanisms so that the fit between what the organization produces and what the customer needs is evaluated.

Second is a focus on action learning. Action learning is a process of learning by doing. The focus is on evaluating not only what is done but how it is done. Time is built into the production process to evaluate, reflect, and learn from experience. Mistakes are viewed as opportunities to learn and opportunities to make sure mistakes are not repeated.

Third, managers have a set of strategic skills that makes it possible for them to manage the learning organization, including scanning and monitoring the competitive environment, constantly striving to improve, building collaboration and networks, and maintaining flexibility and responsiveness. Figure 9–5 provides a questionnaire you can use to assess yourself on the strategic skills necessary to manage the learning organization. Only by developing and maintaining the skills in people can organizations hope to cope with the tremendous amount of change and complexity they face.

FIGURE 9–5
Strategic Leadership Skills©

To What Extent Do You:	Not at All				Very Much

SCANS AND MONITORS THE
COMPETITIVE ENVIRONMENT

Stay in tune with customers by attending User conferences, using focus groups, and/or use other methods of talking with customers	1	2	3	4	5
Know and monitor competitors, use competitive benchmarks to evaluate own success	1	2	3	4	5
Understand and stay in tune with key business indicators	1	2	3	4	5
Project and anticipate key business trends	1	2	3	4	5

FRAMES APPROPRIATE STRATEGIES

Develop and communicate focused strategies	1	2	3	4	5
Focus attention on key strategies	1	2	3	4	5
Constantly am asking "Are we doing the right thing?"	1	2	3	4	5

ENERGIZES AND MOTIVATES

Instill a need for action and urgency	1	2	3	4	5
Create a sense of ownership and commitment to accomplish the strategy among employees	1	2	3	4	5
Arouse, excite and challenge employees	1	2	3	4	5
Develop and appropriately use subordinate talents and competencies	1	2	3	4	5

BUILDS COLLABORATION AND NETWORKS

Create cohesion and collaboration across organization units	1	2	3	4	5
Build alliances and networks to enhance performance	1	2	3	4	5
Manage conflict and build cross-functional integration	1	2	3	4	5
Keep my eyes focused on the overall strategies of the corporation	1	2	3	4	5
Drive collaboration to eliminate duplication and optimize efficiency	1	2	3	4	5

FIGURE 9–5 (*concluded*)

	Not at All				Very Much
CONSTANTLY STRIVES TO IMPROVE					
Foster a climate of risk-taking to improve performance	1	2	3	4	5
Have a relentless pursuit of excellence	1	2	3	4	5
Encourage intellectual honesty and a willingness to accept and deal with negative information	1	2	3	4	5
Constantly look for a better way and learn from failure	1	2	3	4	5
CREATES STEWARDSHIP AND ACCOUNTABILITY					
Develop and implement appropriate performance standards	1	2	3	4	5
Expect and require honest evaluations	1	2	3	4	5
Hold myself and others accountable for results	1	2	3	4	5
MAINTAINS FLEXIBILITY AND RESPONSIVENESS					
Anticipate change and react quickly	1	2	3	4	5
Effectively manage the change process	1	2	3	4	5
Recognize varying performance demands of different situations	1	2	3	4	5

Source: © Lloyd Baird, Leadership Institute, Boston University School of Management, 1991.

A WORKBOOK EXERCISE FOR ANALYZING AND ESTABLISHING TRAINING AND DEVELOPMENT PROGRAMS[5]

As we discussed in Chapter 1, future organization environments will be quite different from the present ones. Technology changes, new information systems, time to market requirements, and customer demands will all increase complexity and the push for quality and speed. New management skills will be needed, skills that must be developed in managers

---

[5]Adapted from Lloyd Baird, "Developing Skills to Implement Manufacturing Strategy," Manufacturing Round Table, Boston University, 1992.

of the future. We have created the skill development matrix to provide a method for identifying skills that will be needed and to provide guidance for selecting and implementing the training and development programs for developing them. The skill development matrix is built on the assumption that you must not only understand future performance requirements but also the fundamentally different skill sets necessary at different levels of responsibility. Let us consider future performance requirements first and then the different skill sets managers need. These two components can be combined to specifically identify training needs and show how programs should be designed to meet them. The following explains the steps you should go through.

Step 1: Identify Future Performance Requirements

Future performance requirements are a combination of the two fundamental requirements on any job: effectiveness (doing the right thing) and efficiency (doing things right). This creates four different performance requirements that the organization may have to meet in the future (see Figures 9–6 and 9–7).

Performance Requirement I: Maintain Performance. The organization or unit may be on track, providing what customers want and doing it very efficiently. All that need be done in the future is to maintain the current levels of performance.

Performance Requirement II: Enhance Execution. The organization may be providing the right products and services but not at minimal cost and resources. It will need to enhance execution.

Performance Requirement III: Refocus Efforts. Some organizations accomplish their objectives very well; they just happen to be the wrong objectives. To succeed in the future, they must refocus their efforts on correct objectives.

Performance Requirement IV: Fundamental Change. Some organizations are so far off track they are neither doing the right thing nor are they doing it well. These organizations will require fundamental changes both in their focus and ways of doing business if they are to be successful in the future.

FIGURE 9–6

Future Performance Requirements

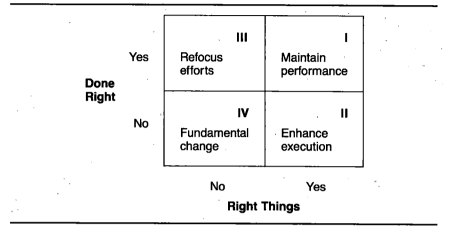

FIGURE 9–7

Future Performance Requirements

Situation I: Maintain Performance
- Customer needs are being met.
- Quality is good.
- Production is efficient.
- Employees have and use the needed skills.

Situation II: Enhance Execution
- Customer needs are identified but not met.
- The strategy is correct but not implemented.
- Employees need new skills to implement strategy.

Situation III: Refocus Efforts
- Employees are motivated but focusing their efforts in the wrong direction.
- Employees' skills are appropriate but not being used to implement the strategy.
- Employees do not accept or understand the strategy; their focus is wrong.

Situation IV: Fundamental Change
- Customer needs are not correctly identified or understood.
- Employees do not have the skills to implement appropriate strategies.
- Employees do not accept or understand appropriate strategies.

Step 2: Identify Skill Sets Needed

The second component that determines how training and development programs should be focused is the skill sets needed. Skills can be seen as organized around a hierarchy of responsibilities: first self-management, then management of the unit within which the individual works, then integration of the unit work with other units within the organization, and finally, the fit of the unit with the external environment. Each set has a different focus on management control, interpersonal relations, use of information, and interaction with the environment as illustrated in Figure 9–8 and explained below:

Skill Set 1: Individual Performance Skills.   The primary skill set requisite in any environment is individual performance and self-management. If the individual cannot perform, he or she will make little or no contribution to the unit or organization. Skills include:

- Technical capability.
- Interpersonal skill.
- Understanding operating procedures.
- Analytical capability.

Skill Set 2: Unit Management Skills.   Work in organizations is done in units: team, group, division, and so on. The second skill set relates to managing unit performance. The focus is on improving everyone's performance so that the units' objectives are accomplished. Skills include:

- Functional skills.
- Integrating subfunction areas.
- Unit goals and effectiveness.

Skill Set 3: Integration Skills.   Work units exist within the context of an organization. What one unit can accomplish is determined by how well it can coordinate its efforts with others. Work groups need supplies and services from some units (internal suppliers) and deliver services to other units (internal customers). They must fit with these internal suppliers and customers. Skills include:

FIGURE 9–8
Dimensions of the Various Skill Sets

	Skill Set I Individual Performance	Skill Set II Unit Management	Skill Set III Integration	Skill Set IV Strategic
Management Control Focus	Accomplish my objectives	Accomplish our objectives	Help many units (including ours) accomplish their objectives	Accomplish and improve objectives within context of shifting environments
Nature of Interpersonal Relations	Delegation and control	Shared responsibility, team building	Internal customer/ supplier relationships, negotiations	Empowerment, value-added, partnering
Use of Information	Record keeping, tracking, standards and evaluation, project measures	Cost-benefit analysis, unit metrics, process and product measure	Integrated organizational databases, systems, dynamics, lags, and flows	Scanning, what-if questions, long- and short-term analysis
Awareness of Environment	As affects personal performance, usually frustrating	Aware of functional shifts, looking for state-of-the-art programs	Environmental shifts identified and incorporated into planning process, aware of need for process efficiencies	Systematically anticipating, customer responsive, shape environment, alliances

- Managing cross-functional integration.
- Organization development.
- Project management.
- Managing organization systems.
- Ability to fit administrative procedures to cross-functional problems.

Skill Set 4: Strategic Skills.   Not only must units fit within the context of the organization but they must also fit their external environment. They have to have mechanisms for scanning and responding to environmental changes. They must make sure all administrative, operating, and technical systems fit with and support each other. They must anticipate change and manage it. Skills include:

- Environmental scanning.
- Strategic fits.
- Anticipation.
- Organization responsiveness and learning.

The skill sets come as building blocks. Unit management skills are built on a foundation of individual skills. The success of the unit is first and foremost determined by the skills of the individuals comprising the unit. Likewise, integration is most effective between units that are well run. If your unit can clearly articulate its strategy and what it needs from other units to accomplish that strategy, you are more likely to get what you need. Also, those you supply are more likely to work well with you if you can clearly specify what you can and cannot do for them. Strategic skills are best used in organizations that are well knit together and functioning. Responding to the environment is quicker in organizations where units are already clear about who they are and how they fit together.

Step 3: Use the Skill Development Matrix to Identify Training and Development Needs

By combining the performance requirements with the skill sets, the skill development matrix is created. The matrix can be used to identify the current status of employees' skills as well as their future desired state. Comparing the present status with the future desired state, the development gap is identified (see Figure 9–9).

FIGURE 9–9
Skill Development Matrix: Assessing Present versus Desired States

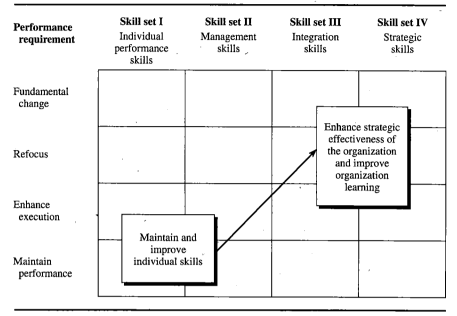

Performance requirement	Skill set I Individual performance skills	Skill set II Management skills	Skill set III Integration skills	Skill set IV Strategic skills
Fundamental change				
Refocus			Enhance strategic effectiveness of the organization and improve organization learning	
Enhance execution	Maintain and improve individual skills			
Maintain performance				

Unfortunately, no matter what they claim, most development programs in American industry are focused on individual skills to maintain performance. Strategic skills aimed at creating a fundamental change in the organization cannot be developed solely by having managers study cases and discuss situations in organizations; they require massive organization development efforts integrated with management education thrusts, and structural and systems changes that support and drive the educational thrusts. In fact, the educational programs become the basis for identifying the needed organizational changes and driving them into implementation. That is far different than developing individual skills.

Step 4: Implement the Development Program

Basic rules for movement exist whenever you are trying to implement programs to move individuals and the organization along either or both dimensions of the skill development matrix. These rules exist because of the inherent nature of skill development and performance requirements. Understanding them identifies the constraints, challenges, and opportunities you will face implementing a development program.

Rules for Movement through Performance Requirements

Rule 1: Improving within a Performance Requirement Is Much Easier than Changing Performance Requirements. For example, helping people improve their ability to maintain performance (*maintain performance*) is much easier than convincing them they are doing the right things but their effort and motivation are just not high enough (move from *maintain performance* to *enhance execution*). They have to increase the time and energy they spend. Likewise, if people believe their focus and efforts are correct and all they must do is maintain performance, it will be very hard to convince them that *fundamental changes* are necessary.

Rule 2: Shifting to Do Right Things Is Much Harder than Simply Improving What You Are Already Doing. Improving what you are already doing is simply a matter of improving skills regarding something you have already accepted as your responsibility. What you are doing is seen as important and necessary; the job of development programs is to help you do it better. However, shifting to doing the right thing necessarily involves recognizing that what you are doing is the wrong thing. Humans do not like to admit to themselves or anyone else that what they are doing is wrong. Before a development program can help participants improve skills and refocus on different performance requirements, people must first accept the need to refocus. Employees with no felt need to change will not change. Only after they have admitted they were wrong can they begin to refocus and do what is right.

Rule 3: The Bigger the Performance Step You Have to Take, the Harder It Is Going to Be. Imagine the following scenario: Competition is stealing customers. Development times are twice as long as they should be. Customers are becoming even more sophisticated. Technology is causing most of your products to become obsolete. Costs are too high. In short, you are in real trouble. You not only have to totally shift what you are doing but you need to improve the efficiency of the total organization (fundamental change). However, your work force firmly believes times are not too bad; sure, competition is heating up, but they firmly believe they have the right skills, are working hard, and producing the right products. All they need to do is to improve their efficiency; that is, get better at doing what they are already doing (enhance execution).

Can you imagine the challenge you will face convincing people that massive changes are necessary? Getting better at doing the wrong thing will simply exacerbate the situation. But psychologically, employees may need to blame someone else. They may say, "We worked hard, we did the best we could. Too bad some other unit did not do their share."

Rules for Movement through Skill Sets

Rule 1: Movement to a Higher Skill Set Requires a Shift in Conceptual Frameworks. For example, developing unit management skills is not simply doing individual skills better. The focus of attention must shift from "I must improve" to "We must improve." Management shifts from a foundation of delegation and control so that *my* objectives are met to shared responsibility and a team orientation to accomplish *our* objectives.

Rule 2: Development within a Skill Set Is Much Easier than Movement to a New Skill Set. Because new frameworks are needed, movement to new skill sets is very hard. We develop our ways of looking at work over long periods of time and through much experience. A good example in many organizations is the difficulty functional heads have making the shift to executive responsibilities. As functional heads, they are responsible for their unit's performance, their focus is functional, and their management practices focus on their unit. When promoted to executives, they will be responsible for coordinating the work of many functional areas and making sure the organization meets the demands of the competitive environment. Their focus must shift from functional unit performance to integrating multiple units, sensing and adapting to the needs of the environment and organizationwide performance. That is a shift many good functional unit managers find very difficult to make.

Rule 3: Each Successive Skill Set Is of a Higher Order than Previous Skill Sets. By higher order, we mean they encompass and include previous skill sets. For example, unit management skills are built on a foundation of good individual skills. It is impossible to be a good unit manager without good individual skills. On the other hand, it is possible to have good individual skills—technical, analytical, and self-management competencies—without having good unit management skills—coordination skills, team management capabilities, and project planning.

A more extreme example will help clarify this rule. It is very possible to approach individual skills from a strategic perspective. In fact, the only way strategic skills of monitoring, adapting, and anticipating will work is if individuals already have the capabilities to manage themselves and interpersonal relations so strategy can be developed and implemented. However, it is not possible to approach strategic skills from an individual perspective. Strategic questions cannot be asked or answered if the focus is limited to the individual—making sure that *I* accomplish *my* objectives—without regard to other people or units or what is happening in the environment.

Rule 3a: Each Skill Set Is Built on the Foundation of Previous Skill Sets; This Makes It Necessary to Always Return to Previous Skill Sets to Make Sure They Are Properly in Place from the New Perspective. For example, individual skills from an individual perspective are very different than individual skills from a unit management, integration, or strategic perspective. At the individual level, skill development focuses on technical competence, operating understanding, and analytical capability. At the strategic level, individual skills take on a new perspective. Technical competence must include an understanding of competition and customers. Operating understanding must include an understanding of how the organization monitors and adjusts to the environment. And analytical capabilities must include the ability to do long- and short-term analysis, ask what-if questions, and include the capability to analyze and scan the environment.

Another example: If you are designing a program to enhance strategic skills, you must include the development of individual skills for monitoring, adjusting, learning, and so on. You must also be concerned about developing the total organization so it includes monitoring, adjusting, and adapting capabilities.

Rule 3b: Progression through the Skill Sets Is a Shifting of Frameworks, Not a Shifting of Responsibilities; That Is, You Can Do Supervisor Work from a Strategic Skill Set. We find that a main problem in organizations is that managers assume the sequence of management skills—individual, unit, integration, and strategic—matches the organization hierarchy. Not true. Many problems are created by workers who do not understand the competition and the customers. A main thrust of organization development is to decentralize and move toward more participative decision making. This will be disastrous if those lower in the hierarchy do not develop their integration and strategic skills. In fact, our argument is that development programs need to be designed to give everyone in the hierarchy higher order skills. That will be the difference between organizational success and failure in today's fast-changing complex environments.

Step 5: Use the Skill Development Matrix to Design and Implement the Proper Development Programs

Many types of development programs exist. Which you should choose depends on what you want to accomplish. Figure 9–10 shows the positioning of some popular development programs. Many quality programs, (A) for example, are aimed at improving individual and group management skills so current levels of productivity that are meeting customer needs can be maintained and enhanced. Total quality management programs (B), on the other hand, more often focus on improving organiza-

FIGURE 9–10
Development Programs

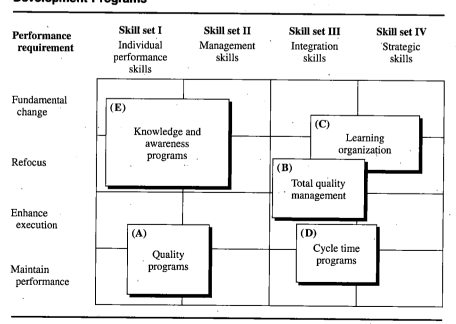

tion performance, enhancing organization processes as well as individual skills. These are very different than programs focused on creating learning organizations (C), where employees and the organization as a whole are constantly identifying what skills they need and developing them to create fundamental changes in the total organization.

Other examples: Many programs aimed at reducing cycle time (D) are focused on improving integration and coordination across departments to improve current levels of performance. Many executive programs run by universities are knowledge and awareness programs (E) aimed at improving the skills of individual executives for monitoring and understanding what is happening in the environment and why fundamental changes are needed in management practices and organization functioning.

The skill development matrix can be used to develop not only one program but a continuum of development programs having different purposes but still coordinated together (see Figure 9–11). Too often in organizations, programs overlap so much they are simply the same pro-

FIGURE 9–11
A Continuum of Management Development Programs

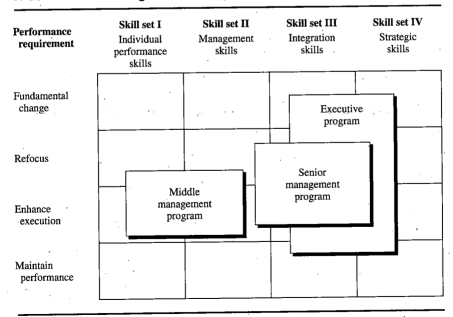

Performance requirement	Skill set I Individual performance skills	Skill set II Management skills	Skill set III Integration skills	Skill set IV Strategic skills
Fundamental change			Executive program	
Refocus		Middle management program	Senior management program	
Enhance execution				
Maintain performance				

gram aimed at different audiences. The skill development matrix allows you to design programs with very different purposes, building them one on another in a continuum of development.

Middle management programs can build individual and group management skills to enhance unit performance and begin building an awareness of how to monitor and adjust to changing environments. Senior management programs can focus on building integration and coordination skills: skills necessary to weave the organization together, improve organization functioning, and drive strategy implementation through multiple units and functions. Executive programs can then focus on monitoring and adapting to the changing environment. Topics would include environmental scanning, strategic fits, and how to anticipate environmental shifts and respond.

APPLICATIONS

1. Determine whether or not a training program is necessary to help improve overall performance.

2. Help employees see their present job as a learning experience in their career so they develop long-term commitments to the organization.

3. Involve workers in decision-making processes so they will be more accepting of change.

4. Develop a system of open communication so you will know how employees feel about proposed changes.

5. Trust that your employees will use the information and authority given to them effectively.

6. Provide employees with information comparing actual behavior to performance objectives. But in order to produce desired results, provide this information in a believable and usable form. It must be seen as an aid to better performance and not as a threat.

7. Manage change effectively by first reducing the resistance to change by increasing skills, reducing peer pressure, or by obtaining new equipment. Then, if necessary, increase the pressure for better performance by increasing monetary incentives, setting higher goals, or providing more recognition for achievement.

8. After individuals and groups have identified problem areas and realize the need for change, decide whether technical, people-oriented, or structural changes should be made.

9. Once the changes have been implemented, help employees maintain the new behavior and new attitudes learned by providing opportunities, feedback, and support on the job.

10. Develop and maintain the skills in people so your organization will be better able to cope with the tremendous amount of change and complexity it faces in the future.

11. Identify training needs and show how programs should be designed to meet them by taking the following steps:

    a. Identify future performance requirements.

    b. Identify skill sets needed.

    c. Use the skill development matrix to identify training and development needs.

    d. Implement the development program.

    e. Use the skill development matrix to design and implement the proper development programs.

CHAPTER 10

CASE 4   LEARN FROM THE BEST: USING TRAINING AND ORGANIZATION DEVELOPMENT TO IMPLEMENT A TOTAL QUALITY PROGRAM*

INTRODUCTION

Total quality programs are excellent examples of how training and organization development can be used to implement organization strategy—in this case, improvement in quality and customer satisfaction. A look at those who have excelled in total quality provides current examples of how implementation of development concepts enhances organization success.

Reflect for a moment on the world's most coveted awards. Better yet, compose a list. Include only the prizes that are universally revered—honors that have meaning throughout the world, and awards that identify a select few individuals or groups as the very best at what they do. What comes to mind?

Our own list was surprisingly short: the Nobel Prize and the Olympic gold medal. Most of the other possibilities we came up with were, for one reason or another, disputable.

*Adapted with permission from George H. Labovitz and Yu Sang Chang, "Learn from the Best," *Quality Progress*, May 1990, pp. 81–85.

Our point? Universally accepted standards of excellence are rare. The few that do exist are valuable because everyone can learn from them. By studying those who earn credible recognition for being the best in a given endeavor, pathways to achieving excellence can be identified. With just this rationale in hand, we undertook our study of companies that have won the Deming Prize.

AN OVERVIEW OF THE DEMING PRIZE AND THE BALDRIGE AWARD

Awarded annually by the Union of Japanese Scientists and Engineers (JUSE) since 1951, the Deming Prize recognizes outstanding achievement in quality strategy, management, and execution. Separate categories of the Deming Prize are awarded to individuals, corporate firms (companies, divisions, and small enterprises), and factories. There are other tributes to total quality excellence, but the Deming Prize is clearly the best known and most universally coveted of such awards.[1]

The prize is named after an American, W. Edwards Deming, who helped guide Japan's post–World War II industrial redevelopment. Yet American management has not been competitive for the honor. Only one U.S. firm, Florida Power & Light Company, has ever won the Deming Prize.[2]

The most obvious explanation for American's modest record in the pursuit of the Deming Prize is that U.S. and European companies have rarely bothered to apply for it. Until recently, the Deming Prize was not well known in the West, and the application process itself is rigorous.

In fact, non-Japanese companies were ineligible to seek the honor until 1987. But most informed observers agree: Very few U.S. corporations could have qualified for the Deming Prize, even had they been eligible. American management has just begun to demonstrate the requisite commitment to total quality principles and practice.

---

[1]An even higher honor, The Nippon Quality Medal, can be earned by companies that have previously won the Deming Prize and thereafter demonstrate five or more years of ongoing improvement.

[2]Three U.S. corporations were previously associated with the Deming Prize, but each was recognized for operations run either by a Japanese subsidiary or through a joint venture with Japanese partners. They are Texas Instruments Japan, Ltd. Bipolar Department; Fuji-Xerox Co., Ltd; and Yokogawa-Hewlett Packard Co., Ltd.

Today, a handful of U.S. corporations might be ready to follow in Florida Power & Light Company's footsteps and apply for the Deming Prize. But a greater number of companies appear to be setting their sights on a goal much closer to home: the Malcolm Baldrige National Quality Award.

The criteria used to select winners of the Baldrige Award are in some ways different from those used in selecting winners of the Deming Prize. However, the two awards are essentially similar in that "both look for quality commitment throughout the organization, from the top down, including anyone with a relationship with the company, such as suppliers, distributors, and customers.[3] This similarity suggests that U.S. corporations now aspiring to the Baldrige Award can profit from an analysis of the quality management practices of Deming Prize winners.

BUSINESS SUCCESS

For most companies, winning a prize is, at best, a secondary mission. The primary missions of the modern corporation are to compete, win new customers, and prevent the competition from winning away one's own customers. This is every bit as true in Japan as it is in the United States and Europe.

In fact, the Deming Prize and business success are closely correlated. Companies honored for achievement in total quality also tend to be leaders in their industry and conspicuously successful in competitive markets. Four companies that have won the Deming Prize are Toyota Motor Co., Ltd., NEC IC/Microcomputer Systems, Ltd., Shimizu Construction Co., Ltd., and the Kansai Electric Power Co., Inc.

Toyota Motor Co., Ltd. This is the largest and most profitable auto and truck manufacturer in Japan. Favorable consumer perception of the quality and value of Toyota products has helped the company capture nearly 10 percent of world automotive market share. In the years ahead, Toyota appears likely to gain as much as 15 percent of world market share, a stake comparable to that held by General Motors.

---

[3]David Bush and Kevin Dooley, "The Deming Prize and Baldrige Award; How They Compare," *Quality Progress*, January 1989.

NEC IC/Microcomputer Systems, Ltd. A clear winner in the fiercely competitive semiconductor marketplace, NEC has also earned a reputation for having exceptional quality in a diverse spectrum of electronics and has enjoyed correspondingly dramatic gains in market share. NEC is pioneering the practical integration of computers and communication systems.

Shimizu Construction Co., Ltd. One of the top five construction firms in Japan, Shimizu has recently made impressive inroads in the United States by developing golf courses, condominium communities, and similar projects. Industry observers note that Shimizu is exceptionally adept at managing properties after development is complete. Shimizu builds long-term relationships with its buyers. First, it offers financing and other services that ease the purchasing process. Then, it attends to customer needs that arise after the real estate transaction.

The Kansai Electric Power Co., Inc. The most emulated Japanese utility company, Kansai helped open the floodgates of service sector quality initiatives in Japan with its total quality implementation. Kansai offers electric service at consistently low rates and has managed to shorten service interruptions significantly in comparison with other Japanese electric utilities.

Our research drew on a variety of sources, including data and interviews compiled by Boston University's Asian Management Center, reviews of actual total quality program materials, quality management conference presentations, and informal exchanges with Japanese academicians.

The main source of information and insights for this article, however, was our ongoing series of personal interviews with Japanese companies that have won the Deming Prize. In most of the companies visited by Yu Sang Chang, coauthor of this case, interviews were conducted separately with total quality staff members and senior line managers.

The objective of this research was to identify total quality management training and development programs and practices that are consistently evident in Deming Prize winners but rare in other companies. These distinguishing practices might prove valuable to competitive-minded U.S. corporations now casting an eye toward the Malcolm Baldrige National Quality Award.

A PLAN FOR SUCCESS

To our surprise, one differentiating factor emerged almost immediately: implementation plans as the key element of organization development. Virtually all of the Deming Prize winners can point to clear, detailed, well-communicated total quality improvement plans, the likes of which are rarely encountered in U.S. or European companies.

Further, the award-winning companies tend to communicate and make people aware of their quality plans schematically (i.e., in visuals posted throughout the company) rather than in burdensome volumes of text. Employees actually see the plan every day and learn of the company's goals through a medium they can readily understand and absorb (see Figure 10–1).

The organization development and training plans for implementing total quality are bound firmly by time, covering between three and five years, with specific annual themes or objectives. Examples of annual themes include reliability enhancement, strengthening vendor partnerships, and cycle time reduction.

Significantly, most plans call for a general adjustment to changing conditions at least once each year. Feedback mechanisms on which these adjustments will be based are specifically mandated so the guiding principle of continuous improvement is woven into the fabric of the development implementation plan itself.

Further focus is provided through the designation of a limited number of megaprojects to be completed each year. By stipulating specific megaprojects within the implementation plan, senior management effectively concentrates the organization's resources and energies on a critical few quality improvement objectives.

Finally, award-winning implementation plans tend to designate defensive and offensive quality improvement goals. Defensive goals are similar to those traditionally included in many U.S. quality implementation plans. They are directed at fulfilling the potential of the status quo (e.g., reducing nonconformance, eliminating cost overruns). Offensive quality improvement goals are, as the name implies, more aggressive in nature. They are directed at expanding the company's potential beyond the status quo, thereby improving its position against its competitors, increasing customer satisfaction, and building market share.

Often, the most powerful offensive goals are quite subtle. For example, most construction firms pay a great deal of attention to the

FIGURE 10–1
Communicating Total Quality

COMMUNICATING TOTAL QUALITY

This poster (from a Japanese insurance company) demonstrates that a complex total quality improvement plan can be communicated in a compact visual.

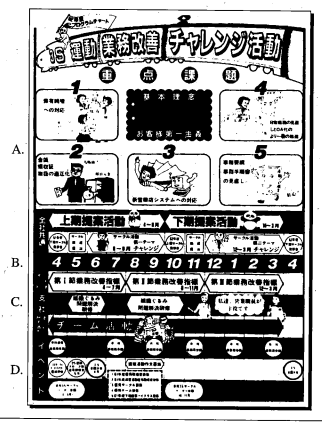

A The guiding vision (black box at top center) emphasizes customer focus and is surrounded by five corresponding goals (roughly translated).
  1. Retain customers through perfect execution.
  2. Achieve error-free processing of cash transactions.
  3. Make computer systems more customer oriented.
  4. Apply office automation to improve internal operations.
  5. Keep standard operating procedures up-to-date with customer needs.

B A central feature of the plan is the time line, which tracks with the fiscal year April to April.

C The two graphic bars immediately below the time line designate activities for senior management (policy deployment) and sales personnel, respectively. The next graphic bar illustrates planning activities of cross-functional teams composed of main office and branch office personnel.

D The bottom section of the poster indicates key events included in the plan, such as steering committee meetings, training schedules, corporate wide recognition events, and team meetings.

durability and conformity (defensive quality goals) of the bricks used in their projects. But the builder who wishes to stand apart adds an offensive goal, using only bricks that weather in a way that is pleasing aesthetically. This subtle difference might not be apparent to customers when they buy the bricks, but, over the years, it will enhance customer satisfaction and set this one construction firm's product apart from all others.

In terms of content, award-winning plans tend to detail training and development in four main areas: senior management activity, customer satisfaction activity, employee involvement activity, and training activity.

THE EXECUTIVE'S ROLE

The Deming Prize–winning plans institutionalize senior management activity, defining an executive role that goes far beyond what one finds in most companies. Training and development must focus on both individual performance and management skill sets. Executives are required to seek out middle managers and solicit their input on quality improvement opportunities and goals. The theory, a sound one, is that middle management's commitment to total quality is vital. That commitment grows when executives take time to ask middle managers, "Where do you think we should go from here?"

In fact, an annual schedule of 30 or more field visits for each senior executive is not uncommon in award-winning companies. This is a significant personal commitment of time, travel, and effort because these field visits involve much more than showing the corporate flag. For one thing, executives typically take time to gather relevant information before each field visit, using tools such as the *jissetsu*. The jissetsu is a report covering each site's quality targets, success in achieving those targets, causes for shortfalls in the total quality effort, degree of interdepartmental cooperation in total quality, and degree of user satisfaction. Plant managers must complete and submit the jissetsu prior to each executive visit, so the executive arrives at the field site with a significant body of data that can be expanded, challenged, and clarified in the ensuing discussions with middle management.[4]

To enhance these discussions, Japanese executives use interactive communication tools and encourage their middle managers to apply the

---

[4]Kaoru Shimoyamada, "The President's Audit: QC Audits at Komatsu," *Quality Progress*, January 1987.

same methods to advance the total quality process. One such communication tool that executives are taught is called catchball (Figure 10–2), in which the executive, manager, or any other member of a department or work group throws out the kernel of an idea for improving quality. For example, someone might say, ''Imagine how happy our customers would be if we never again asked them to fill out a form.''

Chances are, the idea will be impractical when first expressed. The information gathered on forms, to follow this example, might be required

FIGURE 10–2
Catchball

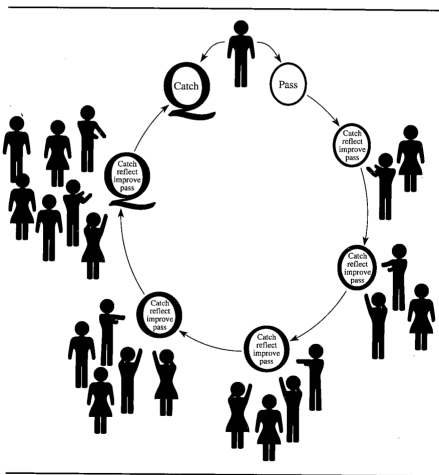

for the company to understand and meet customer needs. But, instead of discarding the idea, Japanese executives ask their people to "catch" it, reflect on it, improve it, and then pass it on to others, who will develop the idea further through the same process.

Catchball takes training and practice, just as a child must practice to become adept at throwing and catching a ball. But, as people learn the technique—and as everyone in the company learns that their ideas will indeed be caught, nurtured, and developed—catchball generates a steady stream of quality improvement innovations.

Within a week after the field visit, the executive writes a commentary for the chairperson and the corporation's total quality department, so each plant manager's performance is very much on the record. As you can well imagine, an executive visit does more to reinforce the importance of total quality than could 100 powerfully worded memorandums.

KEEPING ALL CUSTOMERS SATISFIED

Customer satisfaction activity, the second main area needing development, is distinguished by a high degree of systematization and integration across functions. Managers' integration skills are critical. The implementation and development plan identifies and assigns specific tasks and responsibilities to virtually all departments and sections because the participation of all parts of the company is needed to achieve customer satisfaction. Further, most award-winning companies facilitate integration by having regular gatherings of middle managers to ensure that customer satisfaction breakthroughs (as well as incremental advances) achieved in one area are replicated throughout the company.

Toyota and quite a few other Japanese companies use quality function deployment (QFD) to achieve the customer satisfaction goals articulated in their total quality plans. QFD, which is also used in some U.S. companies, has been described as "a set of planning and communication routines" that "focus and coordinate skills within an organization, first to design then to manufacture and market goods that customers want to purchase and will continue to purchase.[5] Marketing, engineering,

---

[5]John R. Hauser and Don Clausing, "The House of Quality," *Harvard Business Review*, May–June 1988.

manufacturing, and other functions work closely together from the time a product is first conceived to pool their expertise and heed the voice of the customer as they develop new products and bring them to market. Developing both the individual's and the organization's ability to integrate across functions, resolving the likely conflicts, improving cross-cultural communication, and getting everyone to be concerned about jointly delivering customer satisfaction is critical. Not only must they work together to meet current customer requirements but they must develop mechanisms for monitoring and responding to future requirements.

Interestingly, the chain of customer satisfaction activity within award-winning companies often begins and ends with the sales function. The salesperson helps guide the general direction of the company by picking up valuable information about marketplace trends, hidden niches, and the like directly from customers and then passing these insights on to other company functions and the executive leadership.

Perhaps even more important, the salesperson helps each client, in effect, to develop his or her own requirements. So, in Deming Prize–winning companies, product specifications tend to be set in the field rather than in the factory.

STRIVING FOR TOTAL INVOLVEMENT

The award-winning Japanese companies are remarkably proficient at implementing another key to successful organization development: They involve all employees in total quality. Sixty-five percent or more of employees are active in total quality efforts within leading Japanese manufacturing firms, while U.S. Fortune 500 companies report that only about 25 percent of their employees now take part in corporate quality and customer satisfaction initiatives.[6]

The consistently high level of employee involvement in Deming Prize–winning companies is no accident, nor is it purely a reflection of the Japanese work culture. Every implementation plan we studied includes detailed provisions for employee involvement activity.

The emphasis on management's role is especially noteworthy. The plans specifically call on even the most junior of line managers to lead and champion quality improvement teams. The message is clear: Man-

---

[6]ODI Executive Opinion Survey, as reported in *The Wall Street Journal*, Sept. 6, 1988; *Industry Week*, June 6, 1988; and *Quality Progress*, August 1988.

agers must involve their employees in total quality to climb the corporate ladder. Middle managers, in turn, often serve as block advisers who oversee and nurture all quality improvement efforts in their areas.

The employee involvement activity also provides for individual contributions to the quality improvement effort, most often in the form of suggestion systems. It appears that top Japanese companies have far greater success with suggestion systems than do their counterparts in the United States.

Consider, for example, the performance of Toyota's employee suggestion system for the years 1951 through 1986 (Figure 10–3). Toyota's suggestion system got off to a slow start. For the first five years, it generated no more than 0.2 suggestions per employee per year (a rate that nevertheless exceeds the average of 0.16 suggestions per employee now generated by suggestion systems in U.S. companies).[7] In fact, Toyota employees submitted relatively few suggestions until the early 1970s, when, in apparent response to the oil crisis of 1973 and other stimuli, the number of suggestions submitted and the average number of suggestions per employee skyrocketed. A similar leap occurred in 1979–81, the time of the second major oil crunch; thereafter, participation continued to increase at a remarkable rate. In 1986, 95 percent of Toyota employees submitted suggestions, which translates into an average of 47.7 suggestions from each Toyota employee.

How did Toyota foster such a remarkable rate of participation in its employee suggestion system? For one thing, all submitted suggestions receive a response within 24 hours from the employee's direct supervisor. Toyota workers never have to wait and wonder if anyone is listening to their suggestions. Further, good suggestions are systematically rewarded with gold, silver, and bronze medals or with membership in a Good Idea Club or another designation of honor. And, as in most top Japanese companies, a key senior executive is charged with making sure the Toyota suggestion system really works.

But the single most important reason behind the success of Toyota's suggestion system is illustrated in Figure 10–3 under the column Percent Suggestions Implemented. Toyota implemented a full 96 percent of the suggestions its employees submitted in 1986. This reflects both the high caliber of the employees' ideas and the sincerity of Toyota's commitment

---

[7]Yuzo Yasuda, *Toyota's Creative Suggestion Activity*, Japan Management Association, 1989, in Japanese.

FIGURE 10–3
Employee Suggestion System

Year	Total Suggestions Submitted	Suggestions per Employee per Year	Percent Employees Participating	Percent Suggestions Implemented
1951	789	0.1	8	23
1952	627	0.1	6	23
1953	639	0.1	5	31
1954	927	0.2	6	53
1955	1,087	0.2	10	43
1956	1,798	0.4	13	44
1957	1,356	0.2	12	35
1958	2,682	0.5	18	36
1959	2,727	0.4	19	33
1960	5,001	0.6	20	36
1961	6,660	0.6	26	31
1962	7,145	0.6	20	30
1963	6,815	0.5	21	34
1964	8,689	0.5	18	29
1965	15,968	0.7	30	39
1966	17,811	0.7	38	46
1967	20,006	0.7	46	50
1968	29,753	0.9	43	59
1969	40,313	1.1	49	68
1970	49,414	1.3	54	72
1971	88,607	2.2	67	74
1972	168,458	4.1	69	75
1973	284,717	6.8	75	77
1974	398,091	9.1	78	78
1975	381,438	8.7	81	83
1976	463,442	10.6	83	83
1977	454,552	10.6	86	86
1978	527,718	12.2	89	88
1979	575,861	13.3	91	92
1980	859,039	19.2	92	93
1981	1,412,565	31.2	93	93
1982	1,905,642	38.8	94	95
1983	1,655,868	31.5	94	95
1984	2,149,744	40.2	95	96
1985	2,453,105	45.6	95	96
1986	2,648,710	47.7	95	96

to act on the insights and suggestions of it people. Employees at Toyota know that the suggestions they submit will be valued and applied.

CONSISTENT TRAINING

The final area addressed in the award-winning plans is training to develop individual skills. In contrast to the disconnected bursts of quality-related training common in many other corporate settings, the Deming Prize–winners' investment in developing quality awareness and quality improvement skills is steady and ongoing at all levels in the corporation.

Figure 10–4 presents a master quality training schedule from a Japanese manufacturing company that won the Deming Prize. The schedule mandates fundamental quality training for everyone in the company—from top executives through part-time employees—thereby ensuring that all managers and employees understand vital quality principles and can speak the same language. It also stipulates that new employees receive quality training within a few days of joining the company.

At the same time, the schedule clearly recognizes that quality training needs vary by level and function. QC staff members and specialists, for example, are required to complete far more quality training than any of the other groups. There is even differentiation within the QC staff group, with white-collar (clerical) training set apart from the courses for people in technical areas.

Just as important, senior managers in award-winning companies often take a keen interest in training content. This results in quality training that is, more often than not, exceptionally concrete. People are brought together to deal with real issues and to solve real problems that are of concern to senior management. The company simply uses these occasions to introduce new quality improvement skills and techniques.

TAKE THESE LESSONS TO HEART

We do not suggest that U.S. or European companies attempt to implant a Deming Prize–winning total quality scheme into their own operations. Clearly, a total quality process must reflect the realities of the company: its goals, its culture, and its people. On the other hand, it makes sense

FIGURE 10-4
Master Quality Training Schedule

	Object		Course Name	Hours	Instructor
Compulsory training	Directors	All	Executive Course (with company)	1.5 days 11H	External instructor
	Department and section managers	All	Department and section management course	4 days 38H	
		Managers with 5 years (+) experience	Refresher course	2 days 19H	Specialized instructor
	Staff — Technical	All	QC (staff) course	4 days 32H	
	Staff — Clerical	All	QC (staff) course	3 days 24H	
	Line — Supervisor	All	Supervisor course	3 days 24H	
	Line — Group leader and circle leader	All	Group leader course	3 days 24H	Instructor in each plant, division, and office
	Line — Worker	All	QC worker course	one day 8H	
	New employees	All	New employee course	one day 8H	
	Part-time employees	All	Part-time employee course	one day 8H	

FIGURE 10-4 (concluded)

	Object		Course Name	Hours	Instructor
Specialist training	Staff		1. Basic course (A)	4 months at 5 days per month 192H	
		Selected staffs	2. Basic course (B)	3 months at 4 days per month 114H	
			3. Reliability	4 days 39H	Specialized instructor
			4. Design of experiment	4 days 36H	
			5. Multivariate analysis	4 days 36H	
			6. Others		

to draw all the relevant lessons one can from the best known and most honored total quality implementations, especially if a company hopes to gain such recognition for itself.

First and foremost, there must be a plan. Total quality improvement should be structured and scheduled in considerable detail. The plan should include offensive as well as defensive quality improvement goals. It should be communicated through visual media to every employee in the company.

The plan should put the burden of total quality squarely on management. Commitment must be obtained from senior executives to carry the total quality vision out of the boardroom and into the company's everyday operations. Middle managers should focus on unlocking the vast quality improvement potential inherent in the work force.

The quality plan should be used to unite diverse functions and elements of the company in pursuit of customer satisfaction. Quality-related training activities should also be linked directly to both the offensive and defensive goals.

Even if a Baldrige Award or Deming Prize is not in their future, companies should take these few lessons to heart. They could be vital to continued survival and success in an increasingly competitive world.

CHAPTER 11

GETTING PAYOFF FROM INVESTMENT IN HUMAN RESOURCE MANAGEMENT*

INTRODUCTION

We have all heard and given speeches praising people as our most important resource for implementing organization strategy. No manager would say otherwise, at least not in public. As our economy shifts from an industrial to a service base, as complex technology requires increasingly skilled operators, and as more and more information must be sifted and analyzed, people in our operation make the difference between competitive success and failure. Naturally, managers say the human resource management activities introduced in Chapter 1—designing work, human resource and career planning, recruiting and selecting, appraising and rewarding, and developing—must be based on the organization strategy and must be as efficient as possible. But in too many organizations this is simply lip service. There is no payoff from money spent on human resource management.

To investigate how managers can get payoff from their investment in human resource management we visited 50 corporations, ranging in size from 2,000 to 300,000 employees and varying in industry from automobiles to consumer products. Most of the managers we met with were offering excuses: "The payoff is long term, be patient." "You cannot measure results in dollars, they are intangible." "We know what we are

*Adapted with permission from Lloyd Baird and Ilan Meshoulam, "Getting Payoff from Investment in Human Resource Management", *Business Horizons*, Indiana University, January-February 1992, pp. 68–75.

doing, the program will work." "The problem is not the program, managers just are not implementing it right." However, we did find some managers that have no need for excuses. They are getting immediate and very significant return on money and time spent on human resource management. As a summary to our discussions of human resource management, we present our findings as a guide for spending your human resource dollars so you do not waste them.

WHY DO MANAGERS WASTE HUMAN RESOURCE DOLLARS?

We found three reasons why managers waste time and money managing human resources. First, resources are wasted when effort and programs are not focused on pressing business needs. A complex centralized human resource information system is developed around a mainframe computer, when what managers need is a simple system to recruit and develop people at the unit level. A sophisticated career planning system is adopted when what is needed is a counseling program to help people manage themselves. A new performance appraisal form is adopted when what is needed is a feedback mechanism giving employees on-line information about their performance. Far too often, managers are left uninvolved in the process of designing and implementing the human resource management practices they will use. Often these decisions about human resources are driven by specialists who have a desire to be current and have state-of-the-art programs with no consideration given to pressing business needs. Personnel professionals are not the only culprits: operating managers also want to have the latest techniques and programs. Money is wasted on sophisticated programs when what is needed are simple and basic answers to problems.

Second, resources are wasted when programs, information, and skills do not fit together and support each other. A new human resource information system may be exactly what is needed, but managers do not know how to use the information they are given. Or, as we found in many firms, the reverse is true—managers are very skilled at planning but have no human resource information to include in their planning process.

Third, and most importantly, resources are wasted because managers do not manage them. They do not expect payoff and demand cost justification for human resource investments. Common management tools, cost-benefit analysis, strategic planning, and market analysis used for financial and production resources are not used to manage people. Let us look at the causes for waste, how to recognize the warning signs, and what operating managers should do.

WASTE 1: HUMAN RESOURCE MANAGEMENT NOT FOCUSED ON PRESSING BUSINESS NEEDS

We found that organizations and units within the organization can be described by five stages of development, with different human resource management (HRM) needs at each stage. Program or approach do not work the same everywhere; they must be adapted to fit unique business needs. Figure 11–1 briefly describes the five development stages and their human resource management needs.

To get payoff, human resource investments must be made in areas of the most need; then, as business needs change, investments are shifted. If a unit is just beginning (Stage I—startup) managers need simple recruiting systems to help find the right people and get them up to speed on the job quickly; basic compensation systems to pay people; and simple work planning systems to assimilate and manage people. When the business hits the growth curve (Stage II—growth), simple recruiting systems will be outstripped by the demand for new people. Managers need professional recruiting help; computerized information systems to track employee movement; training and socialization programs to get the large influx of new recruits attuned to the organization; and feedback to stay in contact with employee attitudes and ensure that a communication network is in place.

For example, a manufacturing firm we studied decided to double its product lines and increase its employee base by 25 percent. Up until this time, they had been growing at 2–5 percent a year. Promotions were infrequent, promotion paths were clear, and performance appraisals were informal, with recruiting done by managers with minimal administrative assistance. The sudden growth quickly outstripped the HR systems in place. The record-keeping systems could not track new hires. The firm had no training or socialization program to help new employees adapt to their jobs and the organization. These were the areas where investments were needed.

Some businesses are under tremendous pressure for efficiency and cost control (Stage III). Investment should be made in human resource information and accounting systems to evaluate and control human

FIGURE 11–1
Human Resource Management Needs

Nature of Organization	Human Resource Management Needs

Stage I: Startup

Entrepreneurship, founder management, informality, limited products and markets	Recruiting to find key people, basic compensation and administrative systems

Stage II: Growth

Dynamic growth, technical specialization, expanded product lines and markets, added formality and structure, professional management introduced	Advanced recruiting capability, training and socialization programs to adapt new employees to the organization

Stage III: Control

Competition for resources, pressure to increase productivity, controlled investments	Cost control of HR programs, controlled investment in business-related skills, computer used to analyze costs

Stage IV: Integration

Diversification, decentralization, product groups or divisions, project management, focus on coordination and integration	Effective integration mechanisms between the various HR components, planning and organization development capability

Stage V: Flexibility

Adaptability, collaborative teamwork, team action, full integration across functional areas, multiple products and markets	Highly developed monitoring and scanning capability, flexibility to adjust to market and environmental needs

resource expenditures. More often in these situations, the response is to simply mandate head count reductions across the board. What managers need is data that will help them control staffing costs, build critical areas and cut others; what they don't need is mandated across-the-board cuts.

Diversification and decentralization (Stage IV) create the need for coordination. Investments should be made in information systems, task forces, planning mechanisms, and structure, which will help the organization coordinate its diverse work force and units. For example, a large high-technology firm, responding to the needs of diversification and decentralization, pushed most HR responsibilities down to the division level. Corporate personnel was reduced by 80 percent and maintained only integrative and strategy-setting policy functions: It was responsible for long-range strategic planning, information systems, organization development, and major corporate programs such as EEO. The typical personnel functions of compensation, appraisal, recruiting, and training were managed by operating managers within the policy framework established by corporate personnel.

Many organizations have a strong need to be extremely flexible and responsive to environmental changes (Stage V). They need investment in HR systems and procedures that will help them adapt quickly by varying the organizations' size, structure, and skill mix. A bank we studied was faced with growing competition, deregulation, advances in technology, and the ever-changing nature of its service business. Line management recognized the need for flexibility and adaptability. Top management cut their staffs to the bone; generalists in the remaining positions hired consultants as needed in specialized areas and contracted out most staff work.

Successful Human Resource Management Is Built on a Solid Base

We found successful HR systems at all stages built on a solid foundation of previous stages. Basic programs served as the foundation of advanced programs. For example, consider the experience various corporations have had over the years. In the 1970s, Digital Equipment Corporation (DEC) built an automated human resource information system using batch processing (Stage II) on the basic employee profile information collected in Stage I. The computer analysis used for management decision making and the on-line information systems established in 1975–78 (Stage III) were developed using the automated system. The distributed information system that in 1982 integrated information from all personnel areas (Stage IV) was developed using the information systems and computer analysis capabilities developed in Stage II. DEC's strategic HR information system for the 90s (Stage V) is built on the foundation of the distributed information network.

At a large bank we visited, the basic salary and benefits programs characteristic of Stage II were established in 1955 to meet the needs of the merged units that formed the bank. In 1965, measurement and control systems were put in place to manage the costs of compensation, benefits, and other personnel expenditures (Stage III). In 1975, an integrated career management, succession planning, compensation, and appraisal system (Stage IV) was developed based on the systems and cost information from Stage III. In 1981, the integrated systems (Stage V) were further tied together and refined to fit the strategic plans for the organization. By 1990, all managers understood and were held accountable for human resource management.

Many organizations do not have the luxury of developing human resource management practices and systems over a long period of time, so we found that if the basics are not in place first, the advanced systems do not work. For example, a high-technology firm we studied attempted to develop and implement over a short period of time a performance management program characteristic of Stage IV, where performance appraisals, compensation, and training are integrated. Unfortunately, they didn't first put in place the basic performance appraisal systems and job descriptions (Stage I and II) on which performance management systems are built. They developed the concepts for an integrated system but could never get them implemented. The organization had to return to basics and develop the earlier stages before the advanced programs would work.

The performance management experience was an example of what was happening throughout the organization. The president and the executive committee consistently put heavy pressure on personnel to help implement the strategic objectives. They expected Stage IV and V responses, strategic planning, projections, analysis, and organization development. Personnel's orientation was recruiting and training programs characteristic of Stage II. Management recognized the wrong orientation of personnel, and a new vice president of human resources, experienced in advanced programs, was hired from academia. He was given the mandate to implement human resource strategic planning, and integrated systems.

The new vice president, who was very knowledgeable about advanced personnel programs and systems, immediately hired specialists and consultants to develop sophisticated programs. These programs were developed but never implemented successfully because the job descriptions, performance appraisals, and information bases needed to implement and manage them were not available. After a year of frustration and failure, all agreed a new approach was needed. After an extensive search, the academic specialist was replaced by a generalist in human resource management who was given the same mandate but approached the job very differently. He put in place a development plan that first returned to the basics, established them quickly, and then built the advanced programs.

This was not without some frustration from management, it should be mentioned. Management knew what they wanted and were impatient for payoffs from the human resource manager and his new systems. When the latest vice president explained the focus initially would be on training, performance appraisal, and turnover, they were concerned. When he went on to explain the development sequence the firm would be moving through, they became more assured.

The high-technology firm's experience was common among the organizations we analyzed. Unless the basics are in place, more advanced programs fail. This happens most often when state-of-the-art programs are purchased with no clear understanding of what basics are needed to make them work.

Being Reactive Costs Time and Money

We found that most human resource management systems were reactive, lagging behind what managers really needed. Many of the companies show evidence of clear examples of this lag. People management systems and procedures were always reactively developed long after they were needed. A few examples will illustrate this.

Company A began diversifying and decentralizing in 1968. It needed decentralized staff support to deliver services and help coordinate the many new activities of the firm (Stage IV). The human resource function remained centralized, and did not begin offering diversified services or decentralized service delivery until 1982. In fact, in 1981, the personnel function attempted to centralize activities that were already decentralized and being performed by the line. While the organization started strategic planning in 1969 (Stage V), the human resource function provided no input until 1980. Not until 1982 did human resource management put in place a long-run strategic plan. And not until the late 1980s did the company's strategic plans include information about people.

In Company B, the human resource management activities lagged by 10 years the decentralization and diversification efforts of the corporation. It seemed just about impossible to reduce the large central human resource staff and decentralize the responsibility to line managers. In Company C, the introduction of automation to control costs throughout the corporation (Stage III) was not adopted in human resource management for 10 years.

Company D was the sole organization we studied that demonstrated action taken by the human resource function to provide services and prepare the organization prior to the organization's actual needs. The most obvious example was the announcement and appointment of the successors to the CEO and the president of the company a few years before their retirement, to assure continuity and smooth transition. This decision was managed and engineered by personnel. In this corporation, the human resource implications are required as part of all business plans and strategies.

There were real costs associated with being late. Costs of implementation reacting to crises were much higher than if situations had been anticipated and responses planned. The lags also meant that the organizations did not have what they needed to productively manage human resources. Even when they did move to put the proper programs and practices in place, time was lost as everyone slowly learned the new methods.

RECOGNIZE WHEN HRM DOES NOT FIT BUSINESS NEEDS

Just as fever and pain are the body's warning signs, the organization also has warning signs indicating caution and a need to find out what is truly happening.

Warning Sign 1: A Push for State-of-the-Art Programs with No Business Justification

Managers and staff may tend to push for state-of-the-art programs because they reflect current professional thinking. There is something attractive about being on the leading edge, in the forefront of new programs and techniques. Line managers may push for state-of-the-art programs because they want to be current and have the most sophisticated programs available to solve their problems. Instead, they should be pushing for programs that help them respond to business needs—programs that produce business results.

Warning Sign 2: The Budget and Focus of Programs Are Driven by Specialists and Staff Rather than by Managers

Staff specialist will tend to focus on areas in which they are experts. They are very capable of giving advice on specialized programs, but too often they do not have the business understanding to make good business decisions. It is time to take human resource management out of the hands of personnel specialists and put it in the hands of managers. The budget and focus of programs should be driven by managers.

Warning Sign 3: No Budget or Control Mechanism

Managing expenditures for maximum payoff is a basic management responsibility. It applies to technology, materials, and financial resources; it should also apply to human resources. Cost-benefit analysis, payoff, productivity, quality, and customer satisfaction are words that should be commonly used when referring to human resource programs. If they are not, something is wrong.

WHAT SHOULD MANAGERS DO TO MAKE SURE HRM FITS THE BUSINESS?

Managers should understand and anticipate the nature of the business and respond with appropriate human resource management programs and practices. They should not be swept up in the clamor for the new fads such as quality circles, flexible time, flexible compensation, and so on without a clear understanding of what they are buying and how these programs fit. Some units are just beginning; they need basic programs in place. Some units have an emphasis on productivity and need help controlling costs and pushing productivity. Other firms need help integrating and coordinating the work of diverse units. Still others need help remaining flexible and being able to quickly adjust to the environment.

Fit the Situation

No one best method exists. Sophisticated succession planning systems are not productive for everyone. Structured job grading systems that limit flexibility and restrict movement do not fit all businesses. State-of-the-art human resource information systems are a waste of money in firms that do not have the basics in place or a management that can utilize them. Career-planning methods that assume progression up a structured hierarchy do not fit most firms.

Managers often adopt more sophisticated programs than are needed. "Human resource management needs fixing, so buy a program to fix it." Managers get trapped in the "get me one of them" syndrome. "If quality circles seem to be helping others, get one of those." "Human resource strategic planning is in all of the journals, we should be doing it also." Programs work in organizations if they fit the needs of the organization. You cannot expect a human resource program that works in another organization to work in yours any more than you can expect someone else's marketing program to work in your organization.

Put the Foundation in Place First

Performance management programs do not work without standards and objectives in place. Meaningful succession planning is impossible without accurate human resource data. Flexible benefit programs do not work without accurate accounting systems. Programs, information, and skills of later stages are built on the foundation of earlier stages. If earlier stages are not in place, later stages will not work.

There is a learning and developmental curve, one stage after another, that human resource management must follow. Missing one block at the base can weaken and destroy the whole structure in later stages. Invest in the foundation first and do not skip stages.

Operations managers must be particularly diligent if the basics are not yet in place. They will often be pressured to develop sophisticated, state-of-the-art strategic programs rather than concentrating on doing the basics well. They cannot, however, start there. They must put the basics in place first.

Viewing development in sequential stages also provides a way to anticipate human resource needs and prepare for them. HRM need not be reactive. As changes in the organization begin, the pressures to move to higher stages can be recognized and preparations made. Ideally, HRM should lead and pull the organization into higher stages.

Always Return to the Basics

Because the foundation is so critical, always return to the basics to make sure they are current. This is necessary for two reasons. First, once implemented, the basics do not always remain useful. Job descriptions become outdated, and compensation and benefit systems will need revision to match market conditions. New managers and personnel professionals will enter the organization and need training.

Second, the basics needed for Stages IV and V are often modifications of the basics established in Stage I. Even in situations where they are the same, they will be viewed and used from a different perspective. For example, the basic performance appraisal system in Stage II is used to assess performance and give feedback to employees. That same performance appraisal in Stage IV and V is used to identify development needs and career moves. It is used in human resource and succession planning and includes evaluation of potential as well as current performance. Even though the performance appraisal forms and processes may remain substantially the same, they are used from a different perspective. They must be reevaluated.

Build a Business Plan for Any HRM Program

Any newly proposed program must be justified by showing how it fits the business need. What are the expected outcomes, what are the costs, how does it fit managers' needs. A competitive analysis should be done. What are others doing? How much does it cost them? What alternatives are available? Will the program contribute to the business? Before any money and time are committed, a business justification must be made.

WASTE 2: HRM COMPONENTS DO NOT FIT WITH AND SUPPORT EACH OTHER

In our visits, we found a very different perspective among managers and human resource professionals who were successfully managing human resources and those who were unsuccessful. No matter how we defined success—turnover, cost, morale surveys, or management perceptions—it came out the same. When we asked managers and personnel professionals in successful firms to describe human resource management, they talked about producing business results by properly managing many components. We identified six strategic components that must fit with and support each other: management awareness, management of the human resource function, portfolio of programs, information technology, personnel skills, and awareness of the internal and external environment. Figure 11–2 presents a description of these components at the five stages of development.

In unsuccessful firms, the focus was on managing programs. Human resource management is not about programs. It is about producing business results with the most efficient expenditure of time and energy possible. We found human resource management is efficient when all the components—information systems, programs, and skills of managers—fit together and support each other. It is not enough for one of the components to fit the needs of the organization. They all must fit. Performance appraisal systems fail if managers do not have the skills or experience necessary to properly use them. A flexible benefit program does not work without the proper information system. Advanced information systems are useless if no one knows how to implement them.

We found another interesting tendency among managers and personnel professionals in unsuccessful units and firms. They were constantly trying to do better what they already did well. Because their orientation was programs, they were constantly striving to improve the programs. This was particularly true when faced with failure, when they could sense that the programs were not making a contribution to the organization. The tendency was to blame the inadequacy on the programs and to request more sophisticated programs. More time and money was spent on performance appraisal programs, even more sophisticated succession-planning programs were adopted, and a broader range of organization development programs were implemented. The problems, of course, were not caused by the programs but by the other components. The succession-planning programs did not work because the appropriate information technology was not available, performance appraisal failed because managers did not have the skills and commitment to use it, and organization development was not successful because HR professionals were not skilled in implementing it. What managers should have done was focus on what they were not doing well, on the components that were lagging and acting as constraints.

Managers and personnel professionals in successful units took a much more business-oriented approach. They asked, ''What is constraining

FIGURE 11–2
Human Resource Strategic Matrix

Components	Stage 1 Initiation	Stage II Functional Growth	Stage III Controlled Growth	Stage IV Functional Integration	Stage V Strategic Integration
Manager Awareness	Aware of function's administrative role	Aware of function's broad role but not committed	Aware; often frustrated at fragmentation	Cooperative and involved	Integrated
Management of the Personnel Function	Loose, informal; often none	Personnel manager; program orientation; manage, conflicts among subfunctions	Personnel executive; business orientation; control, measurements, goals	Function orientation department goals; planning, long-range direction; line/staff relations; collaborative	Company orientation; consistent and integrated with business strategic direction
Portfolio of Programs	Basic salary and benefits administration; basic record keeping; nonexempt hiring	Many new programs added responding to business needs in compensation, benefits, training, etc.; revisiting basic programs	Management control programs; budgets, ROI; portfolio reevaluated in measurable and analytical terms; advanced compensation	Interdisciplinary programs; focus on department goals and direction; productivity; change management; succession planning	Cultural and environmental scanning; long-range planning; emphasis on effectiveness and efficiency in direct response to business needs

FIGURE 11–2 (concluded)

Components	Stage 1 Initiation	Stage II Functional Growth	Stage III Controlled Growth	Stage IV Functional Integration	Stage V Strategic Integration
Information Technology	Manual employee profile; record keeping	Automated salary and basic profile; Advance record keeping	Automate personnel work; mainly profiles, EEO, tracking: basic metrics	Utilize computer or projection; planning, analysis, and evaluation	Planning tools re-search, and analysis; long-range issues and "what-if" questions linked to the personnel and organizational database
Personnel Skills	Administrative routine and housekeeping	Functional specialists	Increased professionalism in function and managerial skills	Integrating activities; skills in systems, planning, and analysis	High-level involvement in organization; skills dealing with macro issues
Awarness of Internal and External Environment	Not aware	Aware of environment and corporate culture but does not incorporate them into function's activities	Aware of risks and opportunities in environment; address some in programs	Aware of; react and incorporate into planning process; environmental changes identified	Systematically search for impact the environment has on organization; take an active role in making and shaping decisions

us?'' ''What is stopping us from delivering business results?'' Consistently, they would work on strategic components that they were not performing well. Rather than implement even more sophisticated succession-planning systems, they developed basic information systems that would allow them to do succession planning. Rather than implement even more complex performance management programs, they trained managers how to use the existing basic programs.

The matrix created by combining the stages of development and the components (Figure 11–2) can be used to draw a profile of human resource management practices. The profile can then be compared against organization needs to identify deficiencies. Figure 11–3, for example, presents the profile of a high-technology firm that is diversifying and trying to become flexible and market responsive. It needs Stage V human resource management. Clearly it has big gaps in its information technology and its management's awareness and ability to use HR programs.

RECOGNIZE WHEN HRM COMPONENTS
DO NOT FIT TOGETHER

Once again, clear warning signs exist when HRM components are not fitting together and supporting each other.

Warning Sign 4: Nothing Seems to Be Wrong with the Programs, but They Are Still Not Working

Programs may meet all professional norms and appear to be well designed but still not work. The problem is not located in the programs but in how they fit with other strategic components. Maybe managers or human resource professionals do not have the right skills, or the right information is not available. Check the other components: they are more than likely to be the problem.

Warning Sign 5: Everyone Constantly Talks about Human Resource Programs

If managers and human resource professionals constantly frame discussions in terms of programs, you have problems. Programs are solutions to be used in conjunction with the other strategic components. If

252

FIGURE 11-3
High Technology Firm

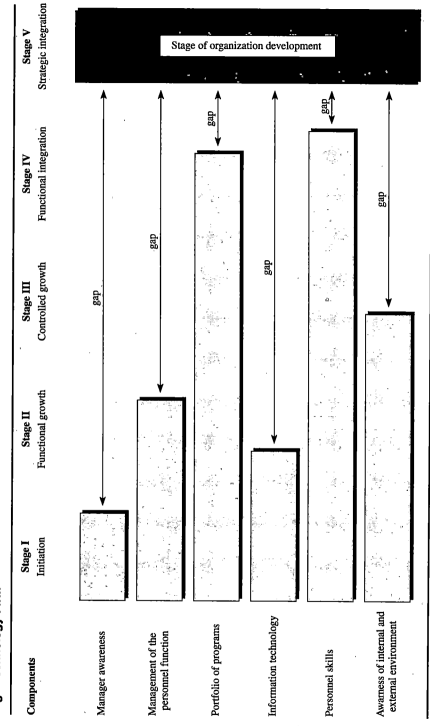

managers only focus on the programs, they will never successfully manage human resources. The other components are most often causing the problem and must be part of the solution.

Warning Sign 6: No Payoff from Program Investment

The ultimate test for a program is the payoff to the organization. It does not matter how professionally sophisticated or state of the art a program is; if it has no payoff, it is useless. That is a hard pill for some personnel professionals to swallow. They think they do their jobs by providing good programs, but often the programs provide no business payoff. Everyone else is measured by results, so personnel professionals should be, too. The sloppiest program in the world that produces results is better than the most elegant program that does not.

The objective of human resource management is to obtain maximum payoff. Human resource management is efficient if all of the components fit with and support each other; that is, if the profile is balanced. Obviously, information systems, environmental scans, sophisticated planning tools, and advanced organization development programs that are not used are inefficient and waste money.

What Managers Should Do to Make Sure HRM Components Support Each Other

Managers must focus on producing business results using the many components of human resource management. A good way to think about the components is as multiple levers that can be pulled; which lever you pull is determined by what is needed to produce business results. Many times, it will not be the program lever. For example, many human resource plans fail because the appropriate information and skills necessary to implement them is not available. Often, assessment and monitoring programs have little impact because managers do not have the skills to use the information. Managers must assess the multiple components and manage them simultaneously.

Do Better What You Do Not Do Well.   You must maintain a balanced profile. The lagging components are preventing you from performing, not what you are already doing well. The tendency, especially for staff professionals, is to try to do better in areas where they are already competent and doing well. They provide even more sophisticated programs, when what is needed is basic information and skills.

Use the Proper Component to Lead the Organization.   A main advantage of thinking of human resource management in terms of developmental stages is that it provides a way of understanding what the organization will need in the future. Advanced stages can be anticipated. As it becomes evident new approaches are needed, human resource management can lead the organization into higher stages of complexity. Thinking of HRM in terms of multiple components identifies many areas that can be managed. You should focus on the component that will have the highest impact on moving the organization. If managers focus heavily on financial reports as the basis of decision making, use information systems to drive the organization forward; if managers are heavily invested in training, use skill building; if the planning process drives the organization, use monitoring capabilities.

APPLICATIONS

1. Make human resource investments in the areas of greatest need: then, as business needs change, shift areas of investment.
2. If your organization or unit is just beginning, make sure the recruiting system provides the right people and get them up to speed on the job quickly.
3. When your organization reaches its growth curve, you will need specialized recruiting help. Make sure you have enough of the right type of people.
4. If your organization is under pressure for efficiency, make investments in human resource information and accounting systems that will help you control costs.
5. When your organization is in the stage of diversification and decentralization, make investments in information systems, task forces, planning mechanisms, and structure to help coordinate the diverse work force and units.
6. If the need in your organization is to be extremely flexible and responsive to environmental changes, make investments in human resource systems and procedures that help it adapt quickly by varying the organization's size, structure, and skill mix.

7. Put basic human resource systems into place before attempting to implement advanced systems.
8. Implement human resource management systems before a crisis occurs. Avoid reactive programs that cost your organization added time and money.
9. Recognize when human resource management does not fit business needs by looking for the following warning signs.
    a. A push for state-of-the-art programs with no business justification.
    b. The budget and focus of programs are driven by specialists and staff rather than managers.
    c. No budget or control mechanism.
10. Understand and anticipate the nature of the business and respond with appropriate human resource management programs and practices. Implement only those programs that will fit with your organization, not someone else's.
11. Build a business plan before implementing any human resource program in order to determine cost, competition, alternatives, and potential contributions.
12. You must manage many components to produce successful business results from a human resource management program. These components are management awareness, management of the human resource function, portfolio of programs, information technology, personnel skills, and awareness of the internal and external environment.

INDEX

OTHER TITLES IN THE BUSINESS ONE IRWIN/APICS LIBRARY OF INTEGRATED RESOURCE MANAGEMENT

Integrated Process Design and Development
Dan L. Shunk

Shows how to design and develop processes that are consistent with the capabilities of the plant and the employees. Shunk introduces process design terminology in reader-friendly terms instead of using the complex jargon found in many manufacturing books.

ISBN: 1-55623-556-9 $42.50

Marketing for the Manufacturer
J. Paul Peter

Explains the marketing role to the nonmarketing specialist. Peter provides a detailed analysis of how marketing fits into various organizational structures and product management systems. He offers methods for researching consumer markets and creating a dynamic strategic plan.

ISBN: 1-55623-648-4 $42.50

Integrated Production and Inventory Management
Thomas E. Vollmann, D. Clay Whybark, and William L. Berry

Explains the use of modern planning and control systems to remove excess inventory investment, save on production and distribution costs, and better integrate organization efforts. The authors give you strategies and systems to optimize customer service through the use of the latest inventory monitoring procedures.

ISBN: 1-55623-604-2 $42.50

Managing for Quality
Integrating Quality and Business Strategy
Howard S. Gitlow

Details how to integrate quality into the heart of a company's business plan and use it to gain a strategic edge over the competition. Gitlow shows how to satisfy customer requirements and reduce the cost of quality. He offers methods for detecting and preventing defects by using a system that minimizes monitoring efforts.

ISBN: 1-55623-544-5 $42.50

Effective Product Design and Development
How to Cut Lead Time and Increase Customer Satisfaction
Stephen R. Rosenthal

Shows manufacturing professionals how to shorten the cycle of new product design and development and turn time into a strategic competitive advantage. Rosenthal helps you use an integrated managerial view of the design and development process, which helps companies catch design flaws early, correct mistakes, and avoid long development delays.

ISBN: 1-55623-603-4 $42.50

Prices quoted are in U.S. currency and are subject to change without notice.

Available in fine bookstores and libraries everywhere.